By late afternoon, time was working against the five Lurps. There was no way the team could cross the river and survive, nor could it hold out until a quick-reaction force arrived. The gunships on station estimated the enemy numbers to be in the hundreds, which likely meant a full battalion or possibly a regiment. There was no way for the division to quickly move in an equivalent-size force to take them on. The division could hammer the area with gunships, artillery fire, and tac air, but the Lurps would have to get themselves out of the trap they were in. Extraction in place was impossible. Their only chance was to run, to escape and evade to an alternate site.

McConnell listened as Bitticks told the gunships to fire at everything outside the smoke grenade he was preparing to throw out. The team would make a dash for the nearest pickup zone through the billowing cloud of smoke. Dropping his heavy rucksacks and getting his people to their feet, the team leader pulled the pin on a smoke grenade and threw it in the direction they wanted to go.

"Go!" he yelled, running at the rising cloud, firing his rifle as he ran. The gunships were already attacking the surrounding jungle as Bitticks, Moline, McConnell, Geiger, and Fatzinger sprinted right up the middle, breaking open a hole in the enemy's defenses. . . .

By Kregg P. J. Jorgenson

ACCEPTABLE LOSS: *An Infantry Soldier's Perspective**
BEAUCOUP DINKY DAU
MIA RESCUE: *LRRPs in Cambodia**
LRRP COMPANY COMMAND: *The Cav's LRP/Rangers in Vietnam, 1968–1969**

*Published by The Ballantine Publishing Group

LRRP COMPANY COMMAND

The Cav's LRP/Rangers in Vietnam, 1968–1969

Kregg P. J. Jorgenson

BALLANTINE BOOKS • NEW YORK

A Ballantine Book
Published by The Ballantine Publishing Group
Copyright © 2000 by Kregg P. J. Jorgenson

www.randomhouse.com/BB/

Library of Congress Catalog Card Number: 00-107752

ISBN 0-8041-1920-1

Manufactured in the United States of America

First Edition: December 2000

10 9 8 7 6 5 4 3 2 1

For our families and loved ones,
whom we often forgot while we were out adventuring

Dragons have been long used in Asian myth to symbolize the primordial fear man has towards the unknown, but it is not the flames he fears the most in the dark, only the unexpected brush against talons and the sound of a dragon's whisper . . .

—HENRY KEITH JORGENSON
Poet/Author, 1917–1993

ACKNOWLEDGMENTS

Academics say that memory is a poor historian; they prefer formal chronology over recollections of incidents filtered by time and emotion. However, I'm not an academic, and I like my history in more human terms, my heroes a little weathered and rough around the edges, defined not only by their chronology but by their times, situations, hopes, fears, joys, and frustrations as well. And that is how I approached this book.

Besides the chronology reconstructed from records, interviews, newsletters, personal correspondence, and official after-action reports of Company E (LRP) and later Company H (Ranger), I am deeply indebted to the following former 1st Cavalry Division's LRRPs, LRP/Rangers, and Apache Troop, 1st of the 9th Cav, veterans for sharing their personal accounts, and for their comments, phone calls, and assistance. Specifically, I want to thank Robert McKenzie, William Hand, Walter James "Spanky" Seymour, Craig Leerburg, Michael Echterling, Bruce Judkins, Michael Gooding, Calvin Renfro, Douglas Parkinson, Dan Roberts, Guy McConnell Jr., Dr. Michael Brennan, Frank Duggan, the late James F. McIntyre, Rick Arden, Robert Gill, Robert Edward Beal, R. B. Alexander, Col. James W. Booth, U.S. Army (Ret.), and the late Kit Beatton, an Apache Troop pilot whose courage time and again proved crucial to those who stood against the dragon.

Special recognition and thanks go to Col. George Paccerelli, U.S. Army (Ret.), who quite literally provided me with an invaluable library of Company E (LRP) and Company H (Ranger) materials, their order of battle, detailed information (including personal notes and letters), and his "commander's insight" that formed the foundation of this book. He was remarkably generous with his time and resources.

Saying that, let me also say that George Paccerelli was determined to take a low profile on this project and urged me instead to focus the story on the men of the company who, he said, "deserved any real credit and recognition for the company's success. They were the heart and soul of the unit. I just had the good fortune to be able to command them."

It was my decision to push Paccerelli into the forefront of the account in order to better tell this story. As you read this book, you will see why.

Thanks also have to go to Gary Linderer, my agent and, more important, my friend, who quite literally helped make it all possible. Finally, to my wife, Katherine, for allowing me the time needed to complete this project.

For the sake of reading ease, I have used the term "Lurp" rather than LRRP or LRP in describing long-range patrols and long-range reconnaissance patrols.

Kregg P. J. Jorgenson

Republic of Vietnam

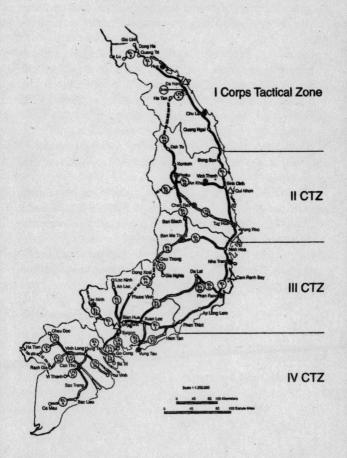

I Corps Tactical Zone

II CTZ

III CTZ

IV CTZ

CHAPTER ONE

On October 18, 1968, Capt. George Paccerelli was selected to take over the 1st Air Cavalry Division's long-range patrol company. He had been handpicked for the job because of his impressive military credentials and because an "experienced" captain was sorely needed in the position. George Paccerelli was experienced, and his personnel file reflected his skill and ability.

He was well read, spoke several languages, and was working on his first masters degree. He was a husband and father and, best of all—at least to the decision makers—he was a professional soldier. Paccerelli had fifteen years of military experience, ten of which had been as an enlisted man. He was Airborne, Ranger, Special Forces, and Jungle School qualified, and had already served two difficult combat tours of duty. He had earned a uniform full of awards, tabs, and medals in battles in Laos, Cambodia, and the Central Highlands of South Vietnam long before he arrived in country for his third tour of duty.

So when G-2, the division-level intelligence arm of the Cav, requested the names of officers qualified to command Company E, 52d Infantry (LRP), at Camp Evans, Lt. Col. Addison D. Davis, the battalion commander of the 2d of the 7th Cav, submitted Paccerelli's name. After all the interviews had been conducted and the selection made, Davis was the first to let Paccerelli know of the outcome.

"Congratulations!" Davis announced with a broad grin. "You're the lucky bastard!"

Until that moment, George Paccerelli had been the battalion's acting S-2, intelligence officer, and he was well suited to run the shop. No one appreciated the intelligence officer's slot more than someone who had had to rely on tactical information in combat. The thirty-two-year-old mustang (former enlisted man) officer had been temporarily filling the slot until a company-command position opened up in one of the battalion's infantry line units, which is where he really wanted to be. Paccerelli was next in line for a combat command and looking forward to it. However, division headquarters had other ideas. Echo Company (LRP) would get priority, not that it really mattered to Paccerelli. In fact, he was genuinely pleased with the idea and saw it as a plum. The concept of small five- to six-man Lurp teams working behind the lines was one of the best ways he knew to beat the Viet Cong and their North Vietnamese commanders at their own game of guerrilla warfare, and with the immense helicopter gunship support the Cav had to offer, he was looking forward to taking command of the air mobile long-range patrol company. There wasn't a veteran Special Forces soldier who didn't subscribe to the logic of Sun-tzu, the ancient Chinese warrior/philosopher, "If you cause opponents to be unaware of the place and time of battle, you will achieve victory."

In the war that preceded the U.S. effort in Indochina, the French had belatedly discovered that commando units working behind the lines could effectively deal with the Viet Minh. The *Groupement des Commandos Mixtes Aeroportes*, better known by their initials, GCMA, were remarkably successful, but deployed too late in the war to turn the tide of their ultimate defeat. Yet, after Dien Bien Phu had fallen and French control over the region slipped into the hands of Communist general Vo Nguyen Giap in 1954, the GCMA commandos managed to fight on effectively for several more years. The "little wars" of the guerrilla fighter were very often effective.

As the S-2, George Paccerelli had often dealt with the division's Lurp teams and was impressed with what he saw and heard during their patrol debriefings. The division Lurps, in his mind, had their act together. Everyone at division knew what they had accomplished six months earlier on Signal Hill, and even if they didn't know the specifics, they sure as hell knew the basic story. It was Custer's Last Stand with a happy ending.

Six months earlier, in Operation Delaware, the Cav had raided the enemy-held A Shau Valley. While seven of the division's nine infantry battalions had roared into the valley and up the surrounding slopes, the Lurps were rappelling onto the five-thousand-foot peak of A Loui, a dark, brooding mountain that overlooked the valley floor. The Lurps, along with volunteers from the 8th Engineers and the 13th Signal Battalion, had been tasked to establish a radio-relay station to coordinate the Cav's operations in the valley below. The radio-relay station was essential to the success of Operation Delaware, and the assault force of Lurps, engineers, and signalmen had to take and hold the mountaintop.

On the morning of 19 April 1968, the assault force departed Camp Evans for the A Shau. The flight was an anxious one for the cavalrymen. Since there was no open space big enough for the helicopters to land, the Lurps had to rappel onto the mountaintop. As the lead UH-1 flared for its short final approach, gusty crosswinds rising over the valley hit the aircraft, forcing it to veer away. The pilot struggled desperately to hold the aircraft steady, but it was a losing battle.

As the first two men hooked up to the ninety-foot rappelling rope and climbed out on the skids, the helicopter's engine faltered, then began to fail. The two Lurps on the ropes, Sergeants Bill Hand and Larry Curtis, had already begun their descent. Too far below the crippled aircraft to be hauled back aboard, Hand and Curtis tried to beat the chopper to the ground, falling the last forty feet into the trees only seconds before the dying aircraft tumbled down behind them.

Injured and dazed from the hard landing, Hand had just enough time to bring his hands over his head, tuck into a tight ball, and roll away before the Huey crashed down through the trees, its main rotor blade digging a trench into the jungle floor just inches from his head. The helicopter itself fell directly on Curtis but, miraculously, did nothing more than trap the injured Lurp beneath its skids.

The second miracle was that there was no fire from the ruptured fuel tank as the helicopter's fourteen hundred SHP Savco Lycoming engine died screaming in place. Those aboard the downed aircraft had also survived, but not without taking a heavy beating against the airframe as it tumbled through the trees. The survivors struggled to climb out of the twisted wreckage, trying to establish some sort of perimeter and assist those too injured to help themselves. Just below the crest of A Loui, the NVA had previously mounted antiaircraft positions to deal with the threat of American helicopters so enemy soldiers were already beginning to turn their attention, and their guns, to the mountaintop above them.

The survivors of the downed helicopter, along with the Lurps who had rappelled in on the second aircraft, laid down cover for the remainder of the assault force as enemy small-arms fire began to find targets among the Cav troopers. By the time all four teams were on the ground and the engineers and signalmen were moving to set up the relay station, the NVA had seized upon the Americans' bad luck to mount an all-out ground assault against them to push them off the mountain. But the American assault force held its ground. By the end of the day, eleven dead or seriously wounded cavalrymen had been lifted off the mountain. Three Lurps—Sgt. Glenn Lambert, Sp4 Richard Turbitt, Jr., and PFC Robert Noto—had been killed in action, along with several of the radiomen and engineers.

Others, including Hand, Curtis, and the air crew of the first liftship, had been badly bruised and battered. As the long day turned into night, the Lurps and other volunteers defended the relay site from repeated enemy assaults and kept it operational.

During the battle, the Lurp company had also lost the services of Lt. Joe Dillinger, the officer in charge of the assault group, who had been seriously wounded by a sniper's bullet. The assault on A Loui was proving to be a costly operation for Company E, but it was one that had served the division well.

Paccerelli knew that Captain Gooding, the Lurp CO at the time, had later led reinforcements onto the mountaintop and secured it to safeguard the vital communications network for the division operations going on five thousand feet below. A handful of men were decorated for gallantry and heroism, and Signal Hill became part of the company's legacy.

Paccerelli had also heard numerous stories of the running battles the small teams had had against the Viet Cong, and he had firsthand knowledge of their ambush patrols, which yielded stacks of VC and NVA unit documents, maps, weapons, and the best intelligence of all—enemy prisoners. In fact, his own first personal encounter with the Lurps had been with S.Sgt. Paul "O. B." O'Brien, after O'Brien's six-man team had ambushed a squad of Viet Cong soldiers along a rural stretch of Highway 1, the coastal macadam road the French a decade earlier had referred to as *"la rue sans joie"—The Street Without Joy*.

Over the decades, the road had earned the name because of the many thousands who had lost their lives on and along it in countless ambushes and small battles, and to mines and booby traps. Not all of the road's many potholes had been caused by weather or traffic, nor all of its stains by transmission fluid and leaky oil pans. While gun jeeps and armored vehicles fought to keep it open during the daylight hours, at night it quickly fell back into the hands of the enemy.

During the Lurps' ambush, O'Brien and his people had managed to capture a Viet Cong political officer, bundle him up, and bring him back to Camp Evans for interrogation. A

Communist political officer was a special prize. His number-three position in an enemy unit's command structure made him an important person and a wielder of considerable power.

Since the site where the Lurp team had captured the political officer was in the 2d of the 7th Cav's area of operations (AO), a line company from that unit was sent out to the area to conduct a search-and-destroy operation. Paccerelli had joined the sweep and had come away impressed with the valuable intelligence provided the battalion by O'Brien and his teammates. The line "doggies" job had been made considerably easier, thanks to the information supplied by the Viet Cong political officer.

For the division's intelligence arm, live prisoners were always better than body counts because of their potential intelligence value, and Captain Paccerelli was pleased that the Lurp team leader understood that. Snatching prisoners was always a risky venture because, while the snatch team knew they wanted to capture an armed enemy alive, the enemy soldier would usually do his best to try to kill or evade those making the attempt. Capturing and subduing him took time, and the presence of a prisoner usually slowed the march, which made the team more vulnerable to pursuit by the enemy.

Paccerelli had debriefed O'Brien and the team after the mission and had liked what he had seen and heard from the Lurps. Sure, they were a little rough around the edges—militarily speaking—but that just meant they needed some spit and polish and to be reminded every now and then that the word "fuck" wasn't a verb, noun, pronoun, or adjective ever likely to find approval as an expression used in army communication. Still, they were impressive field soldiers by anyone's standards.

"It *is* a plum assignment," he said to himself on the way to be briefed at division. Anyone could see it just as anyone could see the spring in his step as he walked.

CHAPTER TWO

But in his appraisal of the unit, the division staff officer was frank, if not brutal, with Captain Paccerelli. "We've had some problems recently with the Lurp company, which is why we're bringing you in," the senior officer said. The look on his face and the tone of his voice only added weight to his words.

"What kind of problems, sir?" asked Paccerelli.

The senior officer launched into a dissertation on "unsoldierly bearing," moved quickly to "low morale," and ended up with what was really the heart of the matter. "There's a question about some of their patrols' faking contact to get out of the field."

Paccerelli didn't view unsoldierly bearing as a particularly great sin. Occasionally, the same had been said of the best Special Forces operators. But attitudes could always be adjusted, and even ragtag soldiers could usually be cleaned up well enough to pass an inspection. Low morale often went hand in hand with whatever was causing the first problem, and that was not something that necessarily worried the captain.

However, the third problem was much more formidable. Paccerelli understood faking it; this was a symptom of something far more serious. Contacts with the enemy compromised the mission and left the team exposed and in danger of being tracked down and surrounded. The standard operating procedure for a Lurp patrol in contact was to abort the mission and call for extraction—before the scheduled end of the mission. Faking contact to end a patrol early was not only strategically stupid, it was dangerous, if in fact it was happening at all. Because a rescue helicopter didn't take fire coming in to extract a team or the pilots hadn't seen any enemy soldiers in the landing zone didn't necessarily mean the Viet Cong weren't there. The accompanying Cobra attack helicopter gunships with their Gatling gun–like machine guns, grenade launchers, and rockets sometimes made the enemy remain hidden for obvious reasons. Still, faking it might happen from time to time. As the new company commander, making certain it didn't would be one of Paccerelli's first priorities.

The staff officer also brought up the desertion of one of the company's Kit Carson scouts, who had taken with him a lot more than one man could carry. The Kit Carson scout was a former North Vietnamese Army lieutenant who had "rallied" to the side of the Saigon government, had gone through the required indoctrination, and had then been retrained and put to work as a scout with the Cav's Lurp company. After additional training in Lurp operations and tactics and appropriate time in the field on patrol, the former NVA lieutenant had apparently "unrallied," returning to the Communists and taking with him all the information, operating procedures, and Lurp intelligence he had recently acquired. He had simply walked away on the mission after convincing the team leader to let him dress in khakis and carry an AK-47.

The former NVA officer was adamant that he should walk point since running into him would confuse the first enemy soldiers they might encounter. Similar tactics had worked in the past. However, on that patrol, the former NVA lieutenant walked farther ahead than normal, and once out of sight of the rest of the team, kept going. Since the patrol was deep in enemy territory, the former NVA officer didn't have to worry too much about making good his escape.

The scout's desertion reflected a far more serious threat to the Lurps themselves as well as to the rest of the division. The NVA officer, obviously planted in the Kit Carson program to spy on American field units, walked away with an incredible amount of tactical information.

There had even been a rumor that the Lurp team had actually killed the Kit Carson scout while out on patrol and had dumped the body in the underbrush. But only a week after his disappearance, enemy gunners targeted the Lurp company area with rockets, dispelling the rumor of foul play. Whoever had plotted the targets for the enemy gunners had known exactly who the Lurps were and the precise coordinates of their tactical operations center, their command post, and their barracks.

While the double agent was viewed as a costly but isolated incident, the Americans had no way of knowing until long after the war had ended that enemy agents had infiltrated most of the South Vietnamese military commands and political offices, and that much more pertinent data than a single company's tactical intelligence information had flooded Hanoi. By 1968, it was no secret to Special Forces, or to the CIA whose OPLAN-34A special teams, which were infiltrated into North Vietnam, had all been compromised or turned. There were security leaks at all levels in the South Vietnamese government, and the magnitude of the infiltration by Communist agents would not be fully understood for decades to come.

However, down at the NVA grunt level, the new and timely information about the Lurps would serve the Viet Cong and NVA who fought against the 1st Cavalry Division.

The Viet Cong and the North Vietnamese Army had suffered much at the hands of the 1st Cav and its Lurp teams, so this windfall of information would provide them with the necessary intelligence to counteract their tactics and strategies. Beating the Cav, and in particular the Lurps, would require more than knowledge of their game plan. As the Communists would soon come to understand, simply knowing how American long-range patrols operated in the field didn't necessarily mean the Viet Cong or NVA could find them. The vast and rugged mountainous jungles that had hidden the Communists so well also hid the Lurps. So, in spite of their scruffiness, the Lurps were doing a good job of gathering intelligence and ambushing enemy units on their own turf.

Paccerelli knew that a number of the Lurps were graduates of the 5th Special Forces Recondo School at Nha Trang, and even the SF "snake eaters" were reasonably impressed with the skills of the young recon soldiers. No one could deny they had potential, but living up to it was another matter.

At battalion, nearly everyone believed that Lurps were elite soldiers who sometimes walked on water, but it was made very clear to the new company commander during his briefing that his new command was sinking rather quickly. Paccerelli's job would be to keep the company from going under, not to make division believe the Lurps could perform miracles.

"You have your work cut out for you, Captain," explained the staff officer as he rose and offered his hand along with a subtle warning. "Good luck. You'll need it."

In yet another briefing before he took command, the squadron commander for the 1st of the 9th Cav made it clear that it was Paccerelli's job to restore the discipline and military bearing of the unit in preparation for its becoming E Troop, 1st of the 9th Cav. That was the first Paccerelli had heard about the Lurps being assimilated into the cavalry squadron. The news caught Paccerelli completely by surprise. Dissatisfaction with a unit was one thing, but shutting it down and taking away its identity was something else entirely.

So the Lurps were to lose their independence and their function! Paccerelli made up his mind that these were two things he would do everything within his power to prevent. He kept the goal to himself as the squadron commander continued with his briefing, explaining how the Lurp company would be attached immediately to the 1st of the 9th for logistical support, mess, and judicial punishment. It was obvious the lieutenant colonel was proud of his command, and rightfully so. Since arriving in country, the squadron had earned several Valorous Unit awards, Presidential Unit Citations, and South Vietnamese Cross of Gallantry with Gold Palm awards.

The 1st of the 9th Cavalry was made up of four distinct troops as well as a headquarters section. Alpha, Bravo, and Charlie troops were comprised of light observation (scout) helicopters, attack gunships, and Huey liftships ("slicks") along with their crews and maintenance sections. In addition, each troop had a thirty-man air-mobile light infantry platoon, known as "Blues," assigned to it. The fourth element, Delta Troop, was a jeep-mounted unit informally known as "The Rat Patrol," which cleared roads and provided convoy escort along the most dangerous stretches of highway in the Cav's area of operation.

The U.S. Army's 1st Cavalry Division was one of the high-profile units serving in Vietnam, and within the division, the 1st of the 9th had been the spearhead for most, if not all, of its operations.

The squadron's legacy began with the near-legendary Buffalo Soldiers, the black cavalry troops who had fought so valiantly to help tame the American Southwest in the late 1800s. Over the decades that followed, with reorganizational changes, the 9th Cav's long and impressive combat history continued, extending to World War II and Korea. By the time they arrived in Vietnam in 1965 under the command of Col. John B. Stockton, the new 9th Cavalry had taken a bold approach to heliborne operations. Stockton, a 1943 West Point graduate, was a controversial figure who sported a black Stetson hat and undeniable zeal for his new squadron. He was instrumental in developing the modern cavalry concept and, in Vietnam, helped shape its future and success. However, it wasn't without its cost. Stockton was relieved of command for what amounted to a daring night assault that saved the lives of over one hundred of his men on a besieged landing zone that was little more than a jungle outpost. Stockton had not received prior approval to commit a reserve force from division headquarters, which proved to be his undoing. After his people on the LZ had received repeated ground attacks, mortar fire, and barrages of rocket-propelled grenade fire that weakened the makeshift jungle base over four hours, Stockton believed he had no choice but to commit additional infantry support. The small base held, and the bold, decisive act saved his people. But Stockton lost his command and was reassigned to a desk job in Saigon. He was called a "Lucky Custer" by his critics. But the enlisted men and the officers who served under his command, and those who had survived the ordeal, remained doggedly loyal to the colonel. His legacy continued because the tactics and loyalty he set in motion served the squadron well.

The unit motto proclaimed them "The Boldest Cavalry the World Has Ever Known," and in Southeast Asia they had been proving it daily.

As the war progressed and the squadron earned more credit and honors, commanding the 1st of the 9th became a major stepping stone to making general.

Paccerelli didn't think the present squadron commander would tolerate anyone tarnishing the squadron's reputation, and said as much. It was clear what would be expected of Paccerelli when he took command.

When the squadron commander finally asked Paccerelli if he thought he could handle the job, the captain nodded once and gave a resounding, "Yes, sir!" He knew that he had probably sounded like one of the ass-kissing officers he so detested, but he wanted the assignment and would say whatever the colonel wanted to hear if it came to that. While some officers might fear to take command of a troubled company in a combat zone, George Paccerelli relished the opportunity.

He was a firm believer that the use of small patrols operating behind the lines was the only way to fight and win a guerrilla war, especially with the side benefits of having the 1st of the 9th as one's all-powerful godfather. The multitude of scout, lift, and gunship helicopters, along with the highly mobile Blues as a ready-reaction force, would provide the Lurps with a distinct tactical advantage.

The lieutenant colonel smiled. Paccerelli suspected that the senior officer was reading his mind, which left him feeling awkward and uncomfortable. But the squadron commander seemed satisfied with the captain's response.

"Welcome to the 1st of the 9th, Captain," the colonel said as he relaxed and offered his hand. Paccerelli took it, wondering if the senior officer could feel his wet palm.

The welcome reminded him of something his father, a career navy officer, had told him when he went off to do his first combat tour. It was a speech about ancient Spartan warriors. How they were exhorted to come back from war "with their shields"—that is as victorious and honorable warriors—or "on them," meaning dead.

In a lesser man, the ominous overtone of the briefing would have clouded enthusiasm for the new assignment, but Paccerelli was happy to have the job, though maybe a little concerned. The new command could certainly prove a double-edged sword. Wielding it would require a certain amount of caution. He'd begin with the unsoldierly bearing. That would start with his own appearance. A company commander must always set the standard by example.

Dressed in highly starched jungle fatigues, spit-shined jungle boots, and the stupid OD baseball cap that some silly shit somewhere decided would make good informal headgear, Capt. George Paccerelli was dropped off at the Lurp company compound and left to his own resources.

Under the usual military protocol, Paccerelli should have been escorted to the new command, formally introduced, and provided with a company formation and a change-of-command ceremony. But this time, the task had been left up to Paccerelli himself. That might have been an oversight, but it could also have been that no one wanted to put the outgoing commander through the stress of conducting a change-of-command ceremony for his replacement.

The Cav's Lurps were Paccerelli's, and he'd either turn the company around or wait until a new commanding officer arrived one day, ax in hand, to replace him.

CHAPTER THREE

In January 1968 the 1st Air Cavalry Division had been rushed to Camp Evans from An Khe to help support the overworked Marines assigned to secure the Demilitarized Zone (DMZ). Shifting the three airmobile Cav brigades into the trouble-plagued region was damage control as well as tactical retribution, and the move, code named Operation Jeb Stuart, paid off.

Camp Evans, a former Marine regimental base camp located just west of Highway 1, lay midway between the Imperial City of Hue in Thua Thien Province, and the always volatile Quang Tri Province in the north. The heliborne division had little time to get comfortable in its new surroundings because just as it arrived, the 1968 Tet offensive exploded throughout South Vietnam, and most notably in the I Corps Tactical Zone. From north to south, the Republic of South Vietnam had been divided into four corps tactical zones, and the fallout from the enemy's Tet offensive was being felt everywhere. The Cav had been instrumental in securing much of II Corps, and I Corps would become their newest challenge.

Early on during the Tet offensive, the 1st Cavalry Division was in the thick of the fighting. Both Hue and Quang Tri were targeted by the Viet Cong and North Vietnamese Army. The enemy had overrun both cities in their New Year's offensive, but they had been pushed back out again in the bitterly intense battles that followed. The Cav proved to be a driving force in the enemy's defeat.

Quang Tri was also on the edge of the DMZ. This inappropriately named imaginary line was supposed to serve as a buffer between North and South Vietnam. In fact, it was the focal point for some of the Tet offensive's worst fighting. U.S. Army and Marine infantry manning the base camps and outposts along the DMZ referred to it as the "Dead Man's Zone," and learned early on that any notion of it being "demilitarized" was purely the figment of some politician's overactive imagination. The DMZ and the Ben Hai River that ran through it were more staging areas for countless attacks into South Vietnam. It was also the home of numerous Communist 133mm artillery batteries and rocket launching sites that were hidden among the rolling hills and dense vegetation of the zone. The enemy positions hammered the American and South Vietnamese bases south of the zone daily.

The only east-west highway in the province, Highway 9, ran from the junction with the north-south Highway 1 in Quang Tri City, west to Dong Ha, then on to Cam Lo, Con Thien, Camp Carroll, the Rock Pile, Khe Sanh, and finally to the fortified Special Forces camp at Lang Vei, which overlooked the Laotian border. The highway was little more than a hole-filled toll road where the growing body count was the price of doing business in the war zone, and in that deadly stretch of frontier during Tet and the months thereafter, business was booming. The Green Beret camp at Lang Vei had been overrun by the NVA, led by an assault of Soviet PT-76 tanks while the Marines at Khe Sanh were encircled and besieged and refused to come to their aid.

Taking the point during relief operations along Highway 9 had been the Cav's 1st of the 9th Squadron and Capt. Michael Gooding's Echo Company Lurps. While the 1st of the 9th was the division's premier aerial reconnaissance and quick-reaction force, E Company was its eyes and ears on the ground.

Besides providing crucial information on enemy locations and tactics, Company E had conducted a number of joint patrols with Marine Force Recon and Reconnaissance Battalion teams in mid-March during Operation Pegasus, when the division fought its way west to relieve the trapped and surrounded Marines at Khe Sanh.

The subsequent operation was successful, as the Cav roared into Khe Sanh in just thirty days, keeping the border base from becoming an American Dien Bien Phu. Mobility had been the key to the division's success in the relief of Khe Sanh, and its helicopter air fleet had forced the Viet Cong and NVA to change their strategy. Now the Americans were able to quickly shift entire platoons and companies around the battlefield as aerial rocket artillery (ARA) and heavily armed gunships provided the punch needed to protect the infantry and send the enemy retreating.

While some recon elements used large, lumbering Chinooks rigged with rope ladders to make their insertions, the Cav's Lurps used the smaller UH-1 Hueys to quickly get in and out of their recon zones.

The joint operations combined Lurp and Marine Force Recon teams, producing a first for army and Marine long-range reconnaissance units in the war, and yielded a bonanza of much-needed ground-level intelligence about the rugged mountain regions being invaded by both services.

In late April 1968, as the fighting moved farther down the Annamite Cordillera and into the infamous A Shau Valley, the six-man Lurp teams continued to serve the division well. The heavily forested valley, where entire Special Forces SOG (Special Operations Group) recon teams had been swallowed up whole, served as an omen to the Lurps of E Company.

Despite the fact that the hotly contested piece of real estate had been bombed by a myriad of B-52 Arc Light missions, shelled continually by innumerable artillery barrages, and strafed and blasted by countless helicopter gunship and tac-air sorties, the lush but heavily scarred valley, surrounded by its dark and foreboding mountains, was still very much in the control of the NVA.

After Khe Sanh, the A Shau became one of the 1st Cavalry Division's primary targets, with the 1st of the 9th spearheading the assault and the division's Lurps providing the other edge of the deadly point. However, by early summer, the Lurp company's once sharp image had been dulled, leaving those in power wondering if the long-range patrol unit could still cut the mustard.

Captain Gooding had long since left the command, and a number of temporary commanders had rotated in and out of the job as the division shifted tactical war zones and the platoons and teams were parceled out among the various brigades. Fragmented, the company's platoons were left to their own resources, which was one reason Capt. George Paccerelli, a Special Forces combat veteran, was brought in to clean up the command, close out Lurp operations and prepare the unit for its new role as E Troop, 1st of the 9th Cav.

Paccerelli, though, had other ideas. He believed he could turn the company around. If he could accomplish that, there would be no reason to shut the company down. But before he could put his plan into operation, the division was presented with yet another challenge, and in the 1st Cav "another challenge" usually meant pulling up stakes and moving to another location. And that is exactly what happened.

The new MAC-V commander, Gen. Creighton Abrams, ordered Maj. Gen. George Forsythe's division to saddle up at once and charge south to defend the Republic's capital of Saigon which, according to intelligence sources, was very vulnerable to attack.

The division's new forward home would be in Phuoc Vinh. The divisional rear would operate out of Bien Hoa. The division's three brigades would work primarily out of Tay Ninh, Quan Loi, and Song Be, with a strategic string of fire support bases set up across the area of operations (AO). That force disposition was designed to block the southern and western approaches to the capital by the estimated four North Vietnamese Army divisions waiting just across the border in Cambodia and by the Viet Cong "main force" regiments hiding in the Tay Ninh countryside. The division's new tactical area of responsibility (TAOR) would take in some of the most heavily infiltrated and fortified areas of South Vietnam.

The Cav's tactical shift, labeled Operation Liberty Canyon, officially began 27 October 1968 and ended two weeks later as the final elements of the division completed the 570-mile journey south to III Corps.

With less than three weeks in command, Captain George Paccerelli received word that all units within the division were expected to be in place and operational by 15 November. The veteran soldier carefully selected several team leaders to accompany advance elements of the 1st of the 9th to Phuoc Vinh and secure a site for the unit's new home.

Like any enterprising company commander, Paccerelli gave the advance party of NCOs a wish list for what he wanted and expected in a new company home, then left them in charge. S.Sgt. Charles Windham and the others were to carry out the new assignment. Paccerelli was hopeful of their success, but hardly naive enough to expect perfection. However, he had to count on Windham's judgment to do the best he could for the unit. Paccerelli's mind was on other matters.

The rest of the company personnel, along with nearly twelve thousand division troopers, was slated to follow the advance elements to Phuoc Vinh by C-130 cargo plane. Moves of that size were always logistical nightmares.

Paccerelli knew that the unit's housing needs were secondary to the move itself, a move that took up the bulk of his waking hours. Remaining behind at Camp Evans, the new company commander concentrated on his part of the task. Nothing could be taken for granted or left to chance, so he planned the move carefully, explained everything he expected of his people, then let his junior officers and senior

NCOs carry it out. Leadership involved delegating authority and then getting out of the way so that people could do their jobs. That was why there were different levels of command.

The company's trucks, jeeps, tents, supplies, generators, and other heavy equipment would make the trip south by sea, embarking from Tan My on the coast and utilizing LST-532, a former U.S. Navy vessel named the *Chase County* and manned by a South Korean crew. It would be the first inter-service move of its kind in country, and the voyage down the South China Sea to the New Port docks in Saigon would take three days, which was all well and good. By that time, the advance party would have a better idea where everything was going to go.

The real challenge would be in having everything packed and ready to load at Tan My for the voyage south. The transportation phase of the problem was still the unknown factor. The entire division was deploying south, and every available jeep, truck, and helicopter would be utilized in ferrying tons of supplies and equipment to the Cav's new home in III Corps. The convoy of naval vessels would sail down the coast, then up the Saigon River past the infamous Rung Sat swamps and into New Port.

The Lurp company's table of organization and equipment (TO&E), the chart that defined its organization and authorized equipment, allowed several vehicles for the company, but as the men were packing up and preparing the move, a *host* of jeeps, trucks, and small "mule" transports suddenly appeared in the area of the Lurp compound. Paccerelli decided that there were times when it was best not to look a herd of gift horses in the mouth. He also avoided looking too closely at the fresh paint on the bumpers or the modified vehicle identification numbers and unit designators. Instead, he turned his attention back to the move itself and to the war that kept getting in the way.

By October 25, Company E was ready. Two days ahead of schedule! Morale was high, and the new Lurp company commander was a little surprised to discover his troops were actually properly dressed for the journey. But then, maybe the icebreaking speech he had given at the informal company formation he had called three weeks before had done some good after all. He had ignored the cold reception from the Lurps and had made known his feelings and expectations in no uncertain terms. He had made up his mind before the formation that if he was going to break the ice, then he might as well shatter it.

As the Lurps had fallen out of their hootches, and the TOC and commo shack were left with skeleton crews, the company's assembly area had turned into a small mass of confused and mingling bodies as the NCOs screamed for the Lurps to fall in.

The impromptu formation had been made up of less than two platoons of field Lurps, a platoon of rear-area personnel and a dozen or so new recruits.

"Is that everybody?" a confused Paccerelli asked a senior NCO who was standing to one side.

"Yes, sir!" the NCO shot back as Paccerelli suddenly remembered that the company had teams parceled out to the various Cav brigades operating throughout the division's AO. Of the more than one hundred soldiers on the company roster, fewer than forty were standing in formation before him at the time. He had just discovered one of the underlying problems with the unit. With no centralized command, there was no real company integrity, which accounted for the commander's lack of control over his personnel. No centralized command and no control also meant no continuing training, let alone feel for morale.

He had noticed that some of the Lurps moved quickly into formation while others took their time or moved cautiously. Their faces were a study in confusion and curiosity.

When the unit had finally been assembled, Paccerelli had taken the first few moments to size up the young soldiers in his command to see what he had to work with. Most were white, slender, and in their late teens and early twenties. A scattering of minorities gave the unit some color, but for the most part Company E looked a lot like a rural high-school football team from a small midwestern town that had just been through a very bad season.

Back when he had arrived to take command of Company E, the outgoing company commander had given him a brief tour of the unit area. It had been easy to spot a few of the more obvious problems in the command. A quick glance at the personnel had told Paccerelli that the shabby, ragtag soldiers loitering around the company area not only needed haircuts and shaves, they also needed focus. A number of the soldiers had long, drooping bandito-style mustaches, while several others had beards growing.

Paccerelli smiled, but the result was anything but humorous, and more than one man standing in formation thought he looked like a cobra ready to strike.

When they had fallen out for the company formation, the men wore a variety of uniforms, or parts of uniforms; some had shown up in shorts and rubber shower shoes.

The motley formation reminded Paccerelli of the scruffy line of transients he had seen standing in the soup-kitchen lines when he was a kid. But the long-range patrol company was supposed to be among the division's best soldiers, its elite. And even though he wanted to give the men the benefit of the doubt, he knew he would have to take charge immediately if he was to be effective. Somebody, more likely a number of somebodies, hadn't been doing the job, and in combat, that attitude wasn't just unacceptable, it was downright dangerous.

Military bearing and pride had been drilled into George Paccerelli over a decade and a half of military service until it was just second nature. He was the son of a career naval officer. He was a professional soldier who had worked his way up through the ranks and took great pride in the accomplishment. He intensely disliked career soldiers who called themselves "professionals" but failed to live up to the standard of the profession.

If first impressions meant anything, in this case they confirmed what Paccerelli had already been told at division and squadron headquarters. The Lurp company needed help. Paccerelli had been selected to be that help, and the troubles, like it or not, were officially his.

Only a handful of older NCOs had served in various leadership roles within the company—"older" meaning late twenties to early thirties; junior NCOs and enlisted men made up the bulk of the formation. Many of the junior NCOs were products of the ninety-day Noncommissioned Officer's Candidate Course (they were derisively called "shake and bakes") and had received little or no formal long-range patrol training. Any patrol expertise they had came from on-the-job training in the jungles. Fortunately, if the man survived the process, the OTJ more than made up for what any Stateside course could ever teach them. Many of the junior NCOs were team leaders or assistant team leaders, and those warriors possessed the self-confidence of much older and more mature combat veterans, even though it seemed that their pride had long ago given way to cynicism.

The Lurp trainees were "green" and still going through the company's ten-day Lurp training course. They seemed very uneasy standing in formation among the veterans.

Paccerelli's gaze came to rest on a young lieutenant standing in front of one of the undersized platoons. He could see that the junior officer was less than satisfied with the formation, and maybe the command. According to the TO&E, there were two junior officers in the company, and Paccerelli wasn't certain which one was standing in front of the formation. He'd make the introductions later when he outlined his plan for the company with both officers present.

He suspected that his junior officers were somewhat underutilized, and he made a mental note that once he was settled in, he'd remedy the situation. Since the junior officers usually spent only six months in the company before rotating to a line unit, the captain would soon be shopping around for new officers. However, two wouldn't be enough for what he had in mind. He would need one more to beef up the command with the kind of leadership the unit needed, specifically utilizing one as an operations officer while leaving the remaining two to serve as platoon leaders.

As the company finally came to some semblance of attention, Paccerelli looked around and felt that something was wrong with the formation. He couldn't quite put his finger on it, but it bothered him. After a brief introduction he began a short speech which left little doubt where he stood on soldiering.

"At morning formation, at 0700 hours, I expect to see everyone in the proper military uniform. I expect proper military haircuts, and shaves as well," he said, letting his gaze traverse the formation and then adding, "You don't have to polish your boots unless you're attached to the rear area, but you do have to brush them. You don't stop soldiering while you're in garrison." Paccerelli paused again as his eyes went from one platoon to the next. Some of the veterans began to squirm uncomfortably.

"Uniforms will be jungle fatigues and soft cap, unless it's a formal presentation, in which case the soft cap will be replaced by a steel pot. PT formations will mean bloused boots and T-shirt."

As the new CO spoke, the Lurps stared at him with more than just a little anger and resentment. The lifer was shaking up their world, and they didn't like it.

After outlining his expectations, Paccerelli closed his speech with the historical reference his father had laid on him as he was shipping out on his first combat tour.

"In ancient Greece, the Spartans were known and feared by all their enemies," he said, scanning the formation again and studying their faces. "They were the best-trained and motivated soldiers of their day, and when they went off to fight they were given a single admonition. They were told, 'You have your shields. Return with them or on them.' As Lurps you're special, and it's time for you to pick up your shields and start looking the part. But if any of you feel that you can't meet these requirements, then I'll be more than happy to arrange a transfer."

As a former enlisted man who had worked his way up through the ranks from private to sergeant first class, George Paccerelli knew there would be grumbling. He expected it; GIs always bitched over a sudden change in the status quo. And he knew some would opt to leave the company because of the change. But due to the nature of the work, an assignment to a Lurp company was voluntary. Patrolling deep behind enemy lines with four or five others was just normal duty, but a change in the status quo always caused losses.

Most of the men would stay. Even if their deportment left a little to be desired, it was evident that they were adventurous young men who not only accepted challenges but responded aggressively to them. That was why they volunteered to become Lurps in the first place. They didn't go behind enemy lines with a team of six men because they wanted to play it safe.

"Any questions?" When no one responded, Paccerelli panned his gaze from one platoon to the next and then back again. It had been a rhetorical question. He hadn't really expected anyone to speak up. But plenty of questions would be discussed among the troops after he dismissed the formation. He was counting on it.

"First Sergeant!" he said, calling the senior NCO forward and turning the formation back over to his control.

The first sergeant marched forward, snapped a salute, and waited for Paccerelli to return it.

"Shields? What shields?" one of the Lurps in formation whispered to Sgt. Bob Gill, who laughed and shook his head at the question. Gill turned and saw the concern on the face of Sgt. David McWilliams.

"No shields," Gill said to McWilliams.

"Yeah, but he said shields, and something about swords!" protested the soldier. "Are we going to be issued swords or what?"

"No, we're not going to be issued shields or swords," Gill replied as the confused Lurp NCO looked alarmed.

"Is he serious about morning formations and PT?"

"He seems to be," said one of the older NCOs.

"Yeah, well who in the fuck does he think he is, John Fucking Wayne?" asked another Lurp, frustrated by the shake-up.

"No," came the response from the older soldier. "John Wayne's an actor. This fucker's for real."

Within the first week, a small number of Lurps requested transfers out of the company. For some the latest change was the final straw. For all they knew, their new gung ho captain was just the latest FNG (fucking new guy) to take command. He might or might not work out, but they weren't going to stick around to find out.

The job of a Lurp was tough enough without having to worry about whether the leadership could pass muster. In combat, people died when new leaders fucked up. All of the Purple Hearts in the world didn't make up for dying or losing a limb.

The new CO was an unknown factor, and some Lurps didn't want to pin their hopes on someone they didn't know. Those Lurps who decided it was time to move on often didn't have very far to go. Most joined the Blues platoons of the 1st of the 9th, literally moving from the proverbial frying pan into the fire. The Blues were light infantry, and they saw more than their share of combat in campaigns stretching from the Bong Son plains to the A Shau Valley. If the 1st Cavalry Division had shock troops, they were the Blues. As airmobile light infantry, they pioneered combat helicopter assault tactics, hitting remote enemy bunker complexes or base camps one day, and rappelling in to rescue downed helicopters the next. In some instances, the missions overlapped. They also served as the heavily armed quick-reaction force for the Lurp teams. They were the cavalrymen who always arrived in the nick of time. They were well equipped and well led, and going from the Lurp company to the Blues was a lateral transfer that to some just made good sense. Only a Lurp could fully appreciate the additional fire power the 1st of the 9th offered.

While some Lurps left voluntarily and were offered a choice of where they wanted to be reassigned, those who were caught smoking marijuana or using drugs were kicked out of the unit or court-martialed. Paccerelli suspected he was losing some good people during the transition, but that couldn't be helped. His own bullheadedness and sometime abrasive manner likely contributed to the problem, but he knew that, once he eliminated the troublemakers and established his authority, things would be better. The talent was there. That was obvious. These were good soldiers. Company E was the only all-volunteer unit in the division, and Paccerelli wanted to make that mean something special.

On the plus side, a surprising amount of talent and potential was showing up among the new recruits. One, a new lieutenant named Robert McKenzie, was a fellow mustang. The former NCO had served four years with the 82d Airborne Division before being selected as one of the army's new drill sergeants. He later attended Officers Candidate School and was commissioned. McKenzie had then spent the following year with the Ranger Department at Fort Benning, Georgia, teaching patrolling. At Benning, he put in so much time in the woods that when he returned home from the field, his young daughter, Tina, hid behind her mother until she could identify the powerfully built stranger. The twenty-five-year-old black officer from Mobile, Alabama, greatly impressed George Paccerelli during his interview, both with his background and his bearing. McKenzie was an articulate, intelligent, physically fit young man, and he possessed the experience and self-confidence that most of the other applicants lacked.

The shape of the company was changing daily, the ranks thinning out as more Lurps requested transfers to other units. It was for the better, Paccerelli told himself. It had to be, there was no other choice.

CHAPTER FOUR

George Paccerelli had known by the age of five that he wanted to be a soldier. At that time, his father was a career naval officer serving with the Atlantic Fleet during World War II, and his family was living in a two-story apartment house just outside the naval base at Norfolk, Virginia. The apartment house was on the beach, and he and his brother and friends spent all of their waking hours playing in the ocean or along the shore.

For a young boy, the beach then was an especially exciting place to be since German submarines were active along the coast. From time to time, cargo and goods washed ashore from ships torpedoed offshore.

Home Guard soldiers were stationed about every five hundred yards along the beach to report sightings and to keep people from looting the cargo as well as to protect the public from unexploded ordnance. The Home Guard had been created to replace National Guard units called to active duty. To the five-year-old, the Home-Guard soldiers, who for the most part were veterans of World War I, looked impressive with their British-style helmets, Home Guard uniforms, and old Springfield rifles.

One day while George and several other boys had been building forts in the sand at low tide, one of the older boys spotted an abandoned lifeboat bobbing in the surf ten or fifteen feet away. He swam out to retrieve it as the other boys waded into the water behind him. The tide was coming in, and the waves were washing over the kids. Even though young George was having trouble standing upright in the shoulder-high surf, he stayed with the others.

As the older youth pulled himself over the boat's bow to peer inside, his face went suddenly white, and he quickly let go and screamed for the other boys to run! The lifeboat hadn't been abandoned; the remains of those who had died in the boat were rotting in the sun. Panic ensued, and the boys scrambled back toward the beach.

As he turned to flee, a wave knocked young George off his feet and tumbled him along the bottom in the rough surf. As he tried to get back to his feet, a second wave sent sand and sea water rushing into his open mouth and nose. He was spitting and sputtering and struggling with the water when a uniformed arm reached down and pulled him out.

"There, there," the old soldier said to the five-year-old. "It's going to be okay. I've got you now. You're okay."

The old veteran carried the boy to the beach, returning him to his frightened mother. He then went back to retrieve the boat, his face ashen and cold as he recognized its contents. By then a crowd had gathered, and the Home Guard soldier kept them back, making it safe for the others.

It was then and there that George knew he wanted to be a soldier.

Later, as an enlisted man in the early sixties, he had served his first tour of duty in the secret war in Laos. He was part of a Special Forces advisory team during Operation White Star. He was an A-team light-weapons specialist who had been cross-trained as a medic, but during White Star his A-team had been tasked with advising the Royal Laotian Army, specifically the 16th Group Mobile, in the use of field artillery.

"Field artillery trainers, huh?" asked a surprised Paccerelli when he found out about his new assignment.

The team sergeant only shrugged. "It'll look good on your

friggin' resume," the senior NCO said. "Besides, it's highly coveted in the civilian sector by business types who want to do more than just stab their coworkers in the back. I understand you can get snotty rich on Wall Street blowing away your competition!"

Before departing to Laos, Paccerelli and his comrades underwent a six-month crash course on the 75mm pack howitzer and the 105mm cannon, and for infantrymen, they came away as fair-to-middling cannon cockers. However, when they arrived in Kho Ka Cham, Laos, in 1962, the advisory team quickly discovered they would actually be training and advising a three-battalion infantry regiment in jungle combat operations. The Communist Pathet Lao and their North Vietnamese allies were wreaking havoc throughout the countryside, and the Laotian Army sorely needed the counterinsurgency skills the SF advisers could teach them. As one of legendary Col. Arthur "Bull" Simons's people, the young staff sergeant soon began to draw the attention of those who recognized his leadership skills.

During Officer Candidate School training back in the States, George Paccerelli was one of the few students who sported a Combat Infantryman's Badge and combat jump wings. The enlisted experience had served him well.

His second combat tour in 1966 saw the then first lieutenant George Paccerelli in the Republic of South Vietnam assigned to the remote border camp at Dak Pek as an A-team executive officer. The officer side of his A-team experience was much different from his enlisted stint, and it took a little getting used to. As a mustang officer, Paccerelli wasn't an average first lieutenant. During the previous year, he had spent some time as an A-team leader in Bad Tolz, Germany, which had further helped him to hone and sharpen his leadership skills.

He had also spent time early in his career as an enlisted man in Panama with the 33d Infantry participating in jungle warfare exercises and, combining that with the practical experience he had picked up in Laos, he had a lot of experience to draw on when it came to jungle warfare. What's more, he had discovered that he really loved the jungle and firmly believed that once a soldier came to know and understand it, he was actually safer there than in other combat environments. In some respects, such as cover and concealment, basic wilderness survival, natural shelters, and availability of water, the jungle had it all.

However, to the uninitiated, the jungle appeared to be just the contrary—a totally hostile and unforgiving environment. It aroused a primordial fear in some soldiers as soon as they set foot into the living maze of tangled yellow-green and matted brown shadows. Man against man was one thing. Man against the jungle only complicated matters.

In Vietnam, there weren't any lions, but there were tigers and bears and dozens of the world's most poisonous snakes and disease carrying insects. Plagues and sicknesses accompanied whatever slithered and crawled through the underbrush or hovered in swarms among the trees. Intense tropical heat allowed opportunistic organisms to fester and grow in the slightest scrape or cut. Bloodsucking leeches would crawl up the thigh and into crotch or armpit before biting the flesh and growing fat on life's blood. There were rabid bats and carnivorous rats and destructive swarms of biting ants that ate every living thing in their path. And there were heart-stopping sudden encounters, point-blank ambushes, punji sticks, tiger pits, and booby traps. Still, if you were properly trained and learned to be at ease in the jungle, the risks were reduced dramatically.

Shortly after he arrived at Dak Pek, Paccerelli had his first encounter with the local Viet Cong. He had gone out on what he thought was a "search and avoid" operation in order to familiarize himself with the AO. But during the patrol, they ran into a like-size enemy unit, and in the brief encounter, the two sides had fired each other up until the Viet Cong broke and ran. The enemy soldiers the SF patrol had wounded and killed were carrying an odd mix of World War II U.S. and German weapons and didn't want to take on his patrol. It was his first successful encounter with the Viet Cong and one that would set the stage for things to follow.

CHAPTER FIVE

By mid-October 1967, George Paccerelli had been promoted to captain and sent down the road to nearby Dak Seang to become the A-245 team leader there. The last camp commander, another Special Forces captain, had been medevacked after stepping on a punji stick and running it through his foot. The job and the camp became Paccerelli's.

Prior to arriving at Dak Seang, Paccerelli was briefed by Col. Francis John "Blackjack" Kelly, the 5th Special Forces Group (A) commander in Nha Trang and told what was expected of him. The big, heavyset former Boston policeman laid down the law in both formal and informal terms, the same way a desk sergeant might lay out the beat to a new street cop.

"You will keep a company-size combat/recon patrol out in your AO at all times. You will keep one company in the camp at all times, and you will train the CIDG yards," the veteran senior officer ordered as he outlined the new captain's responsibilities. The CIDGs—Civilian Irregular Defense Group, "yards"—were the indigenous montagnard volunteers hired by Special Forces to serve at remote jungle camps. Known simply as yards, the native hill people were small in stature but big in heart and loyalty. That is, when their loyalties were not strained by the Vietnamese who employed them on both sides.

The Vietnamese often discriminated against the montagnards and referred to them as *moi*, savages. There was little love lost between the two peoples. Three years earlier, the montagnards had risen in revolt against five CIDG camps in II Corps, killing dozens of Vietnamese soldiers before U.S. Special Forces personnel, acting as intermediaries, were able to bring the revolt to a halt after three weeks. The montagnards were pushing for representation in the Vietnamese National Assembly, positions in the local government, quotas in the Vietnamese officer candidate schools. They also wanted their own tribunals, a montagnard national flag, and, in short, recognition for what was rightfully theirs, whether it was the land they occupied or the languages and culture they shared.

The Vietnamese were racially related to the Chinese in the north, while the montagnards' origins came from the same source as the Polynesians. The majority of the 200,000 or so montagnards who made up the twenty-nine tribes inhabited the Central Highlands of South Vietnam, an area crucial to the Communists' plans for taking over the South. After the war against the French, the Viet Minh sent thousands of montagnards north to bind their allegiance to the Communists, while the French, and later Special Forces, signed agreements with the tribes in the south, which over the succeeding years set interesting dynamics in motion. As for the montagnards, they were more aligned to their individual tribes and their own way of life than to any single political entity.

"For the most part you can trust the yards," Paccerelli had been told by other SF personnel who had worked with them. "But there are some who like to straddle the fence at times."

"Work both sides, you mean?"

"No, just their side," one officer explained. "They fight for their village, their people, the Vietnamese—both North and South—and for us! They're loyal and brave, and most of them will stand beside you even when things go to hell in a hurry."

"And the others?"

The officer shrugged indifferently. "They may just run away, figuring that discretion really is the better part of valor, or maybe they won't want to kill some of their cousins who happen to be on the other side. It's nothing personal . . ."

"Just business?"

"Their business! After everyone has screwed them over for so long, their business has become nothing more than survival."

Paccerelli listened and weighed the information.

In his formal briefing, Paccerelli was also told the camp at Dak Seang would also serve as a "drop out" location for SOG teams that had to be extracted by McGuire rig from across the border in Laos, four to five kilometers to the west.

"SOG?" Paccerelli asked. The briefing officer smiled and quickly changed the subject. Paccerelli had never heard of SOG and, judging from the colonel's response to his query, he probably wouldn't hear anything about it from him either.

Paccerelli guessed that SOG had something to do with running recon teams over the border into neighboring Cambodia and Laos where the North Vietnamese and Viet Cong operated openly and unfettered. Maybe SOG performed other missions, too, but it was probably performing over-the-border recon.

Borders didn't matter much to the Communists in Hanoi, and since they were denying they had even soldiers in Laos and Cambodia, let alone bases, the United States could equally deny that it was sending in recon teams to counter the enemy's actions. It was the only reasonable solution to most of those who were intent on winning the war.

Paccerelli was also ordered not to cause any trouble with South Vietnamese Special Forces personnel ("LLDBs"), who would formally be in charge of the camp. He was to prevent the enemy from using the Kontum/Dak Pek highway along his sector of the mountains. The "highway" was a north-south, two-lane dirt road, potholed and poorly maintained. In any state back home, it would have needed upgrading to be considered a logging road.

"What about the enemy troops in the area?" Paccerelli asked.

Colonel Kelly shrugged. "Local VC," he said, and then added that one year earlier, the local VC had overrun the camp Paccerelli was going to. The senior officer leaned forward in his chair and then looked the captain straight in the eyes to emphasize the next point he wanted to make. "We are not going to have another SF camp overrun. Do I make myself clear, Captain?"

The Special Forces camp at Dak Seang was still under construction, not to mention the few inches of mud that covered everything. The daily monsoon rains had flooded the region, and the camp—little more than a construction site at the time—was an exercise in futility caked in orange ooze.

The fortifications were not yet complete, and the camp had all of the charm of a small frontier boomtown sitting smackdab in the middle of hostile Indian country. Besides the men of the Special Forces A-team and their South Vietnamese counterparts, there was also a half-trained battalion of CIDG personnel and their families. In theory the montagnard CIDGs fought on the side of the South Vietnamese, but since the Vietnamese and the montagnards hated one another, the American Special Forces soldiers served as the glue that held the alliance together.

Besides the light machine guns and crew-served weapons, the camp also sported a 4.2-inch mortar and crew. Wrapped in several strands of barbed wire and a perimeter of incomplete bunkers and fighting positions, Dak Seang had a long way to go before it could be considered a fortified camp.

On the helicopter ride out to Dak Seang, the newly promoted captain had noted that he was sweating more than usual, and when he stood to exit the aircraft, he had to catch himself to keep from falling. Since he had been cross-trained as a medic as an enlisted man, he took his own temperature and wasn't surprised to find it at 102 degrees Fahrenheit.

Even though his temperature was sitting at 102 degrees, with the camp still in disarray, Dak Seang was courting disaster. Paccerelli knew that just as well as he knew that he didn't have time to be sick. The war didn't stop just because you weren't feeling well.

The engineer unit Paccerelli had on loan to help complete the camp was doing a credible job, but there were still a few modifications he wanted made, and he couldn't supervise them from a cot. He'd see the team medic later. Finishing the camp had to take top priority.

Besides the unfinished camp, Dak Seang had a dirt airstrip that was capable of handling C-123 and Caribou cargo planes. It was also useful for picking up SOG personnel after they were dropped off from their McGuire rigs at the camp after having done whatever it was they did.

In November 1967, with the camp now well fortified and reasonably complete, Paccerelli decided it was time to personally take out a hundred-man patrol. Along with an American sergeant and two South Vietnamese Special Forces counterparts, he would go out and see who else was in the AO.

There had been a recent report of elephants and headlights being spotted just west of the camp the evening before. That gave the patrol a direction of movement as the company-size element headed out from camp.

"Elephants with headlights, huh?" Paccerelli muttered to the U.S. sergeant. The NCO shrugged.

"Could be pack elephants or maybe those snazzy sleek sports jobs with leather seats and big trunks. What the fuck, it's a mission," he added, smiling. And it would soon prove to be that and a little more because on their first day out they made contact with a small enemy patrol.

When the contact occurred, the enemy soldiers fired their

weapons, dropped their packs and equipment, then quickly ran west toward their cross-border sanctuaries.

A second, smaller battle quickly erupted within the patrol itself as one of the South Vietnamese Special Forces soldiers began punching and kicking the montagnard point man, all the while swearing and threatening to shoot him. Paccerelli and the American sergeant stepped in quickly to stop the beating as the other montagnards formed a circle around the scene.

"He yell at enemy to run!" screamed the angry South Vietnamese LLDB when Paccerelli moved in. "I hear him! We sneak up on Viet Cong. They no hear or see us, but he say, 'Run away! Quickly!' Him Communist!"

It wasn't uncommon for montagnard tribes to divide their services between the Communists and the Saigon government. For some it was merely a survival tool to hedge their bets against whoever eventually won the war. While the montagnards would shoot Vietnamese or Americans, depending upon which side they were on, they might not shoot montagnards on the other side, which apparently had been the case in this instance. They were loyal soldiers, but loyalty to their families and tribe took precedence.

When the warning from the point man had been confirmed, Paccerelli disarmed the man and had the CIDG commander place him under guard. It was a bad end to a good beginning and an omen of things to come.

The rest of the night passed without incident. Guards were posted, watches set, and the highland jungle settled down for another muggy night. The sky overhead was illuminated by a cloud-covered moon, forcing shadows to dance across the trees and foliage.

The next day, somewhere in the dense jungle highlands that surrounded the Dak Som Valley, Paccerelli made a slight map-reading error that wouldn't become apparent until later. Taking his bearings and compass readings, Paccerelli decided he had the patrol's exact location fixed. Everything on the map matched everything on the ground and the surrounding terrain. The American Special Forces sergeant even agreed with Paccerelli's coordinates, as did the South Vietnamese LLDB Special Forces officer, and CIDG company commander. However, instead of being five hundred yards east of the Laotian border, they soon discovered they were one and a half klicks west of the border, which in layman's terms meant they had invaded a neutral country.

The maps they were using were modified copies of old French maps, which were sometimes merely modified copies of earlier Japanese maps. To make matters even worse, they were also in an area where the border had long been disputed, where armies and government agents had shifted the markers back and forth for centuries. The new war had brought about only the latest shift in the previously recognized boundaries. Footpaths and trails that had been reclaimed by the living jungle, and water courses that had changed their beds made combat patrols in the area a graduate-level exercise in practical cartography.

The terrain was a damp blanket of musky jungle with heavily forested hills paralleling the rich green-and-brown valley. There was ample cover and concealment to hide the well-used road that ran through the valley from the east to the west. They would avoid undue attention by staying off the road and skirting the valley floor via the northern ridgeline.

As Paccerelli was making his latest map reading, one of the montagnard scouts flanking the patrol came running back to the column saying he had spotted an enemy outpost with a squad of "Viet Minh" in occupation.

Within minutes, the patrol had maneuvered silently around the outpost and into position. When he was certain that everyone was ready, Paccerelli gave the command to attack. Surprised by the initial volley of fire, several of the Viet Minh fell dead or wounded. Those caught outside the log-reinforced earthen bunker returned fire but had nowhere to go. Even so, calls for them to surrender were answered by small-arms fire. While an M1919 A6 light machine gun kept the enemy buttoned up in the bunker, one of the CIDGs crawled close enough to toss in several grenades. The explosions, followed by a quick frontal assault, ended all resistance. They found five more lifeless bodies scattered about inside the bunker.

"Viet Minh!" the CIDG commander said, surveying the dead enemy soldiers while Paccerelli knelt to study the dead soldiers' weapons and web gear. Both weapons and gear were new, and while the dead guerrillas were dressed as montagnards, Paccerelli could tell they were definitely Vietnamese. The harsh climate and dense jungle of Southeast Asia had a way of weathering men and equipment, but the 7.62mm Kalashnikov assault rifles and canvas web gear carried by the enemy soldiers had no nicks, scars, scrapes, scratches, or fading. Apparently, it was all new issue.

"No commo with Dak Seang," the American sergeant reported to Paccerelli. "But I managed to reach the 4th Infantry Division south of here."

Paccerelli considered the situation. "Ask them to contact Dak Seang and let them know what we have here. Tell them to contact B-24 and let them know the condition of this equipment." B-24, at the provincial capital of Kontum, controlled the Special Forces A-teams in that sector of Vietnam.

The American Special Forces sergeant nodded and passed along the information over the radio. When he had finished, he asked, "We moving out?"

"That's affirmative," said Paccerelli. "Let's see what these guys were guarding."

The patrol didn't have far to go before they found out. Almost two hundred meters up the ridgeline the CIDG point squad opened fire with their carbines and with the M1919 A6, raking the treetops further up the hill. They kept up such a sustained volley of fire that they were in danger of either running out of ammunition for the light machine gun or burning up the barrel.

Paccerelli ran forward to see what was going on and was soon joined by one of the veteran CIDG platoon sergeants. They found one of the montagnard squad leaders firing straight ahead and pointing up at the crest of the jungle covered ridge. "Viet Minh!" he shouted, continuing to spray the area. "Viet Minh!"

At first, neither Paccerelli nor the platoon sergeant, nor the squad leader could see anything but tree branches dangling where they had been shot to hell. Then they saw them. There had to be fifty or more of the best dressed enemy soldiers that any of them had ever seen deploying against them. However, they weren't Viet Minh but North Vietnamese Army regulars. Dressed in brand-new OD green uniforms, wearing pith helmets and canvas boots, the NVA soldiers were carrying full packs on their backs and brandishing new assault rifles. Even more impressive, their bayonets were fixed and they were beginning their assault downhill. Paccerelli could clearly see the long gunmetal gray spikes on the ends of their AK-47s glistening in the sun.

For the first time Paccerelli realized that there were enemy snipers in the trees and more of them in the tree line ahead. The CIDG light machine gun was still laying down a deadly hail of fire, and it and the carefully aimed rifle fire from the American lead patrol were bringing the NVA soldiers down by the dozens.

"Get your people on line! Get them moving forward! Up the hill! Up the hill!" the SF officer screamed at the montagnard squad leader. But before the man could respond, his neck exploded in a shower of blood and mangled tissue. Then Paccerelli saw the back of the CIDG platoon sergeant's head take a tremendous hit a split second before he fell to his knees dead.

Paccerelli took quick aim, shot one advancing enemy soldier, then turned his rifle on three more as he shoved home another magazine. Calling back to his CIDG force, he tried to urge them forward, yelling at the top of his lungs for them to counterassault. It was their only chance. If they could break the enemy assault, the NVA's momentum would crumble.

He looked back over his shoulder. To his horror and dismay, he saw that most of the montagnards were fleeing. However, the two South Vietnamese Special Forces advisers moved forward and joined Paccerelli and his sergeant, trying to stem the attack and stop the fleeing CIDG mercenaries. Those who remained to fight stood side by side, firing uphill at the charging enemy soldiers, then going hand-to-hand with those who had overrun their position.

"Move to the rear!" the captain yelled to the American sergeant. They had to keep one of the two radios safe as the battle surged around and over them.

A brushfire had started in the thick underbrush, and flames were already climbing high into the dry clusters of bamboo along the edge of the jungle. The loud crackling and popping from the exploding stalks added to the din of battle. The choking smoke from the burning vegetation fed the confusion.

Three times, Paccerelli's patrol tried to take the high ground, and three times, the advisers and the fifteen or so CIDG remaining were pushed back by the heavy volume of enemy fire. By then, the Communists were dug in along the top of the ridge.

Once again they got back on line and mounted yet another bayonet charge. The patrol, or what was left of those who had stayed behind, held on even as the fighting became close and furious. The U.S. Special Forces sergeant took out a group of enemy soldiers that was trying to flank their position just as his South Vietnamese counterparts were battling a similar force on the other side.

Up front, Captain Paccerelli and his steadfast CIDGs tried in vain to get the other montagnards to charge up the hill, only to be pushed back again by the overwhelming numbers; numbers that might very well have been equal had not the majority of the CIDGs broken and run.

All around him, incredibly brave and loyal montagnards were dying from head shots while Paccerelli remained standing. This wasn't by accident; NVA marksmen back in the trees were picking off the small pocket of resistance. But the target they couldn't seem to hit was the montagnard light machine gunner who was still tearing up the center of the enemy assault. It was he who forced the enemy to change strategy.

Paccerelli fired at a line of onrushing NVA, killing several, then found himself surrounded by three or four others who seemed intent on taking him prisoner or using him for bayonet drill. He killed one directly in front of him just as the others charged from the sides. Paccerelli twisted to one side, managing to parry the long, thin spike of the closest NVA as one of the others fired at him at point-blank range. Miraculously, the bullets hit Paccerelli's rifle just as the first soldier turned and tried to bayonet him again. The bullets that struck his rifle had destroyed the bolt mechanism and sent the M-16 slamming hard into his side. Instinctively, Paccerelli had parried again at the very moment the bullets struck his rifle, driving the bayonet and the barrel of the enemy soldier's rifle down into his foot. The spike drove through the top of his jungle boot and impaled him to the ground.

The enemy soldier took the time to grin, a costly mistake. Paccerelli dropped his rifle and decked the NVA soldier with a roundhouse punch to the chin. As the enemy soldier reeled, Paccerelli grabbed his AK-47 and flipped the spike bayonet back up and around and into the stunned soldier's neck, burying it up to the rifle's muzzle. Blood spilled back down the rifle and made Paccerelli's grip on the weapon slippery.

As he tried to extract the bayonet and swing back around to kill the other two soldiers, one of the now thoroughly frightened NVA fired again, hitting the big American in the left arm. At such close range the impact of the bullet sent Paccerelli spinning and sprawling back down the hill.

Seeing his commander's plight, the CIDG machine gunner shifted his weapon and swept away the last two enemy soldiers, then turned the gun back toward the main body of NVA, stopping their momentum dead in its tracks. Dead and dying NVA soldiers littered the hillside while the CIDG grabbed up their casualties and retreated back downhill to better defensive positions.

Struggling to get to his feet Paccerelli retrieved a rifle from one of the dead montagnards and quickly yelled for the RTO to bring up the radio. He immediately called for artillery and air support giving his last known coordinates in the clear. When the spotting round hit a couple hundred meters away, the wounded officer adjusted the fire until he had it where he wanted it. *"Fire for effect!"* he screamed into the radio handset.

Just as the 4th Infantry Division artillery rounds fell on the enemy positions further up the ridge, the Communists began firing mortars on the CIDG positions. The impact of mortar rounds soon turned the hillside into a quaking mass of violent explosions. Both sides scrambled for shelter amid the rain of artillery shells and mortar rounds. With shrapnel flying everywhere, there was no safe haven.

Behind Paccerelli, more of the CIDG were fleeing back the way they had come, and the American officer now realized that any chance of taking the high ground had been lost.

A USAF 0–1 piloted by a forward air controller (FAC) was circling overhead. The pilot soon radioed Paccerelli telling him that his patrol was inside Laos and recommending that they get the hell out. It was good advice.

As the CIDG patrol pulled back toward the border, air force fighter/bombers swept down to cover their withdrawal, dropping five-hundred-pound bombs on the enemy positions. After moving a few hundred meters from the ridgeline, the patrol was out of immediate danger. The men stopped to catch their breath as the earth shook and swayed from the large explosions back in the kill zone.

Many of the CIDG soldiers who had run away when the fighting began rejoined the column as it moved back into South Vietnam. To a man, they acted as though nothing had happened, even though the South Vietnamese Special Forces advisers and the CIDG commander were letting their feelings be known. They continued to move west toward the long valley leading to Dak Seang.

Once clear of the border, Paccerelli radioed for helicopters to come out to pick up his wounded. But a Special Forces Mike Force company engaged in a brutal battle had priority on all the available medevacs, so Paccerelli's patrol would have to wait until the following morning. His wounded people would have to make do on their own.

After the patrol secured a defensive site for the night, Paccerelli moved around the perimeter to survey the damage. There were a half dozen killed and eighteen wounded, counting himself. Of those wounded, several were serious and were being treated as best they could by the field medics, who were struggling to accomplish miracles with emergency field surgery. The moans and cries of the badly wounded echoed over the perimeter, but diminished after the administration of morphine.

Trying to stop the bleeding, a montagnard medic started working on Paccerelli's arm. But when he tried to give the captain a shot of morphine, the officer refused. He wanted to have a clear head in case the NVA came after them.

Paccerelli's wounds were treated with antibiotics and bandaged. The arm itself was already growing cold and numb, and he was having trouble feeling his fingers. His foot hurt like a sonofabitch, too, but there wasn't much he could do about that. The Mike Force had Dustoff priority, and from the sounds of the radio transmissions, they needed it.

"Those were North Vietnamese regulars," the American sergeant muttered, taking a seat in the grass. He looked back toward the Laotian border and added, "They must have been lost or something."

"Or something," the captain said.

"Hard-core little bastards, weren't they?"

"Good shots, too," Paccerelli added, thinking of the CIDGs who had died from head shots and wondering how it was the NVA had missed him. Was he to have been an American Special Forces prisoner of war?

"All things considered, we didn't really do too badly. I mean, considering that it's tough to scrimmage with the opposing side when your offensive line suddenly decides it would rather be a track team."

Paccerelli snorted and nodded. Tough indeed, but nice to know in case he got another opportunity to choose who would or wouldn't get to play next time. When things got tense it was good to know exactly who would hang in there. "You did a good job back there," he said.

"Just doing my job, sir," the sergeant answered, but Paccerelli knew better. In any battle there was always one man or two whose actions decided the outcome. In this case a few determined soldiers had kept them from being overrun and damn near turned the battle around. He decided to put those who stayed and fought in for medals. While waiting for the night to close in, he wondered what it might be like to have an entire company like them.

The CIDG soldiers were making too much noise in their perimeter, and the LLDB were making even more yelling at them to keep the noise down. Paccerelli decided that having a unit of specially selected volunteers wouldn't be a bad idea at all.

But that would have to wait until after he had returned from medevac to Camp Zama, Japan, and had time to recover from his wounds. His wife, Barbara, had flown to Japan to be with him, and her concern turned to horror when her husband decided that he wanted to return to Vietnam to complete his tour of duty.

The young mother of two small children was an army wife, but that didn't alleviate any of the fears that naturally arose around such a decision. All around her, other military wives were folding into themselves when informed that their husbands had been killed in action. Their lives and the lives of their children would forever be changed.

If there is ever a moment in the life of a married professional soldier that hurts more than combat inflicted wounds, it's at that precise second when his decision to return to combat registers in the eyes of his wife. Military life is tough enough on a relationship, but during times of war, the burden becomes almost unbearable.

CHAPTER SIX

Upon his return to Nha Trang just after Christmas 1967, the S-1 informed Paccerelli that they had already replaced him at Dak Seang. From the seriousness of his wounds, no one had assumed that he would be coming back soon, if at all. Now, 5th Special Forces Group had to find the captain a new home and offered him a choice of assignments.

"If you want to take over HHC here at Nha Trang, it's all yours," the officer said.

Paccerelli frowned. HHC, 5th Group's Headquarters and Headquarters Company, didn't appeal to him at all. It was a staff position, but it was not for him. George Paccerelli was a warrior.

"Anything else?" he asked, hoping for something that would get him back out in the field.

"SOG-South," the officer replied.

"What's SOG-South?"

The S-1 officer shook his head. "It's classified."

"The SOG or the South?"

"In this case, both," said the S-1, cryptically.

There was no way that he wanted to spend six months in Nha Trang, so he elected to give SOG a try. "I'll take it," Paccerelli said firmly.

The S-1 nodded. "In that case the S-2 will brief you," he said, referring to the intelligence officer.

However, when Paccerelli showed up on the S-2's doorstep

a short time later, the S-2 offered him little by way of a definition.

"What can you tell me about SOG-South?" asked Paccerelli while the S-2 stood shaking his head.

"Not much, why? That where you're going?" he inquired. Paccerelli nodded.

"Well, it's different," said the S-2. But when Paccerelli pressed further, he was told once again that the mission was "classified" and that he would be briefed more about it at the unit. Obviously it was some sort of special operations.

Paccerelli was given his traveling orders and a handshake and told to pack his bags. He then hopped a flight to Saigon where he was picked up by a "civilian" in an unmarked jeep. The driver wore civilian clothes, but his bearing, demeanor, and haircut said he was military. The man checked his ID then drove him to the B-55 team-house bar for a cold beer or two. The cool beer took the edge off the saunalike humidity and buffered the small talk. Other than the usual pleasantries, little else was discussed, so while Paccerelli still didn't know what SOG-South was, he decided that it was probably better than a staff position at Nha Trang.

After the brief welcome, the man in the civilian clothes drove Paccerelli to a safe house near the Saigon race track and told him to stay put until someone from the B-55 SOG training camp at Long Thun picked him up the following day.

The safe house was an old French colonial structure that had probably once served as a home for some midlevel French civil servant before the first Indochina war. It was a weathered, ochre stucco. A matching stucco wall surrounded the house and offered a degree of privacy from the busy street outside. But it would provide little more than momentary protection from even a halfhearted attempt to get at the occupants.

With .45 pistol in hand, Paccerelli performed a methodical search of the house and grounds just to make sure no unpleasant surprises awaited him. When he was satisfied the place hid no dangers, he holstered the weapon and made himself at home. There wasn't much to the house other than the privacy it offered from the street, which was probably why it had been chosen as a safe house.

To his dismay, there was no food in the kitchen or anywhere else in the house, and since he hadn't eaten all day, the growling coming from the pit of his stomach was likely to give away his location to anyone passing on the street outside. Even worse, the odors of roasting meats and pungent spices from the outdoor bistros and nearby restaurants were wafting in over the walls, making him even more ravenous.

Like any good SF trained soldier, Paccerelli seized the initiative, slipped out the back door, crossed the small backyard, and scrambled up and over the wall. Once out into the rear alleyway, he walked a block or so until he found a street vendor selling fried rice and skewered barbecued meat. He was too hungry to closely scrutinize the meat. After the first taste, he still wasn't certain but guessed that its origins were most likely canine. He finished the meat and downed the accompanying bowl of rice with a bottle of Thai beer. When he was finished he purchased a bag of dried squid, another beer, and some Vietnamese cigarettes to take back to the safe house.

He took a different route back to the safe house, and when he was certain he wasn't being followed, he slipped back into the alley, keeping as small a profile as possible as he moved. When he was behind the safe house, he slipped back safely over the wall.

Upon reentering the house, with his booty in one hand and the .45 automatic in the other, he performed a second house search. When he was satisfied once again that the house was empty, George Paccerelli settled in for his stay.

After determining what he thought would be the safest room in the house, he blocked the front and back doors, and the door to his room, and sat back to wait for his transportation to show up. There was no need to make it easy for any unexpected visitors; trick or treat in his neighborhood could get real nasty.

Three days later another unmarked jeep arrived in front of the safe house. It was driven by another individual dressed in civilian clothing and sporting a Browning 9mm on his hip. Soon they were driving off to some great unknown adventure.

Paccerelli quickly learned that SOG was part of a covert U.S. special operations project. The acronym stood for "Studies and Observations Group," which despite the academic sound of its title, didn't say a whole hell of a lot about the unit's activities.

SOG itself was divided into three commands—North, Central, and South. Its members were the ground-level participants, soldiers in the shadow war that was going on in Laos and Cambodia. Their behind-the-lines operations took them deep into the enemy sanctuaries, where the North Vietnamese and Viet Cong Communists claimed they never operated. SOG also conducted operations against North Vietnam, taking the war into the Communist fatherland.

SOG was indeed "spook stuff," and given the deadly nature of the work each SOG command conducted, it sustained an unusually high casualty rate. Those who had served and survived would come away with a view of the war that few others could share, and many of those who were lost would be listed on another unit's casualty roster to disguise the place of death.

SOG had three designations: CCC—Command and Control Central, based in Kontum with recon teams working northern Cambodia and southern Laos; CCN—Command and Control North, based at Da Nang and operating in Laos and in the DMZ; and CCS—Command and Control South, based out of Ban Me Thuot and running missions into central Cambodia.

The experience Captain Paccerelli acquired during his

time with SOG-CCS would combine with what he had already learned at Dak Seang and in Laos during Operation White Star so that by the time he arrived at E Company, LRPs, the seasoned captain had a well-formed notion of how to conduct successful small-unit operations deep behind enemy lines.

The key, he knew, had to do with the quality of people who served in such a unit, and Company E had the right quality people. But like all diamonds in the rough, the Lurps would require a little polishing before they could really shine.

CHAPTER SEVEN

As the convoy left Camp Evans for the coast, Captain Paccerelli took a last look around the compound and chuckled to himself, more in frustration than in humor. The company area had been a real piece of work when he arrived, but in a relatively short time, it had actually started to take shape. No major improvements had been attempted because long before the move to III Corps had been officially announced, rumor had it that the division was going somewhere. And although everyone seemed to have a different idea as to where they would end up, there had been little doubt that it would not be at Camp Evans.

Wherever they ended up, Paccerelli knew that it wouldn't take long to get reestablished and functioning again. Lurps were never big on neatness and military conformity. They were at their best out in the bush, away from base camp. Everyone in the division knew that and most likely resented it, but there existed a degree of reluctant respect for the young soldiers who operated deep in enemy territory.

Long-range reconnaissance was always viewed as a step beyond macho, but Lurps were also viewed as a step above the average infantry soldier, although not necessarily by the average infantry soldier, who sometimes saw the Lurps as a bit too gung ho for their own interests.

On a base the size of Camp Evans or on any of the fire support bases, Lurps always stood out—small groups of heavily armed men dressed in tiger fatigues or cammies, faces hidden by black-and-green greasepaint. They were pretty hard not to notice.

"That's it!" Paccerelli thought to himself. That's what was wrong with the first formation. The company didn't have a guidon!

A guidon was a unit banner or pennant that identified the unit by its military designation. That along with the unit colors proclaimed its history and lineage with long, thin battle streamers that were attached to the supporting flagstaff. In most units the guidon was a source of pride and honor, but in the Lurp company, it was noticeably absent in the formation.

Later, when he asked about the whereabouts of the company guidon, he was told that the unit was "keeping a low profile," a legacy that had begun when the company had been attached to the military intelligence battalion at Camp Radcliff, in An Khe.

When the original detachment was activated under Capt. James D. Jones in late 1966, the eighteen-man unit was indeed keeping a low profile, and even after Capt. Michael Gooding had been brought in to take over command when the second company commander, Capt. David Tucker, had been killed in action, the unit continued to avoid notice.

Gooding had been an intelligence officer before taking command of the Lurps. He had worked hard to keep from drawing attention to the company and what it was doing. But even before Gooding left Vietnam, through a number of transitional commanding officers, and up to the time Paccerelli arrived, the VC and NVA were becoming increasingly aware of the threat posed to them by the Lurps. They began issuing warnings to their units to be on alert for small American recon patrols. By fall of 1968, keeping a low profile had become a moot point in the company. The enemy knew who they were; why hide from the Americans?

Besides the Kit Carson scout who had "rerallied" to the enemy with vital intelligence, there was also the fact that the company was exposed to constant observation from a nearby mountain that overlooked Camp Evans. All that the Viet Cong or NVA had to do was to post an observer on the crest of the mountain to look down and see who was coming and going in the company area.

During the first two weeks after his arrival, every time Paccerelli left his hootch to walk around the company area, he silently thanked God that the Communists didn't have a decent air force or adequate field artillery. He wasn't able to shake the nagging, unsettling feeling that one day the VC or NVA might set up a mortar or rocket tube on the mountain and take careful aim at the ridiculously easy target. There was no *X* to mark the spot, but the enemy gunners didn't need one with the target-rich environment at Camp Evans.

As for the company's interior defenses, he wasn't pleased at all with the scattering of rundown bunkers around the company area. Besides being inadequate for their intended purpose, some of them would have been hard-pressed to protect the occupants even from flying shrapnel. As fighting positions, they were totally useless. There was no established interlocking fire, their locations offered no tactical advantage, and they were poorly constructed and maintained. Those that didn't have puddles of stagnant rainwater inside looked as though they would collapse under the weight of their own roofs. In the case of an enemy penetration of the perimeter, the bunkers would immediately become poorly defended islands of resistance that offered a determined enemy absolutely no challenge in overcoming and destroying them.

Camp Evans was a large camp, but the Viet Cong had succeeded in overrunning larger and better fortified base camps. Anyone who thought it couldn't happen at Evans was only fooling himself. He instructed the first sergeant to correct the situation immediately.

In theory, the bunkers and fighting positions were there to protect the company compound, which consisted of eight large canvas-and-wood-framed personnel hootches arranged in a squared-off half-moon design along with a shower point, a latrine, and a tactical operations center (TOC).

The eight hootches housed the approximately hundred enlisted men and noncommissioned officers that made up the unit. The hootches reminded Paccerelli of the pictures he had seen of the Colorado mining towns at the turn of the century—sun bleached, weather worn. And the pools of mud grew larger with each new monsoon shower.

Along with several senior NCOs, the first sergeant slept in the easternmost hootch. Of the remaining seven hootches, the CP (command post) also served as the orderly room. The CO's sleeping area was in the back, a small room with nothing more than a cot draped with mosquito netting, a single chair, a wooden footlocker, and several nails pounded into the wall to serve as hooks to hang web gear and extra uniforms. But it served its purpose. He hadn't been assigned to the company to make a nest for himself or get too comfortable in his quarters.

The wood-and-canvas hootches opened up to an assembly area used primarily for formations. A portion of the area doubled as a busy volleyball court and was the site of daily sport and entertainment among the company personnel.

Just down from the volleyball area and north of the hootches stood the former company TOC. The huge dugout structure was a beast and was covered with weathered sandbags and questionable timber. It sat over the company area like a giant sleeping water buffalo. In the rain, the hulking monster appeared to be wallowing in the brown-orange ooze. It was totally inadequate for defense, and it seemed to defy the laws of engineering. A direct hit from an enemy 122mm mortar or a B-40 rocket would collapse the entire mess and quite likely kill everyone inside, which would be a monumental tragedy.

Losing the bunker, Paccerelli judged, wouldn't necessarily be a bad thing, but losing its people would be costly. Two of the people who worked in the belly of the beast—staff

sergeants Rudolfo "Rudy" Torres, Jr. and John R. Barnes—
were two of the company's finest assets. Early on, Paccerelli
came to value and appreciate the unique skills and abilities
of the two staff sergeants. Initial briefings with each had impressed the new CO, but his day-to-day observation of their
performance on the job under stressful situations genuinely
impressed Paccerelli and he was pleased with their talents.

In one hour alone with Torres and his commo section, Paccerelli had come away stunned; he had learned more about
communications and signal equipment from Torres in sixty
minutes than he had learned during the two and a half years
he had spent as an enlisted wire foreman and commo chief!
Torres was phenomenal. Nothing was left to chance, and it
was obvious that Torres had been a field Lurp, understanding
well the value and need for reliable commo on patrol.

Paccerelli subsequently learned from Torres's personnel
file that the man had been one of Captain James's original
selections when the Cav Lurp detachment had been formed.
That meant Torres had to be on his second tour of duty or his
third extension. He not only ran the commo shop—he was
the commo shop!

Staff Sergeant Barnes was the company's operations
sergeant and a solid professional who had "been there and
done that," and had the knowledge and confidence that went
with the job. The two NCOs were the backbone of the company, and their strength and posture were truly impressive.

Both were soldiers who just needed to be told the mission
and then left on their own. This left Paccerelli with little to do
but stand back and offer thanks to some recruiting sergeant
or draft board back in the States.

As he later came to know the team leaders and assistant
team leaders over the course of his first month in the company, he could see the glint of polish begin to shine through
the dull finish as well.

However, these were a nucleus of very special men. For
the most part the team leaders were young NCOs or E-4s,

and getting to know their faces and names would take time. Of those he was beginning to know were team leaders Paul O'Brien, Ronald Bitticks, George Kennedy, Walter James "Spanky" Seymour, John E. Eargle, John A. Schutty, Charles D. Windham, and Sergeant (E-5) Michael Echterling and, among the assistant team leaders, men like sergeants Bruce Judkins and John Hutter, and scores of others who filled out the teams.

The company was authorized sixteen six-man patrols, but from Staff Sergeant Barnes, Paccerelli had learned that the company was rarely able to run more than twelve patrols at a time. Despite combat losses, illness, and individual rotation dates for soldiers completing their tours, the company ran as many six-man teams as possible. When there weren't enough personnel, the teams went out in five-man patrols.

One of his initial changes was the implementation of one-on-one debriefings with the team leaders, right after the team intel debriefing. That was done in order to learn more about the conduct of the individual team members while on patrol, how they behaved under fire and what might be their potential as future team leaders or assistant team leaders.

He also wanted to know when a man's actions warranted a decoration or a transfer from the unit. Paccerelli believed that if the patrols were involved in running firefights with anywhere from thirty to three thousand enemy soldiers, then there were always individuals who deserved decorations. He let his NCOs and officers know his position on the matter and often reiterated the fact.

The issue of awards and decorations was something that upset Paccerelli from his days in the Special Forces. He knew that when a man in SF received a Bronze Star for valor then more than likely that soldier deserved a Silver Star or Distinguished Service Cross.

In reality, most Special Forces soldiers counted themselves lucky if someone remembered to award them a Combat Infantryman Badge, or a Purple Heart if they were wounded!

Paccerelli vowed to himself that wouldn't be the case with his company. The awards system had been put in place to single out for public notice those who had earned recognition for their accomplishments. It was never intended to be a special program for ticket punchers who needed to rack up the medals to further their careers.

If a commanding officer subverted the process, then it created an avenue for dissension and, in effect, told the individual soldier that the officer didn't value him or give a damn about his welfare or his career. Paccerelli decided that wouldn't happen in his company, not while he was the commander.

Writing up awards and obtaining statements from witnesses took time, which he suspected was part of the actual problem, so he offered another approach to his NCOs. "If you think someone deserves an award for his actions, then write something down, submit it, and we'll take it from there," he told the team leaders and senior NCOs. "You're in the position to know and do something about it."

After going over company reports and records, Captain Paccerelli realized that, besides the awards business, a few other matters needed attending to. During a company briefing with his officers and senior NCOs, he shared his concerns with them.

"Gentlemen," the captain said, with a coolness about him that read like the calm before the storm. "I've been going over company records, and let me just say that I'm disturbed by the callous manner in which several key tasks are being handled, if they are even being handled at all!

"Specifically, there are three things that are really bothering me—I mean, besides the lack of a company guidon," Paccerelli offered as several of the senior NCOs suddenly began scribbling madly in their note pads. "First, acts of valor are never to be downplayed as the men's 'just doing their job.'

"In each combat action, the deeds of one or more men always make a difference, and damn it, they should be rewarded!

"Second, the low number of promotions bothers me, too. I've researched the records, and I can find no evidence that there has been any use in this company of impact promotions. Can anyone tell me why we're not promoting qualified personnel?"

Nobody spoke as the storm grew closer. "Okay, let's move on to the third point; there seems to be a lack of an established program for recruitment, nor is there any type of public relations advertising the deeds and accomplishments of the unit."

A senior NCO suddenly stepped forward to protest. "But . . . but sir, we're . . ." the NCO tried to say as Paccerelli raised a hand and cut him off.

"We're what, Sergeant? A supersecret army organization? To hell with that!" he yelled. "I want those sonsofbitches in the north and their Viet Cong buddies to know and fear us! Do you hear me?"

From the silence that greeted his rhetorical question, everyone seemed to understand.

"Three things," he continued, holding up three fingers to emphasize the points he had just made.

"And a company guidon," added one of the senior NCOs.

"Yes, and a company guidon."

There had been a whirlwind of change in the short time Paccerelli had been in command, and the Lurps had adapted rather well. Even the company area was looking considerably better than when the new CO had arrived.

He wasn't sure what to expect when they pulled into Phuoc Vinh, but he suspected that it, too, would take a lot of work, so with a final look around the old Lurp compound at Camp Evans, Capt. George Paccerelli headed for the landing strip.

The war in I Corps was behind them, and the new war in III Corps was just beginning. The Cav Lurps were destined to make their mark under the leadership of their new commanding officer.

CHAPTER EIGHT

One of the lieutenants accompanied the vehicles and heavy equipment on the seaborne leg of the journey south, while the company commander, the operations group, most of the field personnel, and Lurp, the company's mongrel mascot, made the trip by air.

The flight south was accomplished by U.S. Air Force C-130s. The journey was loud, bumpy, and smelled of JP-4 jet fuel. When the plane finally touched down hours later in Phuoc Vinh, Paccerelli stepped down from the ramp, uncertain of what he would find. But the NCOIC of his advance party was standing there. He saluted, a smile on his face. Paccerelli felt a whole lot better about the move.

The senior NCO ushered the Lurps to their new company area, and along the way, the newcomers got their first good look at the former 1st Infantry Division base camp and its backwater, plantationlike surroundings. Phuoc Vinh was in the heart of Phuoc Long Province, the home of the famous Michelin rubber plantation. Unfortunately, the city was directly in the path of any enemy advance moving on Saigon.

Like most of III Corps, Phuoc Vinh was relatively flat. The major exceptions were the five thousand-foot Nui Ba Den in Tay Ninh Province and the slightly lower Nui Ba Ra near Phuoc Binh River in Phuoc Long Province. The region was heavily forested, and to the west and northwest it became dense double- and sometimes triple-canopy jungle. The carefully maintained rubber plantations that dotted the region

floated like manicured islands of civilization in the dense
tangle of bamboo thickets and tropical forests. Operational
landing zones and fire support bases were being established,
at that very moment, to interfere with the enemy's ability to
move or maneuver. LZs Grant, Carolyn, and Eleanor were set
up along major enemy infiltration points to deny the Communists access into the Cav's new area of operatioɪ.s while
artillery batteries on fire support bases Dot, Billy, Buttons,
Phyllis, Jamie, and Ike pounded the point home.

The war in III Corps proved to be considerably different
from that in I Corps. Even the soil in III Corps was different.
The Phuoc Vinh base was built on a fine orange sheet of
powdered clay. It was everywhere and got into everything,
and during the seasonal rains, the dust and loose soil turned
into a sticky morass of orange mud. Paccerelli had experienced that before and knew that walking around the base during the height of the monsoon season would take some
doing.

As for the base camp itself, the design was typical army
tropical flair. The forward base camps were little more than
frontier boomtowns, shantylike in appearance and design,
and as such, they offered no sense of permanence to the eyes
of the beholder. Such camps followed the war, and their un-
stylistic form followed primal functionality. The base camp
itself was laid out to surround the all-important flight line—
the lifeline in and out of Phuoc Vinh. The perimeter was extended outward with the help of giant bulldozers, and ringed
with barbed and concertina wire to protect the aircraft and
the personnel from enemy sappers. Olive-drab sandbagged
bunkers, fighting positions, trenches, and protective gun tow-
ers were erected along the perimeter to oversee the defense
of the base camp that would ultimately house the forward elements of the division. The Cav's rear area would remain at
Bien Hoa, twenty miles northwest of Saigon. It would house
the division's logistical and clerical support, and the Cav's replacement depot. The division's three-day in-country indoc-

trination course for new arrivals provided the replacements with a working understanding of helicopter-based operations and the threats the soldiers faced in Vietnam. The Cav shared the Bien Hoa base with the U.S. Air Force. The differences between the two services' facilities were startling. The air force had all the modern conveniences in its facilities—elaborate clubs, snack bars, tailor and gift shops—connected by paved roads and even a bus system! The army side of Bien Hoa was bleak and dreary. The paved road ended where the army's control began. The 1st Cavalry Division's rear area reflected the dozens of other U.S. Army base camps throughout the Republic of South Vietnam.

Like Bien Hoa, the barracks at Phuoc Vinh were single-story wooden structures set on concrete slabs and topped with corrugated sheet-metal roofs. The basic buildings were surrounded by protective four-foot-high sandbag walls, and access into the hootches was through spring-loaded screen doors located at the front and rear of each building. There were open rafters, torn screen windows with drop wooden shutters, and thin plywood walls. Latrines were four-seat outhouses or open urinals made from empty rocket-packing tubes inserted into the ground at an angle, the open end covered by a piece of screening. Shower facilities consisted of fifty-five-gallon drums or modified fuel tanks elevated over a closet-size outbuilding. The drums and fuel tanks were filled with nonpotable water and offered cold showers in the early mornings and lukewarm showers in the late afternoons. By evening, the shower points were usually out of water.

The new company area was next to the airfield and just east of the new C Troop and the 1st of the 9th headquarters areas. The Lurp compound was situated on what Paccerelli describes as a section of ground shaped like the blade of a butter knife, and surrounded on three sides by dirt roads. The Lurp company commander shook his head, thinking that it made an ideal target for enemy mortars.

A few days later, the first incoming rockets and mortars began slamming into the Phuoc Vinh base camp, a hint of things to come. Luckily for the Lurps, the rockets and mortar rounds fell on the nearby airfield and, of course, the huge aircraft hangar just across the road from their compound. Paccerelli thought their luck would change when the Communists learned where to zero their tubes.

There were two single-story barracks on a trail on the west side of the company area. On the north end was a large bunker suitable only for protection from incoming rockets and mortars. But the bunker would be a death trap during a ground attack. As Paccerelli walked the new company area, he made mental notes and offered comments and suggestions to his senior NCOs.

On the east side of the company area, two wooden barracks were placed side by side, facing east to west. The first one, he decided, would serve as the company command post and TOC. The other would be used as an indoor classroom and the intel center.

Both platoon barracks had protective bunkers attached directly to them, but upon inspection, it was discovered that they were full of stagnant water and in need of major repair. Behind the 2d Platoon barracks, at the far end of the company area, stood a wooden latrine and a separate shower point. All things considered, the new company area was much better than what the Lurps had had back at Camp Evans, but it would still take a lot of sweat and blood to turn it into what Paccerelli had in mind.

As Paccerelli entered the troop barracks, he saw they were a mess. There was dirt and debris everywhere, and only a handful of bunks had been left for his soldiers. However, when he returned a short time later, he was surprised to discover that someone had come up with enough bunks for every man in the company, as well as a few other creature comforts such as lounge chairs and lamps. Several of the

Lurps were busy nailing empty rocket shipping crates to the walls to serve as desks, while others were turning wooden grenade cases into stools and tables.

The November sky was unusually clear and warm during the waning days of the Vietnamese southern monsoon season, and the only storm clouds found to be brewing over the Lurp compound at Phuoc Vinh were behind the angry eyes of Capt. George Paccerelli.

The Lurp company commander stewed silently as he completed his walk through the new company area, surveying the mess. And it was definitely a mess. Dirt, garbage, litter, and debris were everywhere. The sandbag blast walls surrounding all the buildings were collapsed in some places and leaking sand in others.

The Cav was taking over Phuoc Vinh from the 1st Infantry Division, and the Big Red One soldiers had left the base camp in a shambles. Cleaning it would be one thing, but repairing the damage and general state of the place would take time.

"This the best we could do?" the captain inquired of Staff Sergeant Windham and the others in the advance party who had secured the site.

Several of the NCOs nodded, while one of them offered, "Unfortunately, sir, this is as good as it gets."

"Then we make it home, and we make it better," said the captain.

"This your 'when you get lemons, make lemonade' speech, Captain?"

Paccerelli laughed. "Something like that," he said.

"I thought so," said the NCO. "This place seems to have a whole shitload of lemons."

CHAPTER NINE

The ferry service from I Corps to III Corps went off without any major hitches, and by the first week in November, the road convoy wheeled into the company compound at Phuoc Vinh.

The first sergeant went to work immediately, getting things organized, and shortly afterward, the company compound began to take shape. The orderly room was set up in the west end of the building with the first sergeant's desk on the right and the company clerk's desk on the left. A hallway behind them led to the rear of the building and stopped in front of two small rooms. The first would serve as the CO's office with space for a table and a couple of chairs—one for the commanding officer and another for a single visitor. The second room would be Paccerelli's living quarters, set up with a bunk, mosquito netting, and a single footlocker.

Farther on, the building opened into a large area where Staff Sergeant Barnes set up his operations center and Staff Sergeant Torres his commo section. Barnes had also begun work setting up a defensible position atop the large bunker, ringing it with sandbags and gun positions.

The company was an exercise in well-organized activity and the ex-SF captain was amazed at how quickly things were coming together. As the orderly room, operations, and commo sections were being completed, the field platoons were moving into the barracks. The 1st Platoon and communications section personnel were in the northernmost bar-

racks, the 2d Platoon and the remainder of the headquarters
section were getting comfortable in the southernmost barracks. Senior NCO billets were in the rear of each platoon's
barracks.

The trip south brought with it an additional benefit that
none of the previous company commanders had enjoyed. For
the first time since its inception, the entire company was in
one place. Company E was a whole company again. Rather
than have the teams farmed out to the various brigades covering a one-thousand-square-mile area of operations, the
company area at Phuoc Vinh would serve as a single, centralized command.

That meant the Lurps would no longer feel like bastard
stepchildren left to the questionable hospitality of the fickle
brigade commanders. In the past, depending upon their assignments with the brigades, the Lurp teams were sometimes
relegated to pulling guard duty outside base camps or sitting
on LPs and OPs outside the wire at some out-of-the-way fire
support base.

Some of the veteran team leaders complained bitterly
about their misuse, pointing out that the grunts could pull
perimeter duty themselves. While their complaints were
valid, nothing had been done to change the situation. With
the escalation brought on by the Tet offensive and the constant shifting of the division's resources to put out one fire
after another, the complaints of the team leaders naturally
took a back seat to more pressing concerns.

Being attached to the 1st of the 9th helped a lot, as did the
new situation at Phuoc Vinh. Paccerelli worked hard to capitalize on the company's good fortune.

Under the new SOP, the company would provide each of
the brigades with a Lurp liaison team consisting of a staff
sergeant and a radio operator. The Lurps would establish and
maintain two radio-relay teams atop the two largest mountains in the AO—Nui Ba Den (Black Virgin Mountain) near
Tay Ninh to cover the western half of the division's area of

operations, and Nui Ba Ra (White Virgin Mountain) near Song Be to cover the eastern half. The liaison teams would live with the units assigned to provide security at the radio-relay sites, and provide commo to the recon teams out in the field twenty-four hours a day. When a patrol called in a situation report (sitrep), the relay station would forward the information to the company operations center back at Phuoc Vinh, which in turn would pass it on to the squadron operations center, which would then forward the report to division. The stress level on a relay team was no lower than it was on one of the recon teams, but the relay-team jobs usually went to experienced team members who had done their time in the field and deserved a physically less demanding position.

Since the company didn't have its own mess facilities, the Lurps "dined" with the 1st of the 9th. In return for the favor, they helped the Cav with perimeter defense responsibilities at the Phuoc Vinh base camp, manning a series of bunkers and a single guard tower.

The first sergeant and the senior NCOs slept in the company area, but the junior officers were housed with the 1st of the 9th, since the squadron was officer heavy and could easily accommodate two officers in one of its BOQs. An added benefit was that the arrangement allowed the company officers to get to know some of the squadron officers, and that helped to bridge the gap that had existed between the two units prior to the realignment. Good relations and friendships made it easier to ask for special favors, like when a team was in heavy contact at night and needed an emergency extraction. Or, on the flip side, when a squadron helicopter was shot down and volunteers were needed to rappel in to rescue the survivors.

Attitudes were changing, but it was a slow, methodical process. Trust would have to be built between the two units, and that would take time.

CHAPTER TEN

Since Paccerelli saw no need for a company executive officer, he decided to designate 1st Lt. Robert McKenzie as the operations officer and pair him up with Staff Sergeant Barnes. The job would help the young officer develop his knowledge and understanding of the art of patrolling, and Barnes would be a good mentor.

It wasn't anything personal against the other two officers who he had put in charge of the platoons. Lieutenants Donald Keldsen and John Butkovich were both Ranger School graduates, and the Ranger School was a great introduction to combat patrolling and the arts and crafts of movement in the enemy's backyard. But only on-the-job training, reinforced by classroom work, could prepare a man for long-range recon patrolling and offer him a deep appreciation of terrain and the skills of the hunter and tracker. All three lieutenants were fine officers who showed excellent potential, especially McKenzie, and now it was time to help bring out that potential.

But both Keldsen and Butkovich were nearing the end of their tours of duty with the Lurp company, so Paccerelli had already interviewed and approved a couple of new lieutenants to replace them. Lieutenants William Bell and Donald Malcolm would soon arrive in the company area. Paccerelli didn't want Keldsen or Butkovich to go, but the junior officers were typically assigned to the company for a period of six months. That meant that just as they were getting up to speed with their duties, it was time for them to leave. The Cav, like most other combat units of its kind, sorely needed experienced junior officers and NCOs.

The company would also be getting a new first shirt because First Sergeant Dennison had left. Jerry L. Price was brought in to replace him. Paccerelli liked Price immediately and saw him as a strong asset to the company. Price was a veteran paratrooper who looked every bit the part and knew how to make things happen. A good top sergeant was the prime motivator for any unit, its overseer, top dog, and chief shit disturber, and Price appeared to be that much and more. He knew he had a job to do, and nothing else was important.

With the officers' assignments taken care of and a new first sergeant on the way, Paccerelli turned his attention to the company's in-house training program. It was good as far as it went, but it needed to go further to insure the proper preparation of the newly assigned recruits. At seven to ten days in duration, it was far too brief to cover everything that needed to be taught. He went over the training schedule with the team leaders and the training NCO, listened to their comments and suggestions, and then added a few things of his own. Paccerelli didn't order the changes to be made. Instead, he left the development and implementation of the program to his NCOs.

The course was lengthened to twelve days and encompassed every aspect of jungle patrolling he and his NCOs could think of: map reading, commo, ambush techniques, immediate-action drills, Viet Cong and NVA tactics and techniques, enemy weapons and familiarization training, artillery adjustment (both mortar and cannon fire), tac air adjustment, aerial rocket or helicopter gunship adjustment, infiltration and extraction techniques, rappelling, and emergency medical procedures. Formal classroom instruction was mixed with an equal amount of hands-on training and a healthy dose of physical fitness conditioning.

PT began with predawn calisthenics and a three- to five-mile run, complete with individual weapon and "simulated" combat load. The simulated combat load was a thirty-pound sandbag stuffed in the bottom of a rucksack. In the field on a real mission, the actual weight of a Lurp's rucksack ran closer to one hundred pounds so an individual had to be in great shape to successfully hump the jungle. If they were in contact, the Lurps would drop their rucksacks and fight with their weapons and LBE—the load bearing equipment that held twenty to twenty-five eighteen-round magazines, four to five grenades, canteen, knife, McGuire rig rope, and in the case of the team member who packed the M-79 grenade launcher as a backup weapon, a specially fitted vest that carried eighteen or so high-explosive rounds.

Training had to be realistic and was modified from time to time to meet the needs of the team. If there was any disagreement or uncertainty as to exactly what the CO had in mind, then it became clear to all during any one of a number of briefings he held with his NCOs and officers.

During these briefings, he explained there were things he had learned and used in the jungle that the schools seemed to have forgotten or overlooked, such as shaking black pepper on your trail to neutralize the olfactory senses of tracker dogs the enemy might send after you, which the Viet Cong did on many an occasion.

"The men need more knowledge of the enemy's uniforms, weapons, and tactics," he pointed out. "I'm a firm believer that if you know your enemy, then you can defeat him. The NVA and Viet Cong may be brave, but they also have to rank as some of the dumbest soldiers that God ever put on this earth! Their lack of individual initiative, their inability to rapidly change tactics or learn from their mistakes has to be taught to our people and capitalized on.

"Survival in combat isn't merely a matter of luck," he added. "It maybe plays a 20 percent role in the final outcome. The other 80 percent is training, and I mean, good, no-bullshit, hard-core training.

"It's critical to know when to shoot and when to scoot; when to dive and when to charge; when to roll right and when to crawl left; when to calmly aim and squeeze off the shots and when to recon by fire; and when to keep your damn head and butt down! These may sound like trivial clichés, but war makes them deadly clichés.

"On patrol you can never assume it's a monkey, a barking deer, or an abandoned bunker or campsite, just like you never assume that the Rogers' Rangers rules are outdated just because he compiled them in the seventeen hundreds, or that the enemy hasn't read them or the equivalent. I want the men in the company to be able to identify the smell of a fish and rice-flavored latrine or the smell of *nuoc mam* farts because those odors mean Vietnamese!

"I'll tell you right now that the reaction of an enemy soldier to a face-to-face encounter with a fully camouflaged Lurp is absolutely 'nothing'—at least for a second or two—time enough for us to react. One well-aimed shot here is better than a full magazine on automatic fire. Also, never underestimate the intelligence nor the stupidity of the enemy. And finally, never believe your own propaganda nor underestimate its effectiveness."

While the captain's informal "lessons learned" were offered as suggestions and recommendations, Paccerelli insisted that the instructors for the training program be former team leaders or assistant team leaders, men who knew the job.

From the Marine Corps, Paccerelli borrowed the "every Marine's a rifleman" concept and applied it to the entire company. First and foremost, he wanted every man in the company to be an operational Lurp, regardless of the duties he was assigned.

"All headquarters jobs, Captain?" asked one of the officers searching for clarification.

Paccerelli nodded. "All of them. That means successful completion of Lurp training, time on operational patrols, and rear jobs only for those who have danced to the tune of AK-47s."

Turning to his operations officer, Paccerelli said, "I also want a picture taken of every team that goes out."

Lieutenant McKenzie had the sense not to question why. He waited . . .

"In case we lose a team or any member of a team, I don't want any doubt about who we're rushing in to find. An updated picture is critical when it comes to searching for MIAs."

From the unit fund the company commander ordered 52d Infantry crests from Japan and authorized their use on the Lurps' fatigue caps and right breast pocket. While it seemed a trivial thing to some, it was easy to see the impact the unit insignia had upon the men, who wore them with pride and distinction.

Slowly, the company was changing, but the metamorphosis would have a way to go before the changes would be considered SOP. To help initiate the changes, Paccerelli established a company newsletter so that the Lurps could have something to back up instructions and announcements made at morning formation.

On a daily basis, it seemed that most of the CO's battles had been against inertia, and if he was still finding pockets of resistance within the company, he was also battling the sarcasm and doubt of a few officers within the 1st of the 9th during the daily squadron briefings, especially after night contacts during which a team reported contact with an overwhelming enemy force. Usually, by the time the squadron's gunships got on station the only tracers they could see were those of the Lurps.

"Gee, you don't think they were just trying to get out of the field, do you?" one pilot sneered as Paccerelli jumped to his feet to face the critic.

"Even the Viet Cong aren't stupid enough to give away their positions to gunships. Obviously, they had ceased fire or maybe they decided that it wasn't worth it when you showed up on station."

"If they were there at all!"

Paccerelli eyed the pilot coldly, his words careful and deliberate. "If my people said they were in contact, then they were in contact. Maybe you just weren't close enough to the ground to see the enemy."

"*At ease*, gentlemen!" the squadron's sergeant major would snap to interrupt the escalating confrontation. A trained boxer, Paccerelli certainly didn't mind going toe-to-toe with his critics, or even further if need be, and there were times during that first month when the Lurp commanding officer half expected the squadron commander to relieve him for his tit-for-tat defense of the company during those briefings. He was still getting almost daily ass chewings. But that went along with cleaning up the company. The sarcasm and the insults were another matter entirely. Once during squadron briefing, after he had jumped to the defense of one of his teams, a pilot even asked if he drank before he attended the briefings. Paccerelli was up in an instant, turning to face the smart-ass.

"What did you say?"

"Eh . . . nothing, Captain. It . . . it was just a joke."

Paccerelli's eyes narrowed as he pushed up closer to the critic. "I don't like the joke. I don't like it at all," he said as the pilot nodded nervously and a senior officer brought them back to order.

He didn't drink before the briefings, let alone off duty enough to warrant such a smart-ass remark, and he was quick to let the jerk and the others know it. He kept a bottle of Johnny Walker Black Label in his footlocker, and allowed himself a shot a week, but that was it. His anger didn't stem from alcohol but from the abuse his people were taking from some of the hotshots who never, ever stepped foot in the jungle, let alone pulled a long-range patrol. The 1st of the 9th had some great pilots—no question about it—but they also had their share of assholes as well. Every unit did. And it didn't help matters any that men who went into reconnaissance work often held strong opinions.

He was certain he was earning a reputation as a "hard-core sonofabitch," but he shrugged it off; that was business. However, he wouldn't tolerate personal attacks, let alone attacks or cheap shots on his people. The company was changing, and those who had remained with the unit were working their asses off to make it better, which was why Paccerelli defended them.

He estimated that he was getting his ass chewed out by the colonel at least every third day or so, and by Thanksgiving, he half expected to see a 1st of the 9th officer with flight wings and crossed sabers on a black Stetson cavalry hat knocking on his hootch door and saying he was there to take over.

At issue early on was the credibility of the Lurps themselves, which Paccerelli defended on a daily basis. Not once did he hear criticism of an aero-scout's report of contact or actions taken, even while potshots were being directed at the Lurp reports. It seemed to Paccerelli that his Lurps were trapped in the middle of a free-fire zone. While it never came to blows, it sometimes got very heated.

The heat finally began to die down at the end of the monsoon season when the changes in the company, like the change in the weather, became apparent, even to the casual observer.

When one of his company's teams ambushed a squad of Viet Cong soldiers and brought back maps and documents, the Lurp company commander was ecstatic to discover that among them was a VC directive ordering its soldiers not to fire on the division's helicopters since ". . . it invited more trouble and attention."

Paccerelli not only felt vindicated but he actually savored the intelligence analyst's translation of the report as he brought his copy to one of the morning briefings and read it to those assembled.

There would still be the occasional snide comment or remark, which Paccerelli would immediately counter, but any talk of muffling the identity of the company seemed to disappear as Company E (LRP) slowly began to earn back its respect within the squadron and the division.

CHAPTER ELEVEN

Staff sergeants Stan Lento and Guy R. McConnell, Jr., didn't look like poster boy Lurps to Paccerelli, but after making it through the company training the two short, stocky soldiers, along with the other volunteers in the class, were congratulated by the commanding officer and the NCOs before being assigned to one of the company's eight operational teams. Well, Lento and the others were anyway.

McConnell had the misfortune of breaking his wrist on the last day of training. New guys were always an unknown factor, and until they had a few missions under their belts—their "cherry" missions to prove themselves—they were viewed as liabilities, FNGs to be scorned and berated. New guys with broken bones were a whole new subcategory.

It didn't help McConnell either that he was a shake-and-bake sergeant who, with his quiet demeanor and cherubic expression, looked more like a history professor at a midwestern junior college than a would-be death-dealing commando.

"Shake and bake" was the name GIs gave to the graduates of the Noncommissioned Officer Candidate Course at Fort Benning, Georgia, because of the brevity of the course. They were the "ninety-day wonders" of the Vietnam War. The course provided the combat infantry with young, enthusiastic NCOs who, if they didn't have the experience to lead soldiers in combat, at least had the basics. Or so the theory went.

Soldiers who had worked their way up through the ranks held them in lesser regard, as did some officers.

McConnell had done well in the revamped Lurp training program and seemed anxious to prove himself, just as Lento was doing. According to several team leaders who had taken him out on patrols, the freckle-faced potato farmer from Maine had done what was expected of him and had the "feel" and the instincts of someone with a lot more combat experience. One of those team leaders was Sgt. Bob Gill, who knew that Lento would work out well and said as much. Coming from Gill, it was high praise.

Sp4. Craig Leerburg was another recent Lurp training graduate, and the affable blond soldier was also doing well on patrol. His team leaders praised him during the one-on-ones with the CO and said he showed good potential. He was a hunter at heart, and his good woodsmanship showed. What's more, he seemed to like the thrill of going behind the lines and the adrenaline rush it provided. Like many of the other Lurps in E Company, he soon came to view the scrub brush on the mountains and the vast fields of elephant grass in their area of operations with some degree of comfort.

However, if Lento, McConnell, or Leerburg ever entertained thoughts about becoming comfortable with III Corps, their comfort level, like many of the other Lurps in the unit, was tempered by an understanding of exactly what they were facing in the region.

"Up north the area was so steep that we'd have to tie ourselves to trees at times so we wouldn't fall down the hillsides when we slept," offered Sgt. Dwight "Bull" Durham, a veteran Lurp, who was considered by some to be the heart of the company. Durham, an Oklahoma native, had just finished going over the company song, a reworking of the country western classic, "Ghost Riders in the Sky." Durham's version was about a six-man team that had been surrounded by enemy soldiers, the tag line being ". . . with a 16 on their shoulder and a claymore in their pack, six men went out that day, but only he came back."

"The nice thing about it was that the enemy couldn't always just walk right up to you. It took work, and they made noise," Durham said.

"No shit, and it was easy sometimes to tell where Charlie would congregate because there were only so many watering holes!" chimed in another.

"And here?" asked Lento.

"Here the watering holes are everywhere and so are the trails, which means the fuckers can walk up on you by accident and it's 'oh shit!' time real quick. Look at what just happened to the Dirty Half Dozen!"

"The who?" asked one of the new Lurps.

Another said, "What?"

"Three-Four," responded the veteran. "O'Brien's team. They call themselves the 'Dirty Half Dozen.' Anyway, they're in contact, or were. The Old Man just went out to pick them up."

"What happened?"

"They had set up between two trails, when an NVA soldier almost walked right up on them. No shit, he got maybe ten to fifteen feet away when they spotted him and fired him up. O. B. and Echterling got him first, before the others opened up."

"Why did the others open up if the team leader and assistant team leader had already shot him?" Lento asked.

"Because the NVA soldier kept firing, I guess," the veteran said. "The guy is dead, only his body doesn't know it yet, and he doesn't fall down or nothing. One of his arms is gone, but he's still firing back so they *really* kill him. The team is grabbing everything he's carrying when the rest of the NVA begin to close in . . ."

The veteran had the attention of the new guys along with the others in the platoon hootch.

"The company's first kill in III Corps!" the Lurp beamed.

"Better than that!" replied the team leader. "Barnes or someone in the TOC thinks it might be the first kill for any Cav unit down here!"

"NVA?" one of the new graduates asked while the team leader nodded.

"Yeah, and lots of them. Intel says they have whole divisions just sitting a few miles over the border. Our job will be to stand in their way and yell when they're coming."

"Whole divisions, huh?"

The veteran nodded. "You're new, right?"

Stan Lento nodded back.

"So after you yell . . ."

"Yeah?"

"Remember to run real fast."

Everyone in the company was anxious to hear the rest of the story, and after the team's return and subsequent debriefing, the Lurps crowded around them waiting for their chance to talk with the five soldiers. Team 3-4 had been the first team out in the new AO.

Most of those on O'Brien's team were still animated and excited and had yet to come down from the adrenaline rush. When they finally did, it would be instantaneous. Adrenaline only went so far. Like most war experiences, each would remember his role in the event and retell it from his own perspective.

Sgt. Michael J. Echterling of Lowell, Indiana, remembered three things vividly. First, the severed arm with the enemy soldier's finger still on the trigger of the AK-47. Second, he recalled the damaged cigarette lighter that must have been in the NVA's top shirt pocket because the impact of the Lurp small-arms fire had pushed it deep into the man's chest. And three, Captain Paccerelli riding bellyman on the extraction helicopter and yanking on Echterling's arm so hard trying to pull him into the helicopter that he nearly threw the assistant team leader out the other side of the open cabin.

"The captain flew bellyman, huh?" It was more of a statement than a question, and the team leader who had asked was as surprised as the others when Echterling nodded. Extractions were often more dangerous than insertions, and the job of the bellyman took balls.

"You didn't hear him walk up until he was almost there?" asked one of the team leaders from the Second Platoon.

Sp4. Auggie Garcia, the team's rear scout, nodded his head.

"It's thick jungle out there," Echterling replied. "Which means they can't see us either, not until they're real close." If that was supposed to be comforting news to the assembled Lurps, it had less than the intended effect.

The thought of being "real close" to an enemy scared the hell out of many of the new Lurps, and it showed on their faces. But then, it didn't sit real well with many of the unit's veterans either.

The Lurps' new war had just begun.

CHAPTER TWELVE

Paccerelli's daily routine began at 0530 when the Lurp on CQ (charge of quarters) duty woke him. He slept only four hours a night, catnapping at other times when he could. When the CQ walked toward his room the creaking of the dry wooden floor boards automatically brought his eyes open as his hand reached for the loaded .45 automatic which lay on his ammo-box nightstand. The automatic was set on half-cock and always within easy reach.

"First call, Captain," the CQ said before reaching the doorway. The young sergeant knew enough to announce his message rather than physically try to wake the captain. This was not something you wanted to do to anyone in the Lurp company.

Not long before, he had walked into one of the hootches with a flashlight in his hands only to have the man in the first bunk, less than a few feet away, reach for his M-16 then dry-fire it at the intruder. The Lurp was still half-asleep and had reacted out of pure instinct.

"First call, sir," the CQ said again.

"Yes, thank you, Sergeant." The officer sat up and pushed the mosquito netting out of the way as he rubbed the sleep from his eyes.

He had been lullabied to sleep the night before by 175mm guns shooting a fire mission and had begun his early morning routine to the sound of helicopters cranking. The high, piercing whine of the helicopters' turbine engines was followed a short time later by the *whop-whop-whop* of their rotor blades as the air crews went through their first-light pre-flight checks.

After the 0700 morning formation, unless he had an aerial recon to perform, the Lurp CO attended the 1st of the 9th briefing at the squadron's TOC. Then, depending upon the urgency of the information he had received from the squadron briefing, he would pay a visit to the squadron S-3 (operations) to pick up any additional information or to inquire about the status of his helicopters.

From the S-3 shop, he then went to visit the MI or S-2 shop for any last-minute updates on new intelligence, at times joining Staff Sergeant Barnes and the operations officer, who were there for a more detailed briefing.

Back at the company, he would be briefed by the first sergeant, then take care of any internal matters that had to be attended to immediately. When that was completed, he'd get briefed by his own operations on the latest status of the teams in the field, those preparing to go out, and those due to come in.

Paccerelli would review the mission requests that the company had received from G-2 (division intelligence) and the brigades and take information on the operational readiness of the teams on stand-down.

Barring no unforeseeable problems, he would next check with intel to see how the team briefings and debriefings were coming along, studying them for new patterns developed by the enemy or the Lurps that might be relevant to future missions.

If a new training class was starting up, he would drop by to say something to the men, not the Patton "blood and guts" crap; he figured that by the time the new volunteers had finished training, they would be fully aware of just how dangerous their work was going to be.

Next, he would walk through the company area, not to check or double-check on the first sergeant's performance but, instead, to see and be seen by the men, to talk with them and see how they were getting along. Since a number of the teams had previously served the division's three brigades and operated away from the company when it was at Camp Evans, becoming familiar with their faces and names would take several weeks.

A few minutes here or there wasn't much, but it was a start. After the walk-through, Paccerelli would return to his office, talk with the first sergeant about recruiting efforts, and then begin to wade through the steady stream of paperwork that accompanied the job of CO. There were leave, R & R, and hospital status reports to read and respond to, as well as award and promotion recommendations to review and consider.

If there were no hospital visits to make or Special Forces camp to visit, there was always someone from operations or commo to work out the details of a future mission. After dealing with all that, *then* he would sit at his field desk, light up a cheap cigar from the PX, and burrow into the mountain of paperwork.

Among the material cluttering his desk was the worthless trash from book, car, or ring salesmen informing him that PFC John Doe or Sergeant Whosoever had not sent in his monthly payment on time and asking him to check into it.

It never failed to amaze him why there was always a pack of gutless ass kissers, waiting to retire, sitting up at corps level stressing that such incidents be "looked into," and God help the commander who didn't call in Private First Class Doe or Sergeant Whosoever and shoot one or both in the kneecap for not making that payment to some rip-off artist who preyed on the young soldiers every payday.

Paccerelli responded with the kinds of letters he thought the collection letters merited, which were not exactly what the ass kissers had in mind.

However, when it came to letters claiming nonsupport of family, Paccerelli adopted a different posture. He felt that if a man was not trustworthy enough to take care of his wife and children, then he wasn't trustworthy enough to be on a Lurp team. Sometimes the problem wasn't that the soldiers didn't want to write to their loved ones back home, but was something else entirely, something he would never have expected. More than once some embarrassed young Lurp explained to him that he didn't know how to write or how to write well enough not to embarrass himself even further. On such an occasion, Paccerelli would write the letter for the soldier to the soldier's dictation.

Once in a while, he received letters from school children or packages from high-school cooking classes that required a reply, so he would pass them on to selected NCOs or to the other officers. Some he answered himself.

At times, there were letters from parents wondering why "their boy" hadn't written in a while. He would immediately call those "boys" in to his office and "order" them to write a letter home, requiring them to show it to him when it was done. He would then have them seal the letter in front of him before handing it to the mail clerk.

Some of those letters that Paccerelli wrote could be annoying or time-consuming or a distraction but they were not hard. The *hard* letters would be the ones he would have to write to the families informing them that their hopes had just been shattered on some stinking jungle trail or along some nameless river. Even though there was a prepared format to follow, George Paccerelli knew he would turn to his Bible for some sense of solace, if only to remind himself that some good had to come from all of this waste. He knew he would labor over the letter, knowing that while the parents or family was reading "Dear Mr. [or Mrs.] So and So" they would be thinking about that little boy whose diaper they had changed; or who they watched disappear into a classroom on the first day of school.

That wasn't a task he would enjoy, and he would do everything within his power to make certain such letters were few.

If he was accused of being a hard-nosed commander, that was the reason for it. For honorable men, long after the din of war had ended, there would always be the echo of conscience and the second guessing that grew with time and distance. "Could I have done something different? Could I have done something more?"

He had not yet had to write one those letters, but he knew it was inevitable. There were few combat commanders who would leave Vietnam without having lost soldiers or having to write those terrible letters. That was a luxury few would enjoy.

To that end he established an order of battle (OB) for the company, a record of the enemy units, their locations, and their commanders, executive officers, and political officers they were facing. From team sightings and captured documents and prisoners, he learned the specifics and patiently recorded them in the official record. G-2 and S-2 would provide the key intelligence for the patrols, but at company level, Paccerelli wanted to insure that his own intel NCO had the most up-to-date and reliable information for the team leaders' briefings prior to the patrols' going out. Knowledge of the enemy was key to defeating him, and the order of battle would provide some of that hard-earned information.

There would always be interruptions to the paperwork as teams readied to go out or helicopters were sent in to bring other patrols back.

He informed Staff Sergeant Barnes and Staff Sergeant Torres to notify him immediately if the teams got into contact, and in the first thirty days, interruptions were frequent as patrols were making contact throughout their area of operations. Sleep was catch-as-catch-can as the war maintained its own schedule.

The captain also put together a rear-area team that would serve as a small quick-reaction force for patrols that needed "immediate" assistance. This special unit was also available to the 1st of the 9th if they needed it. He also stood ready to lead any "special" patrols that he considered too dangerous for the team leaders to take out. He felt that good team leaders were invaluable to the company, and he wasn't about to ask his team leaders to do anything that he wouldn't do himself.

At the conclusion of the afternoon briefings and updates from the squadron, as well as company briefings and updates on the status of the teams in the field, the day wound down, and the night settled in. Only then would the tall, lanky officer go to the 1st of the 9th Cav mess hall for a bite to eat. Sometimes, too tired to make the trip to the Cav mess hall, he would just open a can of C rations. When he had finished eating, he would turn his attention to his own personal paperwork—reading his mail or writing letters home to Barbara and the kids, and to his mother and stepfather, his father and stepmother, in the glaring illumination of a single bare lightbulb and accompanied by the low drone of an overworked generator.

The local Viet Cong and NVA were just beginning to welcome the division to Phuoc Vinh with occasional rocket or mortar rounds. The explosions set off sirens and a flurry of activity the closer they got to their targets.

The war was never that far away, and any sense of normalcy was only temporary and restricted to a handful of reasonably quiet moments.

CHAPTER THIRTEEN

Requests for patrols originated at division G-2, the three brigade S-2 shops, or from division artillery (divarty) S-2. The number 2 after the letter designation meant that the request came from the intelligence office of the requesting authority. The *G* in the alphanumeric designation meant divisional level, while an *S* meant it applied to the brigade or battalion level units.

At G-2, the G-2 plans officer delivered the mission request to the Lurp company operations section, which would then notify the 1st of the 9th Squadron for the necessary helicopter and gunship support as well as designating one of its four troops to serve as a ready reaction force if it came down to that. The Lurp company operations section—Lieutenant McKenzie or Staff Sergeant Barnes—would also notify the Lurp liaison sergeant at the appropriate brigade tactical operations center and give the brigade S-2 the mission specifics on the patrol going out in his brigade's tactical area of operations.

At brigade S-2, the S-2 officer would hand the mission request to the Lurp company's liaison sergeant at the brigade TOC. The liaison sergeant would then transmit the request to Lurp operations, which would alert a patrol while notifying both squadron and division.

Finally, at divarty, the S-2 officer delivered the mission request to Lurp company operations, which would notify squadron and division G-2. At division, the assistant chief of staff, G-2, retained final authority to approve or disapprove the various mission requests to insure that the missions were consistent with divisional interests.

It was Paccerelli who insured that the missions were also consistent with Lurp company interests. Early on, he had gone on record at one of the briefings arguing that he felt the patrols were misused when the requesting authority used the teams as overnight patrols outside the perimeter to watch for rockets being launched, as blocking forces, or even as economy of force missions. "That's not long-range reconnaissance," he argued, "and that won't accomplish the mission we were tasked to do."

He had been brought in to shake things up, and that's what he had done, and it was what he was still doing. He had done some careful and selective weeding to raise the company's level of performance, and he would do a lot more before it was over, but not at the expense of the Lurps he commanded.

Going on record verbally was one thing but following that up with a report to the division's commanding general through the appropriate chain of command also meant that he was putting his career on the line. But then George Paccerelli understood long-range reconnaissance, which was why he had been picked to command the Lurp company in the first place. So he naturally assumed that helping division better understand the company's role was his job, and it was a job he took seriously.

In his report he stated, "The concept of proper utilization of the long-range patrol was either misunderstood or ignored completely by the brigade level S-2s and S-3s."

In the same report to the commanding general he also praised the command's decision to centralize the Lurp company. Paccerelli wrote that ". . . the centralization of the company has reduced the number of control personnel required; increased the number of deployable patrols; insured that personnel losses through battle, illness or DEROS can be more readily compensated for; allows for retraining of patrols during stand-down, and allows training on special equipment and lessons learned. It has made patrols available to saturate divisional areas of interest, and insures speedier dissemination of gathered information; increases proficiency of patrols, decreases administrative difficulties, and maintains control of personnel."

In his closing, Paccerelli added, "It is imperative that only highly motivated competent and mature officers and noncommissioned officers be assigned as company commander, platoon leaders, first sergeant, platoon sergeants, operation sergeant, intelligence sergeant, and communication sergeant. Proper leadership and know-how by the aforementioned personnel will insure the commanding general of well-trained and highly skilled personnel and patrol members. The assignment of first-tour personnel and personnel with no Vietnam War experience should be avoided."

Paccerelli underlined the words Vietnam War for additional impact, not that he needed it since the report itself probably had the effect of a hard-right punch. He was taking his hits at the daily briefings, and he was countering with a few jabs of his own. But they were hard jabs he had experienced in jungle combat and lessons learned from his two previous tours. There are always more fronts to a war than many military leaders like to admit, little fronts with little battles, and not all of them were against the designated enemy.

"Well, George, what's your next career?" Paccerelli asked himself after he had aired his latest "constructive" comments. Each briefing seemed to be a sparring match, with the 1st of the 9th's sergeant major or squadron commander acting as the referee. Much to his own surprise, and maybe even to some in the squadron, he remained in command.

When the Cav moved south into III Corps, the Viet Cong and NVA were well aware that the long-range patrollers had arrived with the division, and a new approach was taken in dealing with the threat long-range patrollers made to the security of the NVA's operations.

When the enemy suspected a team was operating in the area, they would sweep through the target area with soldiers on line. As the enemy element moved, they would fire signal shots to keep their sweep on line, and when the Communists picked up the trail of the team and began closing in, their signal shots would come closer together.

To counteract that tactic, the team leader would immediately call in artillery on the areas where the signal shots originated, breaking up the sweep and forcing the Viet Cong and NVA to try another approach. Other team leaders carried an AK-47 along on patrols to answer the signal shots in an attempt to confuse the enemy. Both methods seemed to work well.

One of the enemy's new methods of tracking the teams was discovered on 17 November when Team 3-6 was operating northeast of the Minh Thanh Special Forces camp.

As Team 3-6 moved through the jungle, the team leader suspected they were being followed and circled back the way they had come to see if anyone was trailing them. A few minutes later they had their answer as the first three Viet Cong soldiers came into view, but that was not what rattled the team. The enemy soldiers were using a tracker dog to sniff out the Americans' trail. The team engaged the Viet Cong dog team with an HE round from an M-79 grenade launcher. The resulting explosion took out the dog and several of the enemy soldiers.

Later, after the team's debriefing, Paccerelli ordered the rear security man on all future patrols to carry a bag of black pepper. They were to spread it on their back trail if they suspected they were being tracked with dogs.

Another problem that wasn't as easy to deal with came when the Viet Cong ran across a Lurp patrol and fired a shoulder-mounted B-40 rocket into their formation. B-40s were usually used against fixed positions, helicopters, or tanks. The effects of the weapon against troops in the jungle was devastating. Most of the six-man team had been wounded, but miraculously none had been killed. Extracted later under heavy small-arms fire, the hard-hit patrol brought back a new lesson to the company.

To counter the B-40s, the Lurp patrols used M-72 LAWs. The LAW, a light antitank weapon, was used against the Viet Cong and NVA soldiers to break contact. The first patrol to try it in a firefight discovered that, tit for tat, against a B-40 rocket, it had a distinct psychological advantage.

The frequency of contacts shortly after the teams were inserted soon brought to light the probability that the enemy was employing a counter-Lurp operation that involved monitoring potential landing zones at first light between the hours of 0530 to 0630 and at last light from 1730 hours to 1900 hours when the sun was just setting over the jungle.

The Viet Cong knew that the patrols were deploying at first and last light, and they assigned a single soldier to cover the suspected landing zones, ordering him to report back immediately if an American team arrived.

Once the pattern became clear, the company changed its insertion times and methods. Instead of first-light insertions, the teams deployed between 0700 and 1100 hours, while what had been last-light insertions were moved to between 1400 and 1700 hours.

As often as possible, Lurp teams performed walk-off missions from the various fire support bases in the AO. Sometimes they joined up with the firebase security patrols and, once they were safely into the jungle, dropped off to move to their designated patrol area. Paccerelli also approved of insertions that involved going in on combat assaults with rifle platoons by helicopter. When the rifle platoon was lifted out after their mission was complete, the Lurps remained behind in the jungle, lying dog until the team leader determined it was safe for the patrol to move out.

A third method was also begun, the use of fake insertions. As many as three to four landing zones were selected, and the team helicopters made a realistic run on each, dropping down into the various sites. The team would exit the aircraft only at its selected landing zone; the others were merely decoys.

There were four distinct infiltration routes into the region, each with a nickname: Adams Road, the Jolley Trail, Serges Jungle Highway, and the Northwest Route. Throughout November 1968, Lurp contacts increased dramatically as patrols sought to identify the Communist forces moving into III Corps and to provide "hard" intelligence on enemy operations in the division's AO. Contacts were also increasing as the enemy became aware of the new threat on the ground. No longer did the enemy just have to worry about Special Forces SOG teams from CCS working over the border in Cambodia. Now they had to worry about the Lurp teams hiding in ambush just over the Vietnamese border.

However, if the Viet Cong and North Vietnamese Army units were beginning to understand the methods of the Cav's long-range patrols, then the Lurps of Company E were scoring little victories of their own and getting to know their enemy personally.

From the uniforms, weapons, maps, documents, and private papers removed from the bodies of the Viet Cong and NVA soldiers they had ambushed or captured, the Lurps and the division's infantry companies became more intimate with their enemy, his strengths and numbers, tactics and weapons, and, more important, his direction of movement beneath the vast sea of green-and-brown jungle.

Lying hidden in the underbrush just off the canopy-covered trails, the recon teams monitored the Communist forces as they maneuvered into III Corps from Cambodia. While the Viet Cong or NVA moved cautiously in small groups during the day, larger concentrations of their forces flowed through the provinces at night. The Viet Cong and

NVA infantry units operated in three-man cells with three cells to a squad, three squads to a platoon, three platoons to a company, three companies to a battalion, and three battalions to a regiment. That did not include the combat support elements that provided the heavy mortars and recoilless rifles.

It wasn't uncommon for platoon-size elements or larger to be spread out over miles of thick jungle to avoid detection from the sky and the massive losses to B-52 Arc Lights missions. Often, elements came together only at a given time at a given place for a specific attack. And it was precisely the times of their coming together that was the critical intelligence needed by the 1st Cav Division. Only the long-range patrols could gain immediate access to that information.

The Lurp teams monitored the trails, and when they could, they would ambush the three-man cells that came their way. The teams would also locate and map out the larger hidden jungle bases for future B-52 strikes, especially prior to the annual Tet holiday, when the VC and NVA often took advantage of the festivities to mass for large-scale attacks.

From their patrols and ambushes, the Lurps learned that the 1st and 7th North Vietnamese Army Divisions were operating in the region as were the Viet Cong 5th and 9th Divisions, including the battle-hardened 95C Regiment. Their 122mm rocket and 82mm heavy mortar support came from the 69th Artillery Command. The 122mm rocket carried a hundred-pound high-explosive warhead and could be fired from up to six miles away by three- to five-man rocket crews. Ambushes against those units not only helped curtail attacks against the Cav's bases but identified enemy forces operating in III Corps. Occasionally the Lurps were able to capture documents that provided the names of unit commanders, executive officers, and political cadre.

Like the surface of the ocean, the jungle canopy seldom gave anyone watching from above a real look at what was going on beneath. The vast stretches of jungle in Tay Ninh,

Binh Long, and Phuoc Long provinces bordering Cambodia
became the safe haven for four enemy divisions. Just across
the ill-defined border that separated the Republic of Vietnam
from Cambodia, COSVN—the Viet Cong's Central Office
for South Vietnam—managed the war from Cambodian
sanctuaries less than three miles away, using the dense, ver-
dant jungles of the three South Vietnamese provinces to
carry out their offensive operations against U.S. and government forces.

Advance warning that large numbers of enemy soldiers
were moving to attack, and learning the locations of their
hidden jungle bases were vital to the Cav's tactical success.
The Lurp teams were providing the division with hard intelligence, but it was intelligence that wasn't always believed or
acted upon at first report.

Despite Paccerelli's improvements and the Lurps efforts,
their reports were still being greeted with skepticism.

CHAPTER FOURTEEN

The Slashing Talon team had been inserted just prior to last light and had worked its way into position to cover an open area along the remote border area northwest of Tay Ninh. Slashing Talon was the company's new radio call sign. The team's target was an old smuggler's route that was a suspected crossing site for Viet Cong and NVA into and out of the province.

The "crossing site" was a natural grass field separating the Cambodian jungle on one side from the Vietnamese jungle on the other. The clearing was fifty meters or so across and little more than a natural sump, a depression that, during the rains, reverted back to wetlands. It also served as a temporary watering hole for the animals of the forest. As the dry season set in, the water receded, and the lime green grass that had grown to several feet in height while nourished by the sump began to wither and die in the staggering heat.

The field of thin brown strands rippled in the late afternoon breeze and might have looked tranquil to a civilian, but not to the six-man long-range patrol studying it with keen interest. The team leader, S.Sgt. David Mitchell, had set out the claymore antipersonnel mines and had hidden the team in a dense bamboo thicket amid thick underbrush. They had settled in their observation site just as the sun disappeared over the horizon. There wasn't much moon, and what illumination there was caused the gently swaying grass to take on a grayish cast. From their vantage point, the Lurps had a good view of the crossing site and the Cambodian jungle beyond.

Sgt. Calvin Renfro, the team's medic, was the first to spot the flashlights flickering inside the wood line on the far side of the field. Set against the black backdrop of night, the flashlight beams immediately caught his attention, scaring the hell out of him. It was Renfro's first mission and first combat experience, but he knew enough to realize the flashlights were too big to be fireflies.

Renfro reached over and grabbed Mitchell's arm and pointed toward the lights. As the team medic slowly came up with his rifle in hand, he watched Staff Sergeant Mitchell calmly eyeing the flickering flashlights that were now bouncing out of the jungle and into the grass field, slowly working their way toward where the patrol lay hidden. Mitchell whispered something to his assistant team leader that Renfro couldn't hear. Out in the field, silhouettes of the enemy soldiers were clearly visible, and even the dim moonlight couldn't hide the outline of their helmets or of the assault rifles they were carrying.

Eagerly waiting for the go-ahead to shoot, Renfro turned back to his team leader. When it didn't come, he felt a sinking feeling in the pit of his stomach. His adrenaline was surging as the NVA drew closer.

Amazingly, Mitchell still seemed to be relaxed and composed. The thin, wiry team leader had his hand on the claymore firing device, and was patiently waiting for the enemy soldiers to move into the kill zone. There were five claymore mines daisy-chained together to the team's front, which meant that when Mitchell squeezed the "clacker," all five of the antipersonnel mines would detonate simultaneously. Several additional claymores hooked to separate detonators had been positioned to the rear and flanks of the team.

Each mine contained over a pound of C-4 explosive and seven hundred steel ball bearings. When detonated, the force of the explosive would send the ball bearings out in a deadly arc that would shred anything and everything in its path up to 40 to 50 meters away, and still cause injury up to 250 meters out. The recommended safe distance from the mine's back-blast was sixteen meters—about fifty feet—however, a Lurp team in a tight perimeter in dense jungle didn't have the luxury of that kind of distance; the Lurps learned early on in jungle fighting to set them in close but angle the book-size mines away from their positions.

During Lurp training Renfro had watched as the instructors had placed the mines at the shorter distance before ordering the students down. When the mines were detonated, Renfro and the other Lurp trainees were lifted up by the force of the explosion and violently slammed back down as dust and debris washed back over the thoroughly impressed but stunned student audience.

"That's how it's done," said Lieutenant Bell, who had been monitoring the instruction. "You keep the claymores in sight so the enemy can't turn them around on you. Used in this manner they're an extremely effective weapon."

Now as the flashlights bounced closer toward the team, Renfro steadied his aim on the base of one of the beams and the shadowy figure directly behind it. The enemy soldiers were halfway across the field, and at that range, there was no way he or any of the others could miss. Not that they'd even have to fire their weapons, since the claymores wouldn't miss either.

When the NVA were within five meters, they suddenly spread out and scurried into the jungle on the Vietnamese side of the clearing. The Lurps could hear a single enemy soldier checking out the area before he turned and walked back to the edge of the clearing. Standing just outside the trees, he held up his flashlight and waved it over his head.

Within seconds, the far side of the clearing lit up with dozens of flashlights as a seemingly endless line of NVA soldiers stepped out of the jungle and made their way quickly across the field. Renfro's heart was pounding in his chest as Mitchell signaled for the team to hug the ground.

Out in the field, an NVA officer or NCO was yelling at the soldiers. It took a few moments before the Americans understood what was happening as the line of soldiers broke formation. The NVA weren't just spreading out, they were settling in.

It was a company-size element, and they didn't look like they were in a big hurry to continue on. They were spread out over several hundred yards huddled in small groups. They were talking in hushed tones, and every so often someone's laughter broke through the evening calm that had settled over the forest. One of the soldiers turned on a transistor radio and tuned into AFVN. When the Rolling Stones' "Satisfaction" came over the tinny speaker, Renfro wanted to laugh at the absurdity of it all, especially when several of the NVA walked precariously close to the bamboo thicket they were hidden in looking for a more comfortable place to rest. But Renfro didn't laugh. He was too frightened to laugh. If he had ever entertained any thoughts of being a "hero," those thoughts quickly disappeared.

He had heard somewhere that soldiers who served in Vietnam seldom saw an enemy soldier up close. Well, whoever had made that statement had never served on a Lurp team. It was only Renfro's first mission, and dozens of them were goofing off just a few meters in front of him. Hell, one of the NVA walked to the edge of the trees to empty his bladder, narrowly missing one of the claymore mines. It made for an interesting few seconds until the NVA swore and found his way back in the dark. It was right about then that Renfro decided he had seen the enemy about as close as he ever wanted to.

He was new to the Lurps, and when he got back to Phuoc Vinh—*if* he got back to Phuoc Vinh—he swore to himself that he'd quit the company. Throughout the NVA's rest halt, that was what Renfro kept telling himself he'd do, but when the enemy company reassembled, his thoughts quickly turned back to the problem at hand.

As the NVA finally moved out, Mitchell was on the radio calling in an artillery fire mission, and soon had one round at a time exploding in the direction the enemy formation had taken. With one round at a time, the enemy might mistake it for harassment and interdiction (H & I) fire—random artillery fire at preselected sites conducted by fire support bases throughout the war zone.

When the first round roared across the sky and slammed into the open field, the impact of the explosion sent the Lurps tumbling. After the team leader made certain everybody was okay, he adjusted the coordinates and ordered another 105mm round on the target.

Years of jungle fighting had taught the Communists a few hard lessons, and after several rounds had impacted, the NVA viewed what was happening as more than just a mere coincidence or a case of bad luck. Someone was targeting them. On command, the NVA officer in charge put the company back on line and sent them assaulting through the jungle to find the artillery spotter. Their search was short-lived as more rounds fell into the jungle, this time well away from the team.

Frustrated by the fruitless search or, perhaps, reacting to a rigid timetable, the NVA soon melted away into the forest as Mitchell continued following them with artillery.

By first light a Cav "Pink Team," consisting of a small light-observation helicopter ("White") and a sleek but deadly Cobra gunship ("Red") armed with rockets, miniguns, and an automatic 40mm grenade launcher, were on station, searching the jungle for signs of the enemy troop concentration. The smaller helicopter scoured the treetops, looking for NVA casualties around the impact areas of the artillery rounds, but when no bodies were found, the pilots once again began to doubt the team's story. The doubt had a ripple effect all the way back to the squadron, which in turn sent waves rolling all the way to brigade.

"They don't believe us!" Mitchell whispered to the rest of the team as he turned in disgust back to the radio handset.

"Yeah, well . . . fuck them! We'll find them again!" said one of the other veteran Lurps. Renfro wondered if they were all crazy. Packing up their gear, the patrol set out after the enemy. Mitchell would prove the disbelievers wrong and maybe prove Renfro right. They were surrounded by the enemy all night and barely managed to remain hidden and remain alive. Now they were going to see if they could do it again!

The Lurps moved slowly through the jungle, and after several hundred yards, they finally found signs along a trail that looked promising. The NVA boot prints were fresh and plentiful, and as Mitchell set the team back into an ambush position, he spread out the claymores along the trail and all around the team, hoping it wouldn't be necessary.

Not long after, five NVA soldiers came down the trail. They walked cautiously, but seemed unaware of the danger that lay a few meters in front of them. Mitchell waited until they had entered the kill zone, then detonated the antipersonnel mines. The simultaneous explosions shattered the early morning calm. All five enemy soldiers were killed instantly. The Lurps hurriedly stripped them of their weapons and equipment, then called for an extraction. Seconds later they were slipping back into the jungle toward their designated pickup zone. They now had all the evidence they needed, and their satisfaction was evident in their smug smiles.

On the long flight back to Phuoc Vinh, Renfro was still visibly rattled, and he told himself again that when they landed he was going to quit the company. But after landing, one of the veteran team members threw his arm around Renfro's shoulders and said, "Don't worry, newbie, not everyone is cut out to be a Lurp. Why hell, you'll probably make one hell of a grunt!"

Renfro smiled and swore, salvaging some of his ego. Staff Sergeant Mitchell helped, too, by telling him he had done just fine for his first time out. On the road to the company area, Captain Paccerelli and the operations officer were waiting for the team leader and assistant team leader with a jeep, while one of the clerks had a flatbed mule to ferry the rest of the team back.

"Is it always like that?" Renfro asked, helping to carry the NVA weapons and equipment to the mule.

It was the team leader's turn to smile. "No," Mitchell said with a broad grin. "Sometimes it gets scary."

CHAPTER FIFTEEN

On 8 December, Captain Paccerelli sent a request to Major General Forsyth requesting that Company E (LRP) (AM), 52d Infantry be authorized to wear the black beret as the "distinctive mark of a long-range patrol member." The company was reaching for its new identity.

In the two-page request, the Lurp company commander detailed his reasons for the proposal, outlining the strategies behind it, and even provided a standard operating procedure for wearing the beret.

"As the eyes and ears of the 'First Team'," wrote Paccerelli, "the brave young soldiers of the Long-Range Patrol seek out the elusive enemy on his own ground with only their own resourcefulness to rely upon. These elite troops are the only all-volunteer force in the 1st Cavalry Division (AM) and deserve the recognition and distinction afforded by the black beret as proud members of the First Team, accomplishing a vital, unique mission.

"In addition, the distinctive black beret would attract the attention of the Skytroopers to the Long Range Patrol. Men who are willing to face the challenge of long range patrolling would be able to distinguish a Lurp from others and inquire about the unit. This would be invaluable in recruiting and maintaining the Long Range Patrol company at full strength while retaining the high quality of personnel."

It was politicking and a reminder of what kind of job the young Lurps faced in combat. Besides, the Lurp teams didn't wear helmets in the field. They wore floppy bush hats, and wearing helmets in formations seemed a little absurd anyway in light of that fact, and the fact that in the 1st of the 9th the black Stetson cavalry hat was an approved form of headgear during their own formations.

The black Stetson was the trademark of the 1st of the 9th, and not only added to its esprit de corps but to the men's self-esteem as well. They wore the Stetsons not only with a great deal of pride but as a mark of distinction.

The Lurps were the only all volunteer force in the division, which was its own mark of distinction within the Cav, too. The beret would only add to their own pride and sense of accomplishment. The beret would indeed be a strong selling point.

Paccerelli's proposal continued, "To be eligible to wear the black beret, enlisted personnel must have successfully completed the twelve-day course of instruction presented by the company, and have performed in accordance with acceptable standards on his first three combat operations."

He then explained the proposed procedure for wearing the beret:

    A. Worn centered on the head with the regimental crest centered on a triangle pointing downward towards the wearer's left eye and two fingers above the left eye.

    B. Officers will wear a subdued badge of rank over a blue triangle.

    C. Enlisted personnel will wear the regimental crest over a triangle of green for patrol platoons, brown for communications section, or blue for headquarters section."

Paccerelli then suggested that the berets would be purchased by the individual, and uniformity would be maintained. He closed by adding "a mark of distinction is necessary to maintain the high esprit de corps of these few men who face the challenge and responsibility of the precarious that others avoid. Recognition has paid valuable recruiting dividends to the Long Range Patrols of the 1st Infantry Division, 25th Infantry Division, and the 9th Infantry Division. Even though the 9th Infantry Division has a waiting list of volunteers, the First Team Long Range Patrol far exceeds the accomplishments and records of the other division. Yet, our potential is hardly developed due to lack of sufficient qualified applicants."

Captain Paccerelli sent the request for action through the squadron commander to Major General Forsyth, hoping for quick approval, and when it came, he knew he had just raised the performance stakes. But then the men had raised the standards themselves, and Paccerelli knew it. In just two months, they had come a long, long way. He had already ordered 52d Infantry crests from Japan, and until the berets were authorized, he had each member of the company wear a 52d Infantry crest on both his soft cap and his uniform pocket flap.

Paccerelli was smart enough to realize they hadn't come all this way by themselves, and he began citing others for their assistance and support. In a recommendation for awards to the commanding officer of Battery C, 2d of the 20th, the Lurp CO cited two "Blue Max" gunship pilots for their bravery during a night extraction of one of his recon teams.

On that particular mission, Team 3-9 had quietly worked its way into a well-concealed enemy base camp just prior to sunset. There were dozens of well-maintained earthen-and-log bunkers and interconnecting fighting positions along with a number of open-pit structures with bamboo supports and thatched roofs. As the team leader spread the patrol out, he slipped quietly into one of the bunkers only to find a startled Viet Cong soldier. The VC looked up just in time to see an American with a black-and-green face coming through the opening. As the VC reached for his assault rifle and screamed for help, the Lurp let loose a burst from his CAR-15, killing the man instantly and bringing the entire bunker complex to life.

As the patrol fought back the initial enemy assault, the

team leader was calling for gunship support. Blue Max 67 Mike India and Blue Max 67 November India were the first gunships on station, and at the Lurp team leader's request they covered the withdrawal with rocket, minigun, and automatic grenade fire. The gunship runs bought the Lurps precious time and kept the Viet Cong from flanking the team. The two gunships made run after run, allowing the team to escape and evade.

With the patrol compromised, Captain Paccerelli called for the team's extraction and ordered the men to proceed to their designated pickup zone. By then, the gunships were running low on ammunition, so the Blue Max pilots requested ground artillery support and coordinated its fire from their vantage point in the sky. When the extraction helicopter arrived on station just after dark, the Blue Max gunships directed it in to the team's location under the pale green light of illumination rounds. Then they made a final run over the Viet Cong positions to cover the extraction.

Paccerelli recommended Blue Max 67 Mike India for a Silver Star for gallantry and Blue Max 67 November India for a Distinguished Flying Cross. The recognition and show of appreciation would go far in building cooperation between the two units, as did Paccerelli's presentation to the battery commander of a copy of an ornate World War I German aviator's Blue Max medal, a medal awarded in combat by the kaiser for exceptional feats of heroism.

While reading a military magazine one day, Paccerelli had come across a company that sold replicas of the award and promptly ordered a number of them to have on hand for just such an opportunity. Of course, the presentation was unofficial and the medal couldn't be worn, but it was the recognition that would make all the difference in the world. There were few perks to flying headfirst into light or heavy machine-gun fire day after day, and the 2d of the 20th pilots would fly in support of the Lurps regardless of the medal because that's what they did and who they were.

The official awards and decorations for the Blue Max pilots and the unofficial Blue Max medal would be a concrete expression of the Lurps' gratitude for the efforts of the courageous pilots.

The unofficial expression of gratitude to the Lurp company from division came soon in the form of approval of the black beret as the official headgear of the Lurps. Company E had a new identity.

CHAPTER SIXTEEN

Word had come down from division through the brigades and squadron to the Lurp company that all unit commanders and senior NCOs would be on hand to insure that soldiers did not fire their weapons or explode any ordnance on New Year's Eve.

In the war zone, on major holidays, many GIs reverted to the big kids they had only recently been and used their rifles, grenade launchers, and machine guns, along with signal or parachute flares, concussion, white phosphorus or fragmentation grenades to bring in the New Year or celebrate the Fourth of July. While it was an obvious waste of ammunition and explosives, it also endangered the lives of soldiers or civilians who might be in the path of the falling rounds or shrapnel or secondary fires they sometimes created.

Any veteran officer or NCO knew that at such time there was never a prevailing rule of "common sense," and nowhere was that more evident than in the middle of a war zone, where myriad pyrotechnics were readily available. In a war zone, things never go bump in the night; they go *BOOM!*

There were some who questioned whether there was any such thing as common sense at all when it came to GIs. GIs had been warned not to walk on trails since the VC booby-trapped trails they thought Americans intended to use. Some soldiers disregarded the warnings and walked down the trails anyway, right into the ambushes and booby traps. Soldiers had also been alerted to the dangers of running around to the back of a helicopter when exiting the aircraft, and yet someone was always getting decapitated doing just that. Still others kicked or banged on unexploded five-hundred-pound bombs they encountered during bomb-damage-assessment (BDA) missions only to have horrified NCOs or officers scream orders at them to stop as they shrank back in disbelief.

So it was a given that on the Fourth of July and New Year's Eve all over Vietnam, GIs were going to fire their weapons, even though they had been ordered not to. That was why Paccerelli and the others were standing guard outside of the orderly room on the night of New Year's Eve.

Just prior to midnight several parachute flares blazed through the dark sky as streams of red tracers from small-arms fire erupted around Phuoc Vinh in joyous celebration. Officers and NCOs raced to the suspected firing sites to quell the dangerous disturbances and to confront the rowdy revelers.

To Captain Paccerelli, Lieutenants Malcolm and Bell, the company's first sergeant, and five team leaders all was quiet in the company area, or reasonably so. All over the base camp, GIs were celebrating, and except for some yelling and laughter, all was in order at Company E—until, that is, the lone canister flare arced up and over from C Troop, 1st of the 9th Cav, and landed directly in the middle of the Lurp compound.

The burning fuse left an orange trail from the canister as it billowed out a cloud of gray smoke. In the dark there was no way initially to determine if it was a CS tear gas grenade or merely a smoke grenade.

"It's a smoke round!" someone yelled from near the small burning canister.

"Charlie Troop," added one of the Lurp team leaders to Paccerelli, who was standing nearby. It was the first such incident of the night for the Lurps. The second incident, which occurred less than fifteen minutes later, had far more serious consequences. The sudden explosion tore through the early morning darkness near the Charlie Troop latrine, less than thirty feet from the Lurp orderly room, where the company officers and NCOs were standing watching the sky.

The bright flash of light from the explosion was immediately followed by a thundering boom and hot, flying shrapnel that sent the Lurps diving to the ground and scrambling for shelter.

"Incoming!" one of the senior NCOs yelled. But when there weren't any follow-up explosions, Paccerelli's suspicions turned toward a closer threat. Two of his people had been slightly injured by flying shrapnel, and after inspecting the detonation area, the captain was soon fuming at the cause of the explosion. The blast pattern was unmistakable.

Someone had thrown a grenade, and as the wounded were being treated, the real question was, "Was it an intentional fragging or just a stupid New Year's Eve stunt?" A crowd of company personnel had gathered in front of the orderly room to see what was going on. The answer came when the Lurps were joined by an NCO from Charlie Troop, who said that they had caught the soldier who had thrown the fragmentation grenade, and that he had been taken to the squadron commander, who'd deal with the offender, but not before he went through a very angry squadron sergeant major. A number of the Lurps wanted a shot at him too, but that wasn't going to happen because Captain Paccerelli and his officers and senior NCOs kept the Lurps from retaliating.

The Charlie Troop NCO said that the soldier claimed he wasn't trying to harm anyone, which was why he threw the grenade at the deserted latrine, a story that the Lurps greeted with skepticism since the latrine was close to those who were standing in the company area. They were leaning more and more toward a fragging incident than an accident.

The man who had thrown the grenade said he just wanted to make some noise to celebrate the New Year, that was all. But that wasn't all, and Captain Paccerelli knew it. A certain amount of animosity still existed between the squadron and the Lurp company, and when Paccerelli informed the squadron commander in no uncertain terms that his attitude and that of the 1st of the 9th Cav toward his company was part of the problem, the lieutenant colonel offered a few choice but proper words of his own to the Lurp captain, telling him to cool down and to maintain control of his people.

The squadron's command sergeant major added that he'd take care of C Troop. When he was dismissed, the Lurp company commander knew he had put his head on the chopping block once again. And that time, he expected the ax to fall.

The grenade incident had been, at best, a stupid stunt, and for most in the crowd—especially for S.Sgt. Guy McConnell, Jr.—it was an omen of things to come. His own New Year would start out with a considerable bang.

His broken arm had healed, and on 3 January, the cast had been removed at the squadron aid station. Where the cast had been, the arm was fish-belly white, in sharp contrast to the dark tan that covered the area around it. But the arm felt good, which meant that Sergeant McConnell was "fit for duty," which also meant that he would finally be assigned to a team.

After reporting back from the aid station, he had been told to report to S.Sgt. Ron Bitticks for a mission briefing. Bitticks, his new team leader, was a college art major from Milwaukee. By some accounts, he wasn't comfortable with the military or the war. In fact, when Bitticks was assigned to Sgt. Bill Hand's team after completing Lurp training, Hand wasn't sure what to make of the reluctant warrior. Still, the Georgian liked what he saw in Bitticks. He was quiet, intelligent, and had an affinity for art, which he sometimes tried to share with Hand.

"It took me a good month or so to figure out that when he was talking about Degas, he wasn't talking about a fuel mix!" Hand had later told a buddy.

Time and experience had turned Bitticks into a competent

Lurp, and his own personal convictions had turned him into a responsible team leader. "He's a good TL," Lieutenant Bell had told McConnell. "You're in good hands."

Since it was to be McConnell's first mission, that last bit of news came as a welcome relief. Without firsthand knowledge of someone's competency, new team members had to go on rumor and opinion. Bitticks was well thought of by people McConnell thought well of, so that would have to do for the moment. After meeting with Bitticks and being accepted into the team, McConnell spent the next day going over the pre-mission briefings, drills, weapons and equipment checks with the four others. Five men would be on the mission: Bitticks, Howard Fatzinger, Edward Moline, John "Jake" Geiger, and McConnell. He was the only cherry on the team, and while that usually involved a little ribbing and "fucking with the new guy," Bitticks didn't allow too much of it.

On 5 January, the team was inserted along the river to search for a Viet Cong or NVA unit that had been recently seen in the area. The team's mission was to determine the unit's whereabouts and learn whatever else they could in the process.

Intelligence was timely in this particular instance. The older the information was, the less useful it became because beneath the vast expanse of jungle that made up much of the province, an enemy unit could easily move away to a new location undetected. A day or two made a huge difference.

Upon insertion, the point man came across a small trail, and as they were settling in to monitor it, two NVA soldiers walked up on the Lurps. The first enemy soldier was killed, but the second managed to escape. After gathering the soldier's weapon and equipment, Bitticks called in the kill.

Rather than pull the team out, it was decided that the team would continue the mission, which, somewhat reluctantly, it did. Packing up and moving deeper into the bush, the team soon came to a mud-brown river, and as Bitticks was figuring out his next course of action, the Lurps heard NVA soldiers moving through the jungle along a trail that paralleled the river.

To their horror, over the next twenty minutes, the Lurps counted 150 North Vietnamese soldiers pass by their position. It looked as though the enemy would miss them completely until one of the NVA soldiers halted, and along with several other soldiers trailing behind he started to move in toward the Americans. When they were less than ten meters away and closing, Bitticks ordered the team to open fire. Three NVA fell dead as the early afternoon calm erupted in battle. Bitticks was immediately on the radio, calling for air support.

The gunships were on their way as the TOC advised the Lurps to break contact and escape and evade, but even as that move was being coordinated, the enemy had already shut off all avenues of escape.

Pinned down on three sides and with the river to their backs, the Lurps repelled several direct assaults. As the first Cobra gunships arrived on station, they rolled in on the NVA with rocket, minigun, and 40mm grenade fire.

The area was literally crawling with enemy soldiers, and more gunships were being called in to deal with the overwhelming odds facing the five Lurps. All day, in spite of constant gunship support, the NVA pressed the Lurp team, at one time even trying a well-coordinated three-prong attack. McConnell was wounded by shrapnel in the left arm but quickly treated the wound himself, even as he continued to cover his position. NVA bodies were strung out in a half-moon formation in front of the team where they had fallen, and the Lurps could hear the gasps and cries of wounded men who were dragging themselves back through the brush. But even with their heavy losses, the NVA weren't finished with the Americans. By then they knew who and what they had within their grasp. The individual NVA soldiers knew it too. It was often said that bounties had been offered for members of the American long-range patrols, dead or alive. Captured documents confirmed this and put the bounties at one thousand U.S. dollars for a Lurp and even promised small farms when the war was over, so the incentive was more than mere patriotic zeal.

By late afternoon, time was working against the five Lurps. There was no way the team could cross the river and survive, nor could it hold out until a quick-reaction force arrived. The gunships on station estimated the enemy numbers to be in the hundreds, which likely meant a full battalion or possibly a regiment. There was no way for the division to quickly move in an equivalent-size force to take them on. The division could hammer the area with gunships, artillery fire, and tac air, but the Lurps would have to get themselves out of the trap they were in. Extraction in place was impossible. Their only chance was to run, to escape and evade to an alternate site.

McConnell listened as Bitticks told the gunships to fire at everything outside the smoke grenade he was preparing to throw out. The team would make a dash for the nearest pickup zone through the billowing cloud of smoke. Dropping his heavy rucksacks and getting his people to their feet, the team leader pulled the pin on a smoke grenade and threw it in the direction they wanted to go.

"Go!" he yelled, running at the rising cloud, firing his rifle as he ran. The gunships were already attacking the surrounding jungle as Bitticks, Moline, McConnell, Geiger, and Fatzinger sprinted right up the middle, breaking open a hole in the enemy's defenses.

With unbelievable luck, the five men pushed their way through to the pickup zone. They were extracted a short time later during a running firefight. The Lurps were elated at surviving the mission, but they were also seriously rattled. The gunships were still roaring down over the jungle as red and green tracer rounds tore through the sky and into the forest.

The next day, an infantry search of the area found twenty-seven NVA bodies, and when the report came back to the company, the realization of just how lucky the team had been was just beginning to sink in. McConnell said that it was Bitticks who had much to do with the luck they had, and while there was more than enough recognition to go around for everybody, the stress caused by the ordeal would change the shape of the team forever. The assistant team leader requested a transfer and another team member opted for a rear-area radio position.

McConnell joined Bitticks on two more missions, and on the third time out, the threat of getting killed in the jungle came from a source other than the Viet Cong or NVA; a "friendly" helicopter strafed the team, believing the men Viet Cong. The jungle that had protected the enemy also protected the Lurps from the aerial machine-gun fire as the rounds splintered the tree limbs and were deflected into the forest.

In three missions, McConnell had almost been killed twice: once by the good guys and once by the bad guys.

CHAPTER SEVENTEEN

S.Sgt. Walter James "Spanky" Seymour was on his second year as a Lurp, and probably no one was more surprised to be there than Seymour himself. When he joined the army in 1965, he had originally tried to get into the Special Forces but had been told by a recruiter that he stood a better chance if he had a combat tour of duty under his belt. And while he couldn't guarantee Special Forces training, he could get him jump school if the Bellevue, Washington, resident was serious about his goal. After Basic Infantry Training and advanced training in radiotelegraph operations, Private Jim Seymour was sent to Fort Benning, Georgia, to learn how to jump out of "perfectly good airplanes." The idea of jump school appealed to Seymour, an avid snow and water skier. What's more, he actually liked it.

What he didn't like when he arrived in Vietnam was his job as a rear area radioman, so Seymour volunteered to become a Lurp. He thought that, too, would help his chances of getting into the Special Forces. Somewhere over the course of the next eighteen months, with thirty-plus missions behind the lines in I, II, and III Corps, he had long forgotten about becoming a Green Beret. Instead he concentrated on doing the best job as both a Lurp and a team leader. By January 1969, there were many who believed he had accomplished his goal. Now on his latest extension, he personified the term "grace under pressure" but the grace would become more difficult to maintain as the long-range reconnaissance patrols began to turn into something else entirely.

On 8 January, Seymour's six-man team, Team 3-2, had been inserted into War Zone D on a stay-behind mission along the Cambodian border. The six Lurps—Seymour, Spec Four Tom Chambers, PFC Lewis Davidson, PFC Bruce Judkins, PFC Phil Bailey and Sgt. Robert Ramos (the assistant team leader)—were divided up among the Huey helicopters used to ferry in the grunt company for the ruse.

A stay-behind mission was just what its name implied: 3-2 would ride along with the grunts to the landing zone, the grunts would conduct a short patrol, and when the helicopters lifted them back out, the Lurps would remain behind.

After a brief stopover at LZ Tracey, Seymour's team and the grunts were inserted into the landing zone in the late afternoon in a clearing adjacent to the area they were to patrol. The natural clearing in the jungle that was to serve as the LZ had been prepped by artillery fire before the helicopters touched down. Even so, on the combat assault, the door gunners sprayed the jungle with machine-gun fire. The LZ was actually a sump area in the broken jungle where rainwater collected in the monsoon season and remained long into the dry season. When the Lurps and grunts jumped out of the aircraft, they jumped into an ankle-deep ooze that made the going to the tree line slow and labored.

Once inside the tree line, team 3-2 regrouped and hid while the grunts did a hasty reconnaissance and then readied themselves to be lifted out. Helicopter gunships and low-level scout helicopters continued to work the area as the transport helicopters returned to lift out the infantry unit. Within minutes, the sound of the helicopters was replaced with an awkward silence as Seymour and his team studied the quiet jungle.

After lying dog to make certain they weren't being followed, the staff sergeant moved his team deeper into the jungle toward the patrol area. The going was slow and designed to be slow. Pushing through the jungle, they came to a series of natural breaks in the vegetation that were separated by a long, narrow canal. Seymour studied the area, and when he was satisfied, he gave the order to move out with him in the lead. One by one, they crossed the small waist-deep canal and worked their way through the scrub brush. Behind them, the sun was beginning to set, casting a pale pink wash over the wheat-brown grass. When they came to a second canal, Seymour called for a night halt. The sunset was turning purple, and very soon a primordial darkness would overtake the jungle. Looking over the surroundings and studying his map, Seymour settled on a small clump of trees to hide his team. It was a good choice since the hiding place was bordered by a ditch, the canal, and several natural breaks in the jungle. A depression in the trees offered additional protection. Since the sky was reasonably clear, they seemed in no danger of the depression turning into a small pool.

As the team moved into the trees, PFC Lewis Davidson remained behind to cover their trail. The team's rear scout, his job was to cover their tracks as best he could and keep an eye out for anyone who might be coming up behind the team. Behind the lines, the war came at you from any direction, and when it did, it was always close.

As the others set up in a wagon-wheel formation, their heads to the outside, their feet meeting at the "axle" to give them a 360-degree view, Davidson was still erasing their trail.

The five Lurps were settling in, establishing their fields of fire, when Davidson raced up to the others and pointed back over his shoulder. His face was drawn. "Gooks! They're following us!"

Seymour crawled over to where Davidson had pointed and peeked out of the trees. He could see no one.

"How many?" asked the team leader as he turned to Davidson.

"Six of them!" he said.

"How far away?"

"A few hundred yards, maybe."

Seymour studied Davidson's face and then stared back out at the open field. Experience had taught him caution, so as he watched and waited he grabbed the handset to the radio figuring that if the gooks were moving away from the team, then he'd call artillery in on them without giving away the team's position.

He had established radio contact with the artillery battery by the time the six enemy soldiers came into his view. But they were no longer a hundred yards or so away. At best, they were twenty-five yards and closing the gap. What's more, they were spread out in the grass field and heading right toward the Lurps. Even in the twilight, it was easy to make out the curved banana clips in their Soviet assault rifles and the outlines of their floppy hats. The six NVA soldiers were tracking the Lurps. The knee-high grass gave way under the stalkers' weight as they moved slowly. If six NVA soldiers were in the open, then there were probably others behind them in the woods. The Viet Cong and NVA strategy was always to fight from a position of strength, and if you assumed the only enemy facing you were the ones you could see, you set yourself up for a nasty surprise.

"Hold on," the staff sergeant said, putting the radio handset down and reaching for a grenade. "I'm going to try for an air burst," he whispered to the others. "When it explodes, I want it to sound like World War III!"

Pulling the pin, he popped the spoon and sent the grenade in a high arc over the six NVA soldiers. When it exploded over them, the shrapnel and concussion would have maximum effect and quite possibly take them all out. At the very least, the blast would stun them until the Lurps opened fire. Seymour's aim was on the mark. But the grenade didn't explode. It landed with a dull thump. It was a dud.

"Oh shit!" Seymour said. "Someone give me another grenade!"

Seymour sent two more grenades out trying to anticipate which direction the NVA might go. This time both grenades exploded, and even before the dust and debris cleared, the enemy tried to flank the Americans. Ramos and Bailey kept them pinned down as one used the bank of the canal for cover. Gunfire was also coming from the ditch in front of them, wedging the Lurps in. With nowhere to run, the six Lurps held their position and traded fire with the bad guys. One of the members of the team tossed out a trip flare, lighting up the NVA's hiding place and giving the Lurps a momentary target. When the flare burned out, it set a small fire so more flares were tossed out to deny the enemy ease of movement.

Phil Bailey, the team's radioman, was calling in the contact as the small battle unfolded. Twilight had long since gone and the enemy muzzle flashes blew yellow-orange against a black backdrop. Bailey was also calling in illumination fire, and soon the battle zone was lit up with a pale green glow from the artillery illumination rounds that slowly drifted to the ground.

In the eerie light, the silhouetted figures became darting shadows racing for better cover and concealment, which they found beneath the lip of the canal.

"Use your chunker!" the team leader yelled to Bruce Judkins who nodded and brought the short, compact weapon up to fire. The chunker was actually an M-79 grenade launcher, a six-pound, single-shot, break-open weapon like a fat sawed-off shotgun that could fire a 40mm high-explosive round up to four hundred yards. Four hundred yards was a luxury the Lurps seldom enjoyed, and more often, the M-79 was used at considerably shorter distances. It was a weapon the NVA truly feared.

Judkins was a twenty-year-old from Palmetto, Florida, who was on his first mission as a Lurp. Barely two hours into the patrol, his heart was pounding from the adrenaline, and he was wondering how he would ever make it through a year as a Lurp. His hands were shaking, and when he fired the M-79, the first round disappeared up over the far wood line, somewhere, he figured, into the center of Cambodia, maybe China or Tibet. He swore to himself and reloaded the weapon with another HE—high explosive—round. He'd been carrying forty rounds for the M-79, five or ten of which were antipersonnel rounds. He took quick aim and sent the second round out. This one was closer but still too far away to be effective.

"Bring it down a bit," Seymour calmly said to the nervous Judkins who loaded the weapon a third time. The phrase on-the-job training took on a whole new meaning in combat, and Judkins was becoming a quick study.

"A little more," said the team leader and with the next round out Judkins had found the target. The enemy small-arms fire ceased for a moment then returned with less intensity from that one position as the new Lurp zeroed in on another site. "There you go," Seymour said. He turned his attention elsewhere.

As the small battle wore on, Judkins was amazed at how calm Seymour remained.

They were taking a lot more small-arms fire than Seymour thought six men could lay down, so the men who'd tracked the team weren't alone. In the dark, there was no way of knowing just how many were out there. The low contour of their hiding place made them safe for a while, and maneuvering up to the Lurps in the dark would take some doing and cause some noise. As long as their ammunition held out, the Lurps would hold their own.

A short time later, a gunship arrived on station and, at Seymour's request, began a rocket and minigun run against the NVA positions. The protective fire from the gunship gave the Lurp team leader enough time to check on his people. By then the firefight and sporadic battle had been going on for well over an hour and showed no signs of easing up.

"Everybody okay?" he asked while heads nodded. "How you doing on ammo?"

"Getting low," someone said, which is what Seymour suspected. Each man carried between thirty and forty eighteen-round magazines, three to five grenades, an assortment of trip flares, several smoke grenades, and maybe a "Willie Pete" white phosphorus grenade. Besides the M-79 grenade launcher, which Judkins carried, they also had several claymore mines in their packs. While that was enough ordnance for any sudden confrontation or running battle, it was never enough for a sustained engagement. In the initial exchange, the Lurps had fired on full automatic, which ate up a surprising amount of ammunition. Most of their grenades had been used up trying to get to the NVA who had hunkered down in their fighting positions.

He was fairly sure they had killed or wounded three or four of the six trackers, but the return gunfire told him there were more out there, and as the small battle continued, time was working against them. Even with the gunship offering protective fire, they couldn't hold out much longer.

The team was compromised, any element of surprise gone, so the team leader had Bailey call for an extraction. The response wasn't what Seymour expected. "Talon Six says bring back a body," the radioman said.

Seymour swore, took the radio and requested verification on the last order. Talon Six was the company commander, and the team leader wanted to hear the order from him.

When Captain Paccerelli came on the line he told Seymour that brigade wanted a body, which to the staff sergeant meant that brigade didn't believe they were in contact. There was something more that made Seymour's jaw tighten as the team leader shook his head in frustration but let it go. "Roger Six. Talon Three-Two out," he said back into the handset. Back to his team he added, "They want a body, so I'm going to go out and find them one."

"Are you crazy?" Judkins yelled, grabbing at his team leader's arm. "People in hell want ice water, too, but they're not going to get it!"

"I don't have a choice. We won't get extracted until I produce a body."

What was especially frustrating to Seymour was the knowledge that a platoon of Blues, an infantry platoon from the 1st of the 9th serving as their quick reaction force, was orbiting two klicks to the east. The Blues had come on station approximately twenty-five minutes after the gunships and were waiting for the battle to develop to the point where they would be used on the ground to either reinforce the Lurp team or cover their extraction. Meanwhile, they had a ringside seat to the light-show exploding on the ground below them.

Sudden movement in the ditch in front of them caught their attention and Chambers sent out one of the few remaining grenades. As soon as it exploded Seymour came up firing a full magazine into the ditch. "Cover me!" he said to Chambers and the others. "I'm going to find a body."

Ramos went out after the team leader leaving the four others to secure the makeshift perimeter.

"Be careful!" Judkins heard himself saying. He didn't want to see the team leader or Ramos get killed. Seymour was the one who would keep them all alive. He wasn't sure how he knew this, but he did, and Ramos would help keep Seymour alive. Meanwhile, Chambers would keep them together and alive.

The night was dark, the moonlight nearly invisible, and the darkness quickly swallowed up the two Lurps. After a long few moments, the sudden calm was once again shattered by small-arms fire, only to be followed again by the unnerving silence. Seymour and Ramos soon returned empty-handed. A second attempt with Davidson yielded better results in another area. This time though, they had a guide or guides. Thousands of them. In the moonlight Seymour could make out a cloud of mosquitoes hovering over a shadow. He crept forward, and the shadow became a body. Mosquitoes were feasting on the dead man's blood. Seymour called back to the others over his shoulder. "Ramos, move them out here!" he said. "I got one!"

By the time the rest of the team had scrambled to join Seymour and Davidson, the team leader had a rope tied to the dead Viet Cong soldier. "Get down!" he said, giving the rope a hard pull. Much to their relief, the body wasn't booby-trapped. That solved one problem, but another presented itself. The Lurps were in the open, protected only by the dark and little else.

"Set up a perimeter," he said. "Give me the radio," he added back to Bailey who handed him the handset. As the Lurps improvised a defensive perimeter around the body, Seymour called it in. "Talon Six. We got a body. Request extraction. Over," he said, and when the response came back, he rogered and handed the handset back to Bailey.

A metallic clink from their old position sent the Lurps turning and firing at the noise. Someone was moving in behind them, but not for long. Over the din of their rifle fire, they could hear the whopping noise of the extraction helicopter as it arrived on station.

The extraction helicopter called for something to light up the landing zone. "Wait one," said Seymour popping in his final magazine. The team leader used a magazine of tracer rounds to give the pilot something to zero in on. The magazine of tracer rounds was the "break contact" magazine the teams sometimes used to make good their escape from an enemy ambush. Eighteen flaming tracer rounds fired at him from close range tended to strike fear in the heart of almost any soldier. And while he was ducking, the Lurps would be running. This time though, they would be used as runway lights. "Watch for the tracers," he told the pilot and then fired a steady stream of projectiles across the open field. It made for unusual landing lights, but it was enough.

"Roger. Three-One. Got a Tango visual. Get ready; we're coming in."

When the helicopter touched down, the team rushed to the helicopter, leaving Seymour to struggle with the dead enemy soldier. "You want to help me?" he yelled over the din of the chopping helicopter blades and whine of its turbine as several of the team came back to assist.

The dead soldier was maybe eighteen years of age with a good build and a short haircut. His left arm was blown off just below the elbow, and dark, rich blood stained the front of his uniform shirt and ammunition.pouch. Judkins studied the dead soldier and realized how pitifully easy it was to die in combat. It didn't help matters any that it was also his first mission.

The extraction helicopter touched down at LZ Tracey again, and the Lurps and the NVA body were loaded onto another helicopter and flown to brigade headquarters. On their arrival, a jeep ferried the team and the NVA soldier's body to whoever it was who demanded to see it. An officer in starched fatigues was waiting along with the jeep.

"Hey! Who's gonna clean this mess?" the crew chief from the helicopter yelled to the Lurps. The helicopter floor was covered with a mix of dirt, blood, and feces from the dead man.

Judkins shrugged and climbed into the jeep with the others. That wasn't their problem. When the jeep rolled to a stop at brigade headquarters, the Lurps unloaded the body. When one Lurp lost his grip, the dead soldier's head slammed into the ground with a sickening thump, and the escort officer retched. The team was taken into headquarters, debriefed, and when it was done, an officer asked the team to inventory their ammunition.

"Why?" asked one of the Lurps.

"Talon Six wants them counted," was the reply as a second officer watched the six Lurps empty their magazines and open their pouches for inspection. Between the six Lurps, at best they had eighteen rounds. Less than one full magazine.

"That's it?" asked the surprised officer.

Seymour nodded. "Yes sir, that's it."

The expressions on the faces of the staff officers said it all. The expressions bordered on embarrassment to dumbfounded awe. The squadron commander for the 1st of the 9th was the first to praise the Lurps. "Good job, lads!" he said. When he asked who the team leader was, Staff Sergeant Seymour stepped forward.

"You're a plucky lad," the squadron commander added to Seymour who nodded at what he assumed was a compliment. "Splendid job! Splendid!"

While the squadron commander was obviously satisfied, there were still a few skeptics among the brigade officers, who were suspiciously quiet. Even the new guys understood that long-range reconnaissance patrols were tough enough without the job turning into a macabre scavenger hunt, especially when it jeopardized the team's safety because someone sitting behind a desk miles from the fighting wouldn't believe their reports. The job of a Lurp was dangerous enough without someone second-guessing their actions. Slowly more praise for the team began tumbling their way. Finally, "What, eh, what do we do with the body?" a staff NCO asked. Several of the Lurps shrugged.

"You wanted a body. You got him. Our job's done."

CHAPTER EIGHTEEN

On 1 February 1969, Company E, 52d Infantry (LRP), ceased to exist, and like the mythical phoenix rising out of the ashes, Company H (Ranger), 75th Infantry (Airborne), was born.

By order of Gen. Creighton Abrams, the 75th Infantry Regiment (Merrill's Marauders) was activated as the parent unit of the army's fifteen active Ranger companies. The regimental colors were to be maintained by the Ranger Department at Fort Benning, Georgia. Company A was to be located at Fort Benning and serve as the record holding and administration unit for the regiment. Ranger Company B would be stationed at Fort Carson, Colorado.

Ranger Companies C, D, E, F, G, H, I, K, L, M, N, O and P were assigned to the brigade, divisional, and field-force Lurp companies serving in Vietnam. Company E, 52d Infantry (LRP), was to be deactivated and immediately replaced by newly activated H Company, 75th Infantry (Ranger), which would be attached to the 1st Cavalry Division. Any question about the authorization of the black beret to indicate that the company was a special unit had just become a moot point since the black beret became the official headgear of the 75th Rangers. A red, white, and black scroll was approved for wear as a combat patch with the words Airborne and Ranger taking the center of the scroll while the company designation and 75th Infantry formed the two ends of the insignia. Complete uniformity would take a while because several units, including Company H, designed their own scrolls, which varied in detail.

The new companies were authorized to wear the 75th Infantry crest and the 5307th Merrill's Marauders pocket patch to show their lineage. Of course, no one had the crests or pocket patches, let alone the berets or scrolls. When the Company's new first sergeant, Jerry Price, found a picture of the 75th Infantry crests in a book on military heraldry, Captain Paccerelli approved a plan to have several made for each Ranger in the unit. The company that would make the crests was located in Japan, and the order would take a month or so to fulfill but Company H, 75th Infantry (Ranger), would have its crests, and long before they ever appeared at Fort Benning!

The crests were paid for out of the unit fund, and when they finally arrived, they were issued to the company personnel. The scrolls were produced locally, and the large red, white, and black cloth insignia would immediately add a new problem to the uniforms. Since the 1st Cav patch was the army's largest insignia to begin with, the shoulder scroll lowered the divisional patch, which in turn lowered the sleeve rank of the enlisted men.

The berets were to be purchased locally at the Ranger's own expense. The company also had one thousand wooden nickels made with an Indian head on one side and the company's unit designation on the other. The wooden coins would be used as calling cards when visiting the Viet Cong and North Vietnamese Army soldiers working in the AO. Paccerelli wanted the enemy soldiers working in the area to know exactly who they were facing and how their once safe jungle trails and camps had become the hunting grounds for the Rangers. When one of the teams ambushed an enemy patrol, they were to place several wooden nickels on or near the dead bodies so there would be no mistake about who had killed the soldiers. It was psychological warfare, a less than subtle reminder to the Communists that their jungle sanctuaries were no longer safe. An avid student of history, the company commander came up with a French saying that followed along the lines of the tokens: *"Non, je ne regrette rien,"* which meant, roughly, "No regrets." For every casualty and loss the company suffered, George Paccerelli wanted the Viet Cong and NVA to regret it.

About that time, Paccerelli began using historical quotes to help engender a healthy respect for learning among his soldiers. He began by offering them encouragement they could readily understand using references from the ancient Greeks, Shakespeare, and Theodore Roosevelt. Each quote was somehow related to the company to provide the soldiers with a historical perspective that helped them identify with their own situation.

The wooden nickels Paccerelli had ordered were also offered to pilots and crew members as tokens of appreciation from grateful patrol leaders for hot extractions.

Even with the new formal designation, the black berets, new unit crests, and red, white, and black 75th Infantry Ranger scrolls, many in the division still referred to the Rangers as Lurps, and any real change seemed to have occurred in name only. They were no longer Lurps even if some of the veteran team leaders and members of the unit kept their OD green and black Company E Long Range Patrol scrolls.

It was said that the reactivation of the 75th Infantry Ranger concept would bolster the status of the Lurps and recognize their service. Cynics said that it was just Abrams's way of pissing off the Special Forces. Regardless, the 75th Infantry was back, and the Lurps were officially Rangers.

The new squadron commander for the 1st of the 9th Cav, Lt. Col. James M. Peterson, was pleased by his Ranger "lads" and their accomplishments, and the new pride marked by the redesignation would only enhance the squadron as a whole.

The name change didn't change the job, however, which

was still long-range patrol, nor would it decrease the dangers involved. But then, with the element of danger came a certain degree of recognition. Some old Lurps and new Rangers discovered that as they tried to get a peek at the pretty civilian reporter who was interviewing one of their own in front of the orderly room.

"Ooooh baby, baby! Look at them round-eye legs!" someone whispered from behind the small gathering as they checked out the attractive woman.

"They go all the way up to her neck!"

The reporter was dressed in a comfortable blouse, shorts, and sandals, and her trim, well-developed body had succeeded in doing what the Viet Cong and NVA hadn't been able to do to the young Rangers; she was driving them nuts.

"She would love me if she just knew me!" someone else said.

"Not unless you took a two-day shower and put on a ton of Right Guard, she wouldn't!" Sgt. Dwight "Bull" Durham piped in while the group laughed and continued staring at the newswoman. Durham had been polishing a pair of jungle boots when the sudden commotion brought him over to the window to see what all the fuss was about.

"Who is she anyway?" asked Sergeant Gill, who soon moved up to join the hidden audience.

"A reporter doing a local-boy-makes-good story," Durham said.

"So who's she talking to?"

"Wilkie!" someone behind them said, which only caused the two veteran Rangers to smile.

"Then we better go out there and make sure he's giving her the right information!" Gill decided. Durham nodded. After all, he had just been made the company's new intel NCO, and finding out more about who the company was targeting was his job.

"Not to mention getting closer to check out her butt!" Durham grinned.

The two quickly formulated a plan to get in on the interview process. They would apply camouflage paint to Wilkie. The new guy wouldn't have much to say about it; he was new, and Gill was a team leader.

After introducing themselves and offering a demonstration that would make for a great photo opportunity, the two Rangers began applying any and everything they could find to demonstrate proper camouflage technique as they breathed in her perfume and sneaked every glance they could down her blouse or up her legs. Wilkie was taking it all in stride.

"You cover the exposed areas of flesh to blend in with the jungle," Gill offered to the young woman. "You use different camouflage sticks in irregular patterns or streaks; like brown, black, or green, and if you don't have those then you use makeshift items . . ."

"Like shoe polish!" Durham said, retrieving the shoe polish can from his pocket and applying it liberally to Wilkie's neck.

"Carbon paper, dirt . . . anything will do," added Gill. "Just so you reduce the possibility of your skin standing out."

"Right!" agreed Durham. "As Rangers you want to observe without being observed."

"There!" said Gill, the demonstration completed. He and Durham quickly lowered their gaze to her rear as she turned her attention back to Wilkie. The new Ranger was very well camouflaged. The young reporter was getting her story, and the two Rangers were getting what they came after as well. The woman thanked Gill and Durham who added that the pleasure was all theirs.

"To observe without being observed?" Gill said to Durham as they walked back to the platoon hootch.

"Works in a lot of situations, doesn't it?" he replied.

"Yes, but only because we're professionals." Gill laughed. "Goes without saying."

On 4 February, Ranger Team 4-1 had been inserted nine kilometers north of An Loc to recon the busy trails and roads that fed into Cambodia.

The patrol, led by Sgt. Tony Griffith, was to work an area bordered to the north by the Suoi Tonle Trou River, south by Road 304, west by Highway 13, and east of the Prek Ngoy stream. G-2 suspected the enemy was using the area to prepare another Tet attack, and Griffith's patrol was to determine if there was any significant buildup in the area.

On the first day of the mission, although they didn't see the enemy, they knew he wasn't very far away. The Rangers could hear the Communists hunting and cutting firewood, and they could even smell the wood smoke from their fires as it wafted through the jungle.

Griffith called in artillery fire on the suspected enemy locations without giving away his team's position. The jungle was silent afterward and remained so for most of the night. But at two in the morning, the Rangers heard movement on a trail forty meters away. The enemy didn't seem to care about noise discipline, which told Griffith that they had not been suspected of calling in the artillery the previous day. At five in the morning, the Rangers heard what sounded like a truck to the southwest, so later, when the sun had come up, Griffith sent two of his Rangers thirty meters out to scout the area for signs of vehicular traffic. For one of the two, Spec Four Richard Wilkie, it was his first mission, and going out in the dark to check the immediate area where the enemy were certainly lurking was a tough introduction to the job.

Griffith and the other two Rangers remained in their defensive wagon-wheel perimeter, waiting for the two scouts to return. Thirty-five minutes later, the two men turned back when they heard heavy automatic-weapons fire coming from where they had left the team. There was little return fire coming from Griffith and the two remaining Rangers, which only drove the two scouts on.

The NVA were twenty yards from the team and closing in when the two scouts flanked them, surprising the enemy soldiers and driving them off. But not before one of the two, Spec Four Wilkie, had been severely wounded. As the two Rangers struggled back to the team, they found their team leader slumped over his rifle with multiple bullet wounds to the chest. Sgt. Tony Griffith was dead, and another Ranger was seriously wounded.

Griffith had died after throwing back a Chicom grenade the NVA had tossed into the team's perimeter. The seriously wounded Ranger was in danger of dying, as well, unless they got him a medevac helicopter soon.

Within minutes, the Dustoff helicopter was on its way. At Phuoc Vinh, Paccerelli was putting together a Ranger reaction force to go in if they were needed. But word soon came back that the beleaguered team had been extracted. The survivors would return to Phuoc Vinh for a debriefing while the wounded would be flown to the nearest field hospital to be treated. Sgt. Tony Griffith's body would be flown to Graves Registration, which would process the body for shipment home. Home for Griffith had been Butler, Tennessee, and the homecoming there would be anything but joyous.

The company was in a funk, the mood somber. It didn't help when the rumor spread that in the confusion of the jungle battle, the two separated team elements might have fired upon one another. The war was difficult enough without having to fight unfounded rumors, but they couldn't be helped, because when things go bad in combat, everyone second-guesses everyone else's actions and reactions, and the devils that plague the depression dance with abandon.

Captain Paccerelli and his cadre would investigate and dissect the mission and the loss, and immediately work on ways to keep it from happening again. A memorial service had been planned, but not before Paccerelli agonized over the letter to Griffith's family. He hated the process, and when he had finally finished and reread the letter he knew it was not and would never be good enough.

Others in the company were just beginning to come to terms with the loss, and whether they were close to Griffith or Wilkie or not, the realization suddenly hit them that sudden death or a maiming wound could happen to any of them. Some grieved, and others just disassociated themselves from dealing with death or the injuries of others.

Staff Sergeant McConnell was the acting ATL for Team 3-9 and on a mission near Song Be when the five-man patrol walked head-on into an NVA company on a trail confined by thick, heavy brush. In the sudden battle that ensued, the team's point man was shot twice in the leg, and went down. The enemy soldier who had shot the lead Ranger then turned his AK-47 on McConnell who was next in line. At the short distance between them, both the American and North Vietnamese fired at each other. McConnell's canteen was blown from his hip, but that was the extent of his damage as he killed the NVA soldier and two more who were behind him.

The rear scout then helped McConnell with the wounded point man. McConnell picked up the man as the team pushed off the trail and ran for the nearest LZ to evacuate the wounded Ranger. The jungle was dry, and the small-arms fire had ignited a brush fire, and in the confusion caused by the smoke and flames, a medevac helicopter was able to come in and pull the wounded man out.

Even before the helicopter had lifted off, the NVA had regrouped, but they were having trouble maneuvering around the spreading flames. The now four-man Ranger team used the distraction to evade, with the NVA in hot pursuit. It was decided to pull the team, and the Rangers were lifted out under heavy small-arms fire.

Back at Phuoc Vinh, the team unloaded gear and equip-

ment and cleaned and stored their weapons while the team
leader and assistant team leader were being debriefed.

The debriefings were thorough, and by the time they were
done, there was barely enough time to head over to the mess
tent to eat. The Rangers wanted a hot meal and would worry
about cleaning themselves up later, which meant showering
and scrubbing off the camouflage paint mixed with sweat and
grime, and pull off any insects or parasites that had hitched a
free ride out of the jungle at the Rangers' expense. Since the
company was still borrowing mess facilities, the Rangers had
a bit of a walk to reach the mess tent. By the time they arrived
and started through the line, the mess sergeant wanted to
know what they were doing, complaining that it was too late
for them to be served.

"We just came in from the field," McConnell said, patiently. "We were in contact so we had to get debriefed."

"So?" the seemingly indifferent mess NCO said, refusing
the two Rangers a hot meal. "The mess line's closed."

The normally quiet and reserved McConnell exploded and
threw what food he had in his tray at the mess sergeant as the
mess officer hurried over to quell the disturbance.

Ordered before the company commander, the sullen staff
sergeant couldn't explain his actions in the incident other
than just being pissed off and angry at the mess sergeant.
Paccerelli gave the man the room he needed to vent his frustration before he laid down the law and dismissed him. The
incident was totally out of character for the young NCO.

The captain liked McConnell and would go to bat for him.
He was a good Ranger. Combat affected everyone differ-
ently, and McConnell had just caught a glimpse of what it
was doing to him. Turning on the anger during dangerous
close-in fighting in combat was a necessary survival tool, but
turning it off again would take some doing.

CHAPTER NINETEEN

By the second week in February, Staff Sergeant McConnell served his first mission as an ATL on a patrol north of Saigon in the area around the Michelin rubber plantation. One of the few advantages of being an assistant team leader was that he didn't have to carry the radio or medical bag. He also had some say in the decision-making process, but the team leader always made the final call, which simply meant that being an ATL was a good place to be.

For the first two days, there was no sign of the enemy in the area. By day three, the team had set up on an old trail in the heavy underbrush that paralleled a dirt road serving the plantation area. The trail, like the rural road, ran straight for sixty meters or so before snaking its way back into the countryside.

The Rangers were monitoring the trail when they received word that a helicopter working the area just a few kilometers away had engaged a squad of NVA heading toward the Ranger team. Because of the thick underbrush surrounding the area, the NVA would have to use either the trail or the road to make good their escape. The team leader figured they would most likely use the road and decided that's where the team would set up their ambush.

However, when McConnell went out to move the claymore mines, he glanced down the trail and saw the enemy patrol already approaching. The NVA point man was perhaps forty meters away and closing rapidly. The lead soldier saw

McConnell, too, but didn't fire, uncertain as to who or what he was. Since the Ranger was wearing camouflaged fatigues that contained no rank or insignia, McConnell could have just as easily been a Viet Cong guard or reconnaissance sentry. East German camouflage uniforms had been issued to several of the enemy reconnaissance units and the 5th Viet Cong Main Force Division, the Dong Nhi, Phuoc Binh, and the 101st Regiments had also been reported to be wearing camouflage uniforms with the tiger pattern. The enemy soldier elected to wait and see who McConnell actually was before opening fire.

McConnell also held his fire simply because he was in the open and there were too many enemy soldiers to take on by himself. In the meantime, his TL had dropped back into the thick brush and alerted the rest of the team.

Still uncertain of what they had seen, the NVA played it safe and changed directions, leaving a rear guard behind to see if anyone followed. As the Lurp team moved toward the enemy rear guard, the underbrush suddenly exploded with small-arms fire. The Rangers hit the ground and quickly returned fire. In the thick underbrush neither side could see well enough to get a clear target so the gunfire was targeted on nothing more than sound. The team leader called in the contact, and several Charlie Troop gunships were immediately bounced to assist the team. When they arrived on station, McConnell felt surprisingly secure. The gunships usually proved to be the deciding factor in the small battles the Lurps got into because the Viet Cong and NVA units seldom wanted to take them on. Gen. Nguyen Vo Giap's directive was closely adhered to. "Strike only when you are certain of victory," he had ordered, and a squad in the underbrush against Cobra gunships was not certain victory. It was certain suicide. The NVA held their fire and scurried away through the underbrush. However, before they left, they tried one final tactic.

McConnell was covering the area immediately in front of

him when a Chicom grenade suddenly landed inside the team's wagon-wheel perimeter. The ATL saw the threat, yelled "Grenade!" and reached down to grab it and toss it back, but he was too late. As it detonated, the loud explosion sent him tumbling backwards, depositing him in a heap. His ears were pounding, and everything appeared a blurred crimson. When he could finally focus his eyes again, he found that he and one of the other Rangers had been slightly wounded in the explosion. The small wood-handle Chicom grenades didn't seem designed to kill so much as to wound or stun. Dead men could be left behind, wounded men took several soldiers to carry them to safety, which meant a less effective fighting force; stunned men could be overrun.

When the new development had been called in to Phuoc Vinh, Captain Paccerelli was airlifted in with the platoon of infantry serving as the quick-reaction force. A tracker-dog team also joined the search for the NVA soldiers. The dog handler, a young lieutenant, ran his dog along the trail where the NVA had last been seen, and once he had completed the run, he returned to Paccerelli with his report. There were no sign of NVA soldiers, he announced to the Ranger Company commander, and what was more, he doubted if anyone had been on the trail in weeks. The news stunned the Ranger patrol with more effect than the enemy grenade.

The Ranger company commander asked the lieutenant if he was sure, and when the dog handler said he was, the captain accused the team of faking contact to get out of the field.

McConnell was furious, and even though his head was still pounding from the concussion, he marched the group down the trail until he found NVA bootprints in and around a puddle in the narrow trail. The pattern of the tracks was unmistakable, and water was still oozing into the depression. "Then what's that, Lieutenant?" he asked, pointing to the Vietnamese bootprints clearly visible in the mud.

Both the Ranger company CO and the tracker dog officer studied the imprints. The herringbone pattern was definitely

NVA. The Ranger team was out of hot water, but the two officers weren't, especially Captain Paccerelli who, McConnell thought, shouldn't have been so quick to take the junior officer's word over that of his own people. Like the others, McConnell sulked. If they had thought the captain had walked on water before, then he had just gotten his ankles wet. However, had the enemy bootprints not been found, then the patrol likely would have had hell to pay.

At times, it seemed like everyone expected miracles from the Lurps, then a long line of doubters spoke up once they called in their reports. Until they offered concrete proof. The job of a long-range patrol was tough enough without having to be cross-examined and second-guessed by every outsider with a chip on his shoulder.

Later, back at Phuoc Vinh, and after McConnell had been checked out and treated at the aid station, Lieutenant Bell, the 2d Platoon leader, offered McConnell some consolation by telling him that he had done a good job and that he had been put in for a medal for trying to save the team from the Chicom grenade. McConnell shrugged off the pep talk. He was still feeling the sting of having everyone believe he had faked the contact. Bell's comments were meant to soothe, and McConnell appreciated his concern, but the damage had been done. Of all the officers, the lieutenant from New Jersey, who McConnell liked and trusted most, had at least tried to repair the damage caused by the other two officers.

A week later, another outside officer would have significant impact on the morale and attitudes of the Cav's Rangers. The Michelin patrol had provided one scenario, but a long-range patrol working in Tay Ninh Province would provide another entirely different one.

In the early afternoon on 24 February, S.Sgt. Charles Windham's team had moved toward Highway 247 to see who or what was coming down the hard-packed road on a motorbike so close to the Cambodian border. Because it was a great distance away, the motorbike sounded like a pissed-off june bug winging its way down the highway. The closer it came, the more recognizable the sound became, a small Honda or a moped, but nothing larger. As Windham and the rest of his team quietly moved through the underbrush to the edge of the highway to intercept the motorbike, they quickly discovered that the driver was a lone Viet Cong soldier. The surrounding jungle was quiet as only jungles can be on a hot afternoon, and there was no other road traffic, so Windham decided to set up a hasty ambush. When the motorbike entered the kill zone, the Rangers sprang their trap. Both the small motorbike and rider went down immediately, skidding and tumbling along the orange dirt road before finally coming to a rest. The Viet Cong soldier was dead before the motorbike's engine stopped running, and as they searched the body for documents and retrieved the dead soldier's weapon, the jungle across from the Ranger team suddenly came alive with activity.

The ambush had caught the attention of a larger Viet Cong force bivouacked nearby. It didn't take them long to come out of the jungle to see what all of the fuss was about. Spotting the Americans on the road surrounding the body, the VC immediately engaged the Rangers, who returned fire and slipped quickly back into the jungle.

In the initial volley, a number of the Americans were wounded by the enemy small-arms fire. Windham called in the contact and gave a quick situation report as the Ranger relay team atop the Black Virgin Mountain coordinated the necessary gunship support. Minutes later, when the Viet Cong came after the Rangers it looked to be at least a platoon-size force, thirty or so, and when two more team members were hit by small-arms fire and shrapnel from exploding B-40 rockets, it was decided to extract the team.

Windham was ordered to move to the designated pickup zone for extraction. Back at Tay Ninh, the Apache Troop Blues, the quick-reaction force for the Ranger team, was on the flight line waiting for the order to go. Lt. Robert Peterson—call sign Apache Three-Three—and his UH-1H lift-ship crew lifted off from the flight line and picked up air-speed to follow the faster gunships out to pick up the Rangers. The Apache Troop gunships would engage the enemy soldiers and provide supporting fire as the liftship moved in to make the actual rescue.

The slick was twenty minutes out and closing as Peterson and his crew raced to assist the endangered Rangers. The crew chief and door gunner readied their M-60 machine guns, locking and loading the belt-fed rounds and checking the feed trays to make sure the belts were not fouled. The UH-1H liftship helicopters had little in the way of armor or any real protection, but the machine guns helped keep the enemy's head down and provided valuable support to hard-pressed men on the ground.

On the ground, Windham's team was having a tough go of it as the Viet Cong pressed their attack. The Rangers were still taking heavy small-arms fire. But it was the rocket-propelled grenades from the B-40s that presented the real problem. When the rockets exploded in the trees near the team, they sent red-hot shrapnel everywhere. While a heli-copter could survive multiple hits from a machine gun and still remain airborne, a direct hit from a single B-40 rocket would send it tumbling into the jungle in a fireball.

Lieutenant Peterson was monitoring the situation on his radio as he hurried to the pickup zone. As soon as he was on station, he radioed the Ranger team leader to inform him that he was coming in on short final and to have his people ready for pick-up.

"Negative!" Windham screamed into the radio, warning Peterson off. The Rangers were still under heavy attack by the B-40 rockets, and the rescue attempt would be too dan-gerous.

"On short final. Pop smoke," Peterson replied, ignoring the instruction to abort. He brought the UH-1 helicopter in low and fast over the jungle clearing. The Viet Cong gunners turned their attention to the low flying aircraft. Realizing that his warning was not being heeded, the long-range patrol leader quickly popped a smoke grenade to give the pilot something to zero in on.

The aircraft crew chief and door gunner were firing back into the tree line at the Viet Cong, who were bent on bringing the helicopter down. With their flight helmets on, they could only hear the faint *ticks* of incoming rounds ripping through the aircraft as they descended toward the ground.

The Ranger team was still fighting off the VC assault, but just barely. They were heavily outnumbered and outgunned but even though they were running low on ammo, they weren't about to give up. As Lieutenant Peterson brought his helicopter to a hover next to the marking smoke, the Rangers came running and limping out of the wood line as best they could. But they weren't alone. The Viet Cong were still determined to stop them. B-40 rockets flashed across the pickup zone just missing the rescue helicopter, while small-arms fire increased in volume and managed to find its target. Windham and the others were firing back at the Viet Cong, trying to buy time for them all. The crew chief, seeing that some of the Rangers were having a hard time keeping up, left the helicopter to help bring in the more seriously wounded. Peterson's helicopter was now a sitting duck on the LZ, and he knew if he remained in the pickup zone much longer, they would never make it out.

Green tracers suddenly tore through the tail section and fuselage of the fully exposed aircraft as the Rangers began to scramble aboard. But even before they could turn around inside the helicopter to help provide additional cover fire, the Apache Troop pilot was bringing the ship around and dipping its nose to pick up enough forward air speed to get them out of the clearing. Several lines of large green tracers followed their flight path, only to arc past them and fall back into the jungle. Just above the trees, the helicopter suddenly began to shake and shudder. Lieutenant Peterson transmitted a quick radio message to let the Apache Troop TOC know that he had to find a place to set the crippled aircraft down in a hurry. Then he realized that the wounded Rangers on board presented an additional problem, and Peterson opted to stay aloft long enough to bring the crippled aircraft down at a friendly airfield where medics would be standing by.

Windham's long-range patrol team had survived a horrifying mission thanks to the gutsy Apache Troop air crew, and especially to Lieutenant Peterson who overrode the warning about the B-40s and heavy small-arms fire.

Peterson and his entire crew were put in for medals for exceptional valor. Captain Paccerelli provided a two-page commendation to the Apache Troop commander, describing their deeds in great detail. The medals cost a few dollars to make and were nothing more than a token of appreciation by a grateful Ranger company. The real glory and prestige that were represented by those tiny bits of gold and silver alloy and bright ribbon were in the deeds of those who had earned them.

CHAPTER TWENTY

The stretch of Highway 13 from Quan Loi south to Lai Khe was known as Thunder Road by the mechanized infantry units that routinely made the security runs through the region because of the many ambushes and firefights the Viet Cong and NVA had sprung against South Vietnamese and American convoys. Engineers had used Rome plows and earth graders to push back the jungle in a massive effort to help eliminate the deadly ambushes, and for a while, that seemed to work.

Ranger patrols from Hotel Company had discovered numerous bunker complexes, fighting positions, and trench systems all along the corridor. The largest of them was a vast complex of two hundred underground bunkers just off Thunder Road. The large system of interconnected fortifications was deserted at the time of its discovery, and several subsequent patrols were sent in to map the site, while being careful to leave it undisturbed.

Because the bunkers and fighting positions were maintained, Staff Sergeant Barnes and Lieutenant McKenzie suggested that it would make an ideal target for a B-52 Arc Light mission. Ranger Intelligence section knew the bunker complex was a primary staging area for the enemy units operating along the highway. Captain Paccerelli agreed and passed the proposal up through channels.

After several additional enemy attacks against convoys from the 1st Cav and the Big Red One, long-range patrols from Hotel Company began reporting long columns of enemy soldiers pouring into the area. Again the Ranger company recommended an Arc Light on the enemy bunker complex. That time the request was approved at all levels, and as soon as the flight of B-52 bombers dropped its deadly load on the enemy's jungle hideout, an immediate bomb-damage assessment was ordered on the site.

The infantry platoon performing the BDA of the bunker complex combat assaulted into the roadway and began working its way into the torn and tangled jungle. The going was slow and cautious, and when the platoon broke out into the target area they found that it was littered with splintered trees and shattered vegetation. Huge swimming-pool-size bomb craters were scattered across the jungle. Amid the wreckage they found what was left of the large enemy bunker complex and the soldiers who had been occupying it. Jagged parts of human bodies, twisted weapons, and bits of military equipment were scattered about everywhere.

The forest, or what was left of it, was scorched and denuded of vegetation from the sudden violence of the strike, and everything was coated with a fine white residue.

In the total devastation, the infantrymen accounted for sixty-six confirmed enemy dead and discovered numerous blood trails leading away from the target area. Trench systems leading to tunnel entrances had been collapsed and sealed. The fate of those who had been entombed inside the tunnels could only be imagined. However, the attacks and ambushes along that stretch of Thunder Road decreased dramatically after the bombing. Lt. William Bell, the platoon leader of one of the teams that had discovered the bunker complex, was well satisfied. It was a victory for the company and for the platoon.

In addition to his normal duties as one of the company's two platoon leaders, Lieutenant Bell had the task of accompanying the team leaders assigned to his platoon on overflights and aerial reconnaissance missions prior to the team's insertion into its area of operations. The area along Thunder Road had been one of them, which was something more to relish.

On a typical overflight, the team leader and his platoon leader, and often the platoon sergeant, would overfly the proposed recon zone to search for possible landing zones, pickup points, trails, streams, and points of interest, as well as to get an overview of the general lay of the land.

Bell was also responsible for inserting and extracting his own teams, so combat assaults and rescues became a large part of his Ranger company activities. On special missions, and to verify the qualification of a patrol leader, he would accompany the patrol and report back to Paccerelli with his findings. The missions were also designed to give the young officer a better appreciation of the job his teams were doing in the field, which the lieutenant announced upon his return and whenever he had an opportunity. His were good people and he often said as much.

While both platoon leaders checked out their teams' performances, the enlisted men on the teams would, in turn, check out their officers. The lieutenant accompanying the patrol on a mission was required to pull an equal share of the team's responsibilities on patrol and to yield to the enlisted team leader's authority during the mission. Some of the team leaders had been RIs—Ranger instructors at Fort Benning, Georgia—and had, in fact, trained the officers to become Ranger-qualified or "tab" Rangers. Other, younger, team leaders selected from the ranks had learned the art of patrolling in Vietnam and had become very competent jungle fighters.

Few complaints were registered against team leaders by the officers accompanying the patrols in the field. This was primarily due to the efficiency of the team-leader selection process.

To earn a slot as a team leader, the Ranger had to have a certain amount of experience on patrol and have shown some skill and composure in the field under pressure. During the debriefings, the team leaders would report the actions of the various team members. Paccerelli kept a file on each team member and relied on it heavily when it came time to select new team leaders. A TL candidate would be appointed first as an assistant team leader and then studied in that role to determine his capabilities or limitations. The platoon sergeant and platoon leader had a say in the selection process. The ATL would be sent to the Special Forces Recondo School in Nha Trang, if there was an opening, for some fine tuning and graduate work in the fine art of patrolling.

It was Lieutenant Bell who spotted McConnell's leadership skills early on and championed his selection. S.Sgt. Mac McConnell had already shown his skills on patrol, and he was made a team leader after serving only seven missions.

S.Sgt. Stan Lento was of the same caliber, although by the time of his selection, the farm boy from Maine had a few more missions to his credit than McConnell. McConnell noticed a change in Lento, subtle at first, but definitely a change, and others were wondering, too. Lento was no longer showing his buddies pictures of his wife back home. He had once mentioned something about a divorce but had left it at that. He had the war to occupy his mind, and the added responsibility of a team to look after.

McConnell's first mission as a team leader in late February was a disaster. It was a miserable experience, and he felt as though he didn't know what he was doing. What was even worse, he suspected the team felt the same way. On the second day of the patrol, after setting up in a tight defensive perimeter, the radio went out, and McConnell and the team's RTO tried everything they could to get it working again. They changed batteries, fiddled with the radio's handset, put up the long whip antenna, and even shifted locations in case the problem was a natural physical barrier like a hill or mountain that was interfering with the transmission. None of their efforts worked, and soon the other men on the five-man

Capt. George Paccerelli as leader of A-team. (Photo courtesy of George Paccerelli)

Capt. George Paccerelli when attached to SOG. (Photo courtesy of George Paccerelli)

Insertion helicopter at Signal Hill, 1968, downed while LRRP/Rangers Bill Hand and Larry Curtis were rappelling in to set up a radio relay station. (Photo courtesy of Bill Hand)

Left to right, standing: ATL Dan Roberts and medic J. Stein after capturing a Viet Cong first lieutenant. (Photo courtesy of Dan Roberts)

Apache Troop, first of the ninth liftship pulling out a downed scout helicopter in Tay Ninh. (Photo courtesy of Kit Beatton)

LRRP/Ranger Bob Gill at Camp Evans. (Photo courtesy of Bob Gill)

Apache Troop Blue Capt. R. B. Alexander who actively recruited LRRP/Rangers to serve as squadron leaders with his Blues recon platoon. One of his acquisitions was Bob Gill, who would later save Alexander's life. (Photo courtesy of R. B. Alexander)

Apache Troop Blues coming in to assist LRRP/Rangers. (Photo courtesy of R. B. Alexander)

LRRP/Ranger team leader Jim "Spanky" Seymour and montagnard Blol with the team as they ready for an insertion. Seymour served two and a half years as a LRRP/Ranger. (Photo courtesy of Jim Seymour)

LRRP/Ranger team teader Jim "Spanky" Seymour leads his team in from another mission. Assistant team leader Lee Hennings is in center. (Photo courtesy of Jim Seymour)

S.Sgt. Guy McConnell's Ranger team. McConnell kneeling at right. (Photo courtesy of Guy McConnell)

Left to right, standing: Rangers Jim McIntyre, Richard Cramer, and Bill Abbott. Left to right, kneeling: Lee Comstock and Rick Arden. McIntyre would use his rucksack to shield a grenade's blast during a firefight. (Photo courtesy of Rick Arden)

The village of Phuoc Vinh, outside of Camp Gorvad. (Photo courtesy of Jim "Spanky" Seymour)

LRRP/Ranger Jim "Spanky" Seymour performing a rappelling demo. (Photo courtesy of Jim "Spanky" Seymour)

Kit Carson scout Hoc Yan in the field with H Company Rangers. (Photo courtesy of Darrell Smith)

First of the ninth Blues going in to support LRRP/Rangers. (Photo courtesy of Capt. Kit Beatton)

Kregg P. J. Jorgenson (Photo courtesy of Katherine Knapp Jorgenson)

Rangers Jim McIntyre, Kenneth Yeisley, and Richard Cramer at Phuoc Vinh, 1969. (Photo courtesy of Kenneth Yeisley)

patrol had become quiet and distant, making McConnell think they were questioning his ability.

After a long, troubling night, the reluctant team leader finally got a message out to the radio-relay station on their URC-10 backup radio. The mission was scrubbed, and when the team eventually made it back to the company, McConnell was chewed out royally by Captain Paccerelli who warned him that if they had faked a bad radio in order to get out of the field then there would be hell to pay. Putting the lives of others at risk because you were scared was not only dangerous but stupid, and Paccerelli wouldn't tolerate it. Lurp missions tied up a lot of much-needed resources, and pulling out a team sometimes meant taking the gunships and liftships away from another team or unit. Paccerelli also realized that at times his temper got in the way of his judgment, and cooling down became a matter of going over the facts and details once again to determine what had really happened. He also relied on his senior sergeants and junior officers for additional comments and suggestions, and like a judge, he waited until all of the facts were in before finally deciding the case and rendering his verdict.

Until the communications NCO checked out the radio and confirmed that it had malfunctioned and that it wasn't the team leader's fault, Captain Paccerelli refused to talk to McConnell or to any member of the team about the mission.

McConnell said little himself. He knew the real hell was from the self-doubt you suffered while trying to do a difficult job under situational or climatic conditions that were seldom favorable. Being a Lurp/Ranger team leader lost some of its luster at moments like that, especially when you got your ass chewed out for things beyond your control.

His buddies assured McConnell the next mission would go better, and later, lying back on his cot, he told himself that it would have to be. Hemingway once described courage as "grace under pressure" and for a Ranger team leader, the time and pressures always dictated the level of grace. Like the sweltering temperatures they endured, the team leaders got "hot" or "cold" in degrees, the changes gradual and measurable.

One team leader who was hot was S.Sgt. Walter James "Spanky" Seymour, who seemed to have had long-range patrolling refined to a military science. Seymour, a quiet, soft-spoken soldier from Bellevue, Washington, was just beginning his second year as a Lurp/Ranger and referred to missions as "going camping," and the confidence he constantly demonstrated in the field came only with time and experience. At five feet eight inches and 130 pounds, Seymour's diminutive stature stood in stark contrast to his courage as a behind-the-lines operator. It was his remarkable calm in the face of danger and, perhaps, his sense of comfort in the jungle that inspired most of the people who went on patrol with him. He wasn't intimidated by the jungle. He actually seemed to like it. Several of the other team leaders in the company viewed him as a "stone-cold killer," while others who had served on his team knew that the simple truth was that he was just very good at his job, which they admitted often boiled down to surviving kill-or-be-killed situations. Being good at it didn't necessarily mean you liked it, but staying alive on a long-range patrol did mean that you had to be prepared. Seymour was always prepared.

While most GIs in Vietnam would never see a Viet Cong or NVA close up, much less a squad or more, long-range patrols routinely viewed them on intimate terms; usually up close while they were moving through a stretch of jungle or while reconning hidden base camps. The Rangers often got the opportunity to study what the enemy wore and carried, and when they ambushed the enemy, they got to sift through their papers and personal effects as the enemy lay dying. War got to be a really personal thing for them.

The Rangers came to know how the Viet Cong and NVA waited for them, often tracking the teams into the jungle to ambush them or getting on line and sweeping the vicinity of a team after a passing helicopter had given away their position by waving at them or dropping a smoke grenade to mark their positions when an overflight was requested by the team leader to verify the team's map location.

The Rangers were on intimate terms with the enemy, and no one understood the enemy better than those who had extended their combat tours to remain in the field.

Newly arrived Spec Four Dan Roberts from Thousand Oaks, California, served his first three missions with Seymour before he was assigned to another team, and Roberts was impressed by Seymour's woodsmanship and his coolness under fire. His ambushes were well planned and thought out as were his backup plans in case of the unexpected, and from those first three missions under Seymour's tutelage, Roberts came away with a strong foundation that would serve him well through his tour.

S.Sgt. Timothy Greenly was another natural team leader, and the tall, lanky Ranger possessed a gift for Lurp/Ranger field operations. But by the beginning of March, the company would need all of the talent it could muster as the North Vietnamese Army pressed in on the division.

Company patrols had reported recent buildups of enemy activity around Tay Ninh, and on 8 March 1969, the grunts and the artillery battery at Fire Support Base Grant became their next target.

Just after midnight, the jungle outpost was hit by a massive rocket and mortar attack, which was followed immediately by a massive ground assault. In the opening salvos, the fire support base's CP took a direct hit, killing many inside. Among the losses was Lt. Col. Peter Gorvad, the battalion commander for the 2d of the 12th Cav, which was then occupying Grant. With fires burning out of control and secondary explosions reverberating inside the perimeter, the base was in turmoil as the NVA 95C Regiment, under the command of Lieutenant Colonel Dung, swarmed forward, determined to breach its barbed-wire perimeter.

For two hours the battle for FSB Grant raged with little success for Dung's regiment as the Cav grunts and redlegs (artillerymen) fought desperately to hold the base. By sunrise, the enemy bodies littered the perimeter around the firebase, and numerous blood trails led back into the shadows of nearby Black Virgin Mountain.

Less than thirty-six hours later Fire Support Base Grant was hit again, this time by Lt. Col. Bui Ngoc Nuoi's 101D Regiment. But, like the earlier assault, his ground attack also failed.

As additional Ranger long-range patrols were sent into Tay Ninh province, the patrols began reporting heavy bicycle traffic, which meant the enemy was ferrying in supplies and equipment. Truck traffic moving south from Cambodia on several routes was also reported by the patrols, and Paccerelli quickly suggested during a squadron briefing that a special Ranger patrol go in to mine those routes. And, since the routes were closely watched and monitored by the NVA and Viet Cong and because of the danger involved, Captain Paccerelli volunteered to lead the patrol.

With six other carefully selected personnel, including First Lieutenant McKenzie, the minelaying team went through a short but intensive training program in the use and placement of the M7A2 antitank mine. An NCO from the 8th Engineers accompanied the patrol to serve as the minefield recorder.

Following a careful reconnaissance of the targeted locations, the seven-man patrol was flown into position in what appeared to be a typical last-light insertion by Apache Troop, 1st of the 9th Cav.

Under the cover of darkness Paccerelli led the Rangers to the trails and planted four M7A2 mines with an extra two-pound slab of C-4 explosive over each. Covering and camouflaging their work, the seven-man patrol moved out again and were soon picked up by an Apache Troop liftship.

A short time later, two Soviet-style, Chinese-built trucks were destroyed as they tried to infiltrate the region at night.

Company commander George Paccerelli and S.Sgt. George Kennedy then went back into the area with the 11th Armored Cavalry Regiment, riding the lead tank in line, to retrieve the unexploded mines.

On 27 March, Lieutenant Bell was inserting a patrol northeast of Dau Tieng, just north of the Michelin rubber plantation, and all was going well. The Rangers were dropped off in their designated LZ and quickly scurried into the jungle as the insertion helicopter flew away from the area. It was a textbook perfect insertion, but as the helicopter tried to gain altitude it was hit by .51-caliber antiaircraft machine-gun fire from the jungle. The NVA had not spotted the Lurps going in, but had zeroed in on the slow-flying helicopter, raking it repeatedly, hitting everyone on board including Lieutenant Bell.

With no time to react, the helicopter crashed into the jungle and was destroyed. There were no survivors.

CHAPTER TWENTY-ONE

At 0200 hours, Captain Kit Beatton, Apache Three-Zero, entered the darkened hootch in Tay Ninh, switched on his flashlight so as not to awaken everyone in the officers' quarters, and walked down the small corridor to the sectioned-off hootch. His target was the troop's Blues recon platoon leader's bunk. Knowing that Lt. R. B. Alexander probably already had his hand tightly wrapped around the grip of a .45 automatic, he called out to him before he reached his cubicle.

"Blue, you awake?" Beatton asked. The young infantry officer from San Clemente, California, grunted, then sat up slowly.

"What's up?" he asked, not awake enough to comprehend who was standing there. In the distance, the generator next to the troop's tactical operations center droned indifferently.

"A Lurp team's in contact," Beatton announced as Alexander finally recognized the pilot's voice. Usually when he was awakened from a sound sleep, it was only someone from the TOC with bad news. The fact that this time it was the Apache Troop lift platoon commander told him it was something pretty serious. "It looks like they're going to need to be pulled out, so I'm going to the flight line to get ready," Beatton told him. "Just thought you'd like to know. I mean, in case we go down and you have to lose some beauty rest to come out and rescue us."

"It's not beauty rest," Alexander snorted. "It's nasty

dreams, so I'll thank you not to screw it up, Captain!" Alexander stole a quick glance at the luminous face of the Timex travel alarm perched on the rocket box next to his cot. Hell, he thought, it's the middle of the night! Day contacts were bad enough, but the small running battles in dark of night were by far the worst. Not least because of the strong likelihood of encountering an NVA soldier aiming a rocket-propelled grenade at you from only a few feet away in the pitch-black jungle. If he was there, you'd never even see him until he fired the RPG while you were looking his way, and then there'd only be a glimpse of his silhouette in the flash of the backblast a split second before you were vaporized.

"The only black lace you're going to see this morning, Blue, will be on your boots!" Beatton chuckled as he turned and followed his flashlight beam out of the hootch.

Soon afterwards, Alexander heard the helicopters cranking. Beatton's Huey liftship would make the actual extraction while a gunship would provide protective fire.

The infantry reconnaissance platoon leader dressed quickly, then headed across the compound to let his platoon sergeant and squad leaders know what was going on if they weren't already over in the Apache Troop TOC monitoring the situation on the radio. What always amazed the lieutenant was how his squad leaders, sergeants Bob Gill, Tom Chambers, Jim Smart, and Bob Larsen, all of whom had previously served as Lurp/Rangers, always seemed to be one step ahead of everyone else.

He soon discovered them already getting their people ready for an effort to rescue the trapped team. Gill, the former Ranger Team 3-7 patrol leader and intel NCO, had incredible instincts, which Alexander had come to appreciate better after working with him in the field.

The former Lurp/Ranger NCOs in his platoon had strong personal reasons for wanting to participate in the rescue. They had shared experiences—particularly dangers—which had brought them close to the men in trouble. That wasn't the same reason that motivated Captain Beatton to respond. As the liftship platoon leader, it was his responsibility to insert and extract the Ranger long-range patrols, and although each of his pilots shared those duties, Beatton seemed to take more than his share of the hot extractions.

Inside the large sandbag-reinforced bunker that served as the troop's tactical operations center, the room was alive with night-shift personnel who were busy monitoring the radio traffic between Beatton's aircraft, the gunships, and the Ranger patrol. The Rangers already had four wounded, two seriously, and the NVA were closing in. As the helicopters raced out to assist the encircled Rangers, the odds were mounting against their survival. The situation was grim.

By the time Beatton's helicopter arrived on station, the Rangers had suffered two dead and three wounded. Apache 3-0 began his short final, telling the team leader to turn on his strobe light to identify the Rangers' position in the dark.

Back at Tay Ninh, Lieutenant Alexander saw his platoon was ready on the flight line, then he ran back to the TOC to await the word to go. At the contact site, the NVA were turning their attention to Beatton's helicopter, which was just touching down in the LZ. Green tracers began cutting through the underbrush toward the aircraft. The crew chief and door gunner were busy returning fire, being careful to keep their rounds away from the flashing strobe light that one of the Rangers was holding over his head.

"Taking fire!" Captain Beatton announced, surprisingly calm as the distinct *tick . . . tink . . . tick* of incoming rounds sounded through the aircraft. Alexander had always been surprised at how calm Beatton remained under fire, and just prior to taking over the recon platoon, he witnessed the true extent of Beatton's daring and grace under pressure.

Several months earlier, two of the Blue Platoon's three helicopters had been ambushed while coming into a landing zone and shot down, crashing into a burning meadow. Beatton, who was flying the lead aircraft, veered away just in time

with his load of recon soldiers and offloaded them at a safe
area before flying back to the ambush site to rescue the survivors. His aircraft took numerous hits from intense enemy
small-arms fire, but the Apache Troop pilot held his course
and brought the liftship down near the survivors. With ten
wounded infantrymen and aircraft crew members aboard,
Beatton brought the overloaded helicopter out over the treetops—all the while remaining calm and businesslike as he
coaxed the crippled aircraft back to safety.

That was Kit Beatton, and when Alexander took over the
Blue Platoon he knew that whatever happened on the ground,
Apache 3-0 would be there to help or he would certainly die
trying.

The Lurp/Ranger team was finding that out as they struggled to get their dead and dying team members to the rescue
helicopter. "Captain, they're saying they left one behind.
They couldn't carry him out!" the crew chief shouted into his
headset over the din of the battle.

"Say again?" Captain Beatton asked over the tumult.

"One's still back down the trail. He's wounded and can't
make it on his own."

"Roger," Beatton answered, then turned over the controls
to his copilot as he unstrapped his harness. "If I'm not back
in a few minutes, take off!" he shouted over his shoulder, exiting the aircraft.

Beatton pulled out his .38 revolver and disappeared into
the jungle toward the sound of the wounded Ranger's M-16.

The wounded soldier was lying prone behind a fallen log,
holding his own for the moment against an enemy force maneuvering against him. Between rounds, he was gamely trying to bandage his wounds.

"Come on!" Beatton shouted, coming up behind him and
pulling him to his feet as he fired his pistol toward moving
shadows and muzzle flashes. "We're getting out of here!"

The Apache Troop pilot lifted the wounded Ranger over
his shoulders in a fireman's carry and turned to race back

toward the waiting helicopter. Enemy small-arms fire perforated the area where they had just been, and then followed them seconds later in their mad flight back to the LZ. Beatton had fired all six rounds from his revolver and then stuffed it deep into his pocket. There wasn't any time to reload. "Hold on," he shouted to the wounded man as he struggled to the pickup zone. As the two Americans cleared the tree line, Beatton yelled to the crew chief to cover them. He could have saved his breath; the veteran door gunner was already raking the jungle.

A tangle of arms reached out to pull the two men aboard. They were jerked skyward as the helicopter lifted out of the pickup zone and back toward the 45th Field Hospital at Tay Ninh.

When the aircraft returned to the Apache Troop flight line, Lieutenant Alexander and a few others were waiting to greet Beatton and his crew. "So, doesn't that noise bother you?" Alexander asked, looking past the crew members and into the now empty helicopter.

"What noise?" Beatton said.

Alexander smiled. "The sound of your brass balls banging against the cockpit while you're flying."

Beatton merely shrugged it off. "I think the noise my knees make knocking together blocks it all out. They needed some help. I couldn't leave them." Alexander nodded. That was Beatton, and he was proud to have the man as a friend and, more important, glad to have him flying with Apache Troop.

Captain Paccerelli felt the same way after learning of the pilot's daring act. He later recommended Beatton for a Silver Star for gallantry. Just then, however, there were more pressing matters to attend to. Two of his Rangers were dead—Sgt. Dwight "Bull" Durham and Sgt. Loel Largent—and several others were in the hospital. He'd debrief the surviving team members, visit the wounded soldiers, and plan another memorial service. Then he would retreat to his quarters and struggle over the special letters . . .

"I wish to extend to you my most profound sympathy on the recent loss of your son . . ." Paccerelli paused. No school in the army prepared an officer for that painful task, and the more often he had to do it, the less comfortable he became. All soldiers die in battle, whether it is all at once on the battlefield or in bits and pieces late at night in the privacy of the mind.

To keep it from happening too frequently, the captain made a point of continually reminding those higher-ups who were requesting the missions of the job his Rangers were performing. He fought to insure that they wouldn't be sacrificed for nothing.

In a memo to the chief of staff, G-2, on a DD form 95, he made his case for rejecting one such mission. "This officer requests that consideration be given to the attached mission request," he wrote. "It is felt by this officer that the possibility of enemy forces being in the area has been proven by the action of the past several days. The finding phase of the operation has already been accomplished. It appears to this officer that the fix, fight, and finish phases are now in order.

"This officer begs the colonel's leave to request that this mission be postponed until a later date when the question of finding the enemy again enters the field."

He signed and submitted the form and waited for the fallout. Saying "no" in the army was seldom taken very well.

CHAPTER TWENTY-TWO

Throughout the rest of April, the patrols reported numerous sightings within their tactical area of operations and managed to capture large quantities of enemy weapons, documents, and other materials. The patrols were also generating a very large volume of intelligence data. And whether the division thought that the Lurp/Rangers were making up their reports or not, in order to verify the number of sightings and enemy contacts, it was decided that a CID officer would be secreted into the company to conduct an undercover investigation. The intelligence officer was also to investigate the rumor that some Lurp/Ranger patrols were mutilating enemy bodies.

In May, disguised as an enlisted man, the officer joined the unit, went through the company training program, and was assigned as a Lurp/Ranger replacement. After successfully infiltrating the unit, he reported back his findings to division.

He was in the company as a spy for division. Apparently, someone somewhere thought the company was finding too much intelligence material, which had led division to bring in the plant from CID. His assignment definitely cast a shadow on the company's integrity and everything the men had worked so hard to achieve.

Captain Paccerelli complained about the matter, but he didn't really have a say. He bristled at the implication his people were lying about sightings of the enemy or face-to-face encounters and sudden firefights, but he reluctantly accepted the intelligence officer into the company. There was no choice.

On the wall in his hootch, Captain Paccerelli glanced frequently at a quote from Teddy Roosevelt he had brought to the attention of the company.

> It is not the critic who counts, not the man who points out how the strong man stumbled, or where the doer of deeds could have done better. The credit belongs to the man who is actually in the arena whose face is marred by dust and sweat and blood who knows great enthusiasm, great devotion, the triumph of high achievement; and who, at the worse, if he fails, at least fails while daring greatly.

Paccerelli's people dared greatly, and occasionally they stumbled in the arena, but he was certain that the CID officer would only discover what he already knew—that they were very dedicated young men who performed extremely difficult tasks willingly. Though there would always be critics, he felt their numbers were decreasing as was the intensity of their complaints. Soon, he thought, the powers at squadron and division would come to trust the Rangers' field reports.

In early May 1969, the division changed commanders; Maj. Gen. Elvy Benton Roberts took over from Major General Forsyth. Roberts had graduated from West Point in 1943, and in 1944 had jumped into Normandy on D day with the 101st Airborne Division. Later that same year, he participated in Operation Market Garden, the combined Airborne assault on east Holland. The operation was designed to secure four key bridges and was supposed to bring about an early end to the war in Europe. The thirty-five thousand British, American, Polish, and Dutch paratroopers were accidentally dropped far from their intended targets. They struggled to reach their objectives only to run into a crack German tank division that stopped the plan from succeeding just short of its goal.

As a young officer, E. B. Roberts also took part in the defense of Bastogne, Belgium, where the paratroopers held out against enormous odds and helped add to the near-legendary legacy of the famous 101st Airborne Division.

In the early sixties, Roberts became instrumental in the development of the modern airmobile warfare concept. He'd had two tours of duty in Vietnam, in 1966 and 1968, by the time he returned in 1969 and took over the 1st Cavalry Division. Unlike some general officers, who saw Vietnam in conventional tactical terms, Roberts likened the fighting to the Indian Wars in the American Southwest. He saw the Rangers as his scouts, his 1st of the 9th Cav Squadron as his highly mobile cavalry troops who could strike hard and swift, and the heliborne infantry brigades as the pivotal factor needed to destroy the enemy once he'd been found and fixed.

His new approach would be tested early because the Communists attacked Landing Zone Carolyn the day after he took command.

The early morning attack fell again to Lieutenant Colonel Dung's 95C Regiment, and it went better than the two-hour rout he had suffered at LZ Grant in March. In May, after a devastating barrage of rockets and mortars, Dung's soldiers charged forward when the bugles sounded and tore through the camp's perimeter. Hundreds of NVA soldiers rushed the camp from several directions at once and overran enough of the LZ's protective bunkers and fighting positions to split the camp nearly in two, leaving the grunts of the 2d of the 8th Cav and the artillerymen of the 1st of the 30th and 2d of the 19th to counterattack as best they could. Until they finally withdrew at sunrise, the NVA soldiers threatened to obliterate LZ Carolyn.

The fighting was intense and at times erupted into brutal hand-to-hand combat. Artillery positions were overrun, retaken, and overrun again as the battle pivoted back and forth in the predawn hours. Ammunition storage points were blown up, and the smoke from the fires and shrapnel from the exploding rounds fell over Carolyn like a terrible firestorm.

On the ground, cannons were hurriedly lowered and leveled to fire beehive, canister, and flechette rounds at point-blank range into the human-wave assaults, while helicopter gunships and fixed-wing fighter/bombers attacked the Communist forces from above. Each beehive round contained thousands of small naillike projectiles that cut wide swaths through the enemy lines. However, other enemy soldiers leaped forward immediately to fill the ranks of the forward assault waves, only to have their own ranks decimated as the U.S. artillerymen scrambled to load and fire again. Eventually, the North Vietnamese had to climb over the mangled bodies of their slain comrades to get at the Americans.

By first light, the battle for LZ Carolyn was over. Dung's surviving troops withdrew and headed back toward the Cambodian border, while the men still alive on the LZ took inventory.

More Ranger patrols were immediately deployed into the region, and they were soon reporting significant activity as the NVA and Viet Cong geared up for a series of attacks on U.S. fire support bases that began barely one week later.

Ranger teams were sent out to try to determine the latest tactical shifts of the Viet Cong and NVA, which always resulted in more "spontaneous" contacts. As a result, the company suffered another casualty when Sp4. Daniel Arnold was killed on patrol.

CHAPTER TWENTY-THREE

In the following months, Ranger long-range patrols reported that the NVA and VC were using bicycles to ferry weapons, ammunition, and supplies into South Vietnam. Several teams had watched small columns of bicycles stacked ridiculously high with all sorts of military equipment and supplies as they were pushed down trails and along remote jungle paths. The enemy was using wooden extensions attached to the handlebars to push along the heavy bikes. Bicycles were an integral part of the enemy's supply system, and a modified two wheeler could ferry in hundreds of pounds of arms and supplies virtually undetected along the network of jungle footpaths and trails running from Cambodia into parts of South Vietnam. And it looked as though the heavy volume of materials coming into Tay Ninh Province was a pretty strong indicator of the enemy's battle plans.

In an area just north of LZ Grant, the NVA had built a bridge across the river for bicycle and foot traffic, and after an Apache Troop scout bird flying at treetop level discovered it, an accompanying gunship decided to take it out with rockets. But the gunship was driven back by a Soviet-made 12.7mm antiaircraft machine gun before another pilot arrived on station from the troop to make his own run. The 12.7mm heavy machine gun was a crew-served weapon used to protect important sites from American aircraft, but to the pilots facing it, the importance of the site was secondary to the amount and accuracy of antiaircraft fire it produced. The heavy automatic-weapons fire tore holes through the cockpit and fuselage of the gunship as the pilot began his run. The pilot and the copilot died instantly as the aircraft tumbled into the thick jungle.

Lieutenant Alexander's Blues were scrambled to attempt a rescue, which they did by rappelling two squads down through the heavy forest to recover the bodies of the dead crew. But it wasn't an easy rescue as the area they were in was rife with enemy bunkers, trenches, and fighting positions. With his fourteen men, the infantry leader brought out the bodies, fighting the jungle and the enemy every step of the way until reaching the extraction point, little more than a natural break in the jungle that offered enough space to land several helicopters. But the Blues weren't alone when they got there. The NVA were pushing to add to their own body-count figures by attacking in strength from the opposite tree line, effectively pinning down the small reaction force. The Blues were taking fire from two different directions and would soon be hopelessly trapped if they didn't get some serious help from somewhere.

Suddenly, a UH-1B model gunship, flown by Apache Troop pilot WO Swede Erickson, roared into the landing zone. Hovering ten feet above the ground, the gunship unleashed rockets and minigun fire directly into the enemy positions before it, too, was downed. While the Blues provided cover, Erickson and his crew joined up with the two infantry squads until more gunships and rescue helicopters arrived to pull them out.

The bridge, its protective 12.7mm antiaircraft gun, and the extensive enemy bunker complex combined to suggest that the NVA were protecting something major beneath the trees, so two days later, the squadron commander, Lieutenant Colonel Peterson, ordered a beefed-up force of Blues, along with supporting gunships and scout helicopters, to return, to find out what it was.

With Lieutenant Alexander in command of the ground

force, the Blues soon discovered the opening to an underground bicycle factory and a large cache of weapons and supplies. However, the underground factory and tunnels were not empty, and the NVA fought hard to defend their property.

A small but intense battle broke out, and the fifty-man force soon found itself fending off a much larger enemy unit. The fighting was close and furious, and at one point, the NVA attempted to box in the Blues before being driven back by some quick maneuvering.

Alexander, a trained demolitions officer, waded out into the murky river, planted a charge of C-4 explosive, and then scrambled back out of the water and withdrew to safety. The tumultuous explosion that followed rocked the river banks and disintegrated the bridge. At least the NVA would be forced to go miles out of their way to cross the river or rebuild the bridge. Either way would cause them some major delays.

Sensing correctly what was about to happen next, the NVA maneuvered to defend their underground facilities. As the reinforced Blues platoon worked its way into position, securing several tunnels and underground chambers, the enemy attacked. Alexander had been setting C-4 charges in the chambers and tunnels and came out to find himself right in the middle of a major fight above ground. When the charges below exploded, collapsing the tunnels and factory chambers, the enraged NVA increased their efforts while the combined cavalry force was ordered to move to a landing zone for extraction because it had accomplished its mission.

Alexander had several wounded friendlies in front of him, and six dead NVA, and suspected that getting to the pickup zone would take some doing. He was right. Time and again the NVA pressed the Americans only to have Cav troopers force them back. When they finally neared the pickup zone, the fight had shifted once again and this time they found themselves pinned down just short of the extraction site by an NVA machine-gun team. Alexander and the squad with him returned fire, but with little visible effect. The NVA machine gun was well dug in and fortified.

Alexander crawled out to find a better position to return fire and realized too late that he had little protective cover. Worse, the enemy gunner was zeroing in on him, and bursts of machine-gun rounds kicked up dirt to his front.

Lieutenant Alexander rolled onto his left side, retrieved a baseball grenade, pulled the pin and tossed it at the enemy position. The grenade arced toward its goal but was deflected at the last moment by an overhanging tree limb.

After the explosion, the NVA machine gunner rose from his hiding place and leveled the RPD on the officer. But, his attention focused on the American officer, he hadn't noticed that Sergeant Gill had worked his way close to the enemy bunker. Gill had just pulled a grenade to take the bunker out when the NVA gunner suddenly rose.

With no time to pick up his rifle and engage the enemy soldier or even to warn the lieutenant to run, Gill took careful aim, screamed for the lieutenant to get down, and threw the grenade at the enemy soldier's head as hard and fast as he could. The grenade beaned the soldier, who dropped the RPD machine gun and fell unconscious back into the fighting position. The live grenade rolled down behind him. The explosion followed immediately, and Gill ran forward to retrieve the machine gun and make certain the soldier or soldiers in the position were dead.

Back at Tay Ninh after the battle, Lieutenant Alexander thanked the sergeant for saving his life. "You threw a perfect strike," he said.

Sergeant Gill merely shrugged off the accomplishment. "He didn't see me," Gill finally replied, smiling.

"For a minute there I wondered if you had even pulled the pin, Sergeant," laughed Alexander.

"They last longer when you don't," Gill responded, then rejoined his squad.

The lieutenant stared after him, wondering what was it about former Lurp/Rangers that made them stand out? Courageous soldiers, sure, but it was something more than that—something that gave them a definite edge—and made the lieutenant happy to have Gill, Chambers, Smart, and Larsen in his platoon. Whether the Rangers knew it or not, the Cav was fortunate to have them in the quick-reaction force because who else better understood the need for immediate support than those who had relied upon it in the past?

The camaraderie and old friendships were still there, too, and every now and then when Rangers came to Tay Ninh to be inserted by Apache Troop, they looked up the former members of their company.

One of Sergeant Chambers's stories was about the mission he had been on with S.Sgt. Spanky Seymour, when the Ranger on guard duty heard the sounds of something or somebody sneaking around in the dark jungle in front of his position. He had quietly awakened the rest of the team and alerted them to the movement. They listened, and when a twig snapped a few moments later, the Rangers knew that someone or something was moving up on the team and was less than a few feet away.

In their small circular night defensive perimeter, the five Lurps anxiously watched and waited, but when the brush in front of them finally parted and a tiger leaped over the team, a new element of fear entered their jungle warfare.

Seymour and Chambers laughed while retelling the story, while others listened in awe and redefined their list of jungle dangers. Another story involved Sgt. Howard Shute, who after waking up one chilly morning in the jungle, pulled off the small piece of camouflage nylon poncho liner each Lurp was allowed to carry in the field as protection against insects and the surprisingly chilling dew of the early morning. Anyway, Shute discovered a deadly bamboo viper asleep on his warm, dry lap.

"No shit! A bamboo viper?" someone asked in disbelief.

The storyteller nodded and held out his hands in a two-foot display of the snake's size.

"Yep, and it's about yea long," he said, "and Shute is wide-eyed and staring at the deadly snake in his lap, which by the way is only inches away from his pecker . . ."

"No shit?"

The storyteller nodded solemnly. "No nothing! I mean, Shute hasn't breathed in a good minute or two as the snake, whose bite will kill your ass faster than any dozen rattlesnakes, realizes someone just snatched away his warm binky, lifts his head to take an angry 'what the fuck's up?' look around."

"Why didn't he just shoot it?" asked a new arrival. The veterans in the small audience shook their heads or snickered.

"And what? Shoot his dick off?" someone else replied sarcastically as the storyteller finished the tale.

"Besides, he couldn't grab his knife or rifle without drawing more attention from the snake, *and*," he quickly added, "he probably didn't think it was a good idea for anyone else on the team to try to shoot it off his groin, either. A William Tell apple on your head is one thing, but a 'Mister Step-and-a-Half' on your balls is something else. No grazed apple ever decided to bite back!"

Mister Step-and-a-Half was the nickname for the deadly reptile whose toxic venom was said to kill its victim in that short a distance.

"So the snake bit him?"

The storyteller shook his head and grinned. "Nope," he finally said. "The now cold snake decided to slither off Shute's lap, down his pant leg and boot and back into the bamboo. I don't think Shute began breathing again until about a day or two later," the storyteller said.

"You Lurps are crazy!"

"It helps," one of the visiting Lurps responded.

What kind of soldiers repeatedly went behind enemy lines with only four or five others? Some might say foolhardy "hot dogs" or "showboats." Not Lieutenant Alexander. He owed his life to a Ranger sergeant and had learned to trust it in the hands of the three others. They weren't just good soldiers, they were exceptional soldiers, and Lieutenant Alexander vowed to take every opportunity that presented itself to recruit as many of them as he could for his Blues platoon.

"Say, Sergeant?" he asked the Ranger who was telling the war stories. "I think the mess tent might have a few more steaks left over on the barbecue for you and your team."

"Thank you, sir!"

Alexander shrugged. "No big thing," he said. "Later, before you catch a ride back to Phuoc Vinh, we'll see if we can round you up a cold beer or Coke while we're at it. How does that sound?"

"It sounds great! Thank you."

Alexander smiled to himself. "Rangers Lead the Way" was the motto of the Army Ranger, so what did it hurt to tempt their "direction" with a whiff of good steak barbecue? Recruiting was all in the sizzle.

CHAPTER TWENTY-FOUR

In June, Paccerelli wrote a newsletter information piece to the company on the deployment of M14 antipersonnel mines, better known as "toe-poppers." It was time to provide the team with an additional punch.

It is recommended that as an early warning for the patrol, and as a form of deadly harassment to the enemy, patrols will establish unmanned (fake) ambushes away from their LP/OPs during the hours of darkness or any other time that the patrol leader feels he has located a lucrative area. The unmanned ambush will employ M14 antipersonnel mines with "det" cord passing under the mines to a well-aimed and camouflaged claymore(s).

To insure positive coverage of the likely avenue(s) of approach, three M14 mines with det cord passing under each, then running to the claymore(s) should be used. They should be placed in a V configuration to adequately cover the killing zone. Although blasting caps are not needed on the det cord, the use of nonelectric blasting caps will insure positive detonation. Remember to carry new det cord on each mission. Two personnel will be present when the mines are emplaced, and in the event that the ambush is not triggered, then those two personnel will recover the mines prior to moving away from the immediate area.

Patrol leaders will have a fire mission worked up on each unmanned ambush site so when the enemy detonates the ambush, artillery fire can immediately engage the area. Due to the enemy often moving in company-size force, it is recommended that 75 meters be considered the ideal safe distance from the patrol for an unmanned ambush; with 50 meters the minimum and up to 500 meters the maximum. Patrols should bear in mind that when the enemy trips the ambush, he will lay out suppressive fires until he realizes that he is not receiving return fire. Keep low to the ground, don't engage him unless absolutely necessary; let the artillery work him over.

Besides the newsletter piece, Captain Paccerelli reminded those in the company of the importance of setting and checking the rattraps every day. Rats were a plague on the bases. They thrived in the frontier-citylike base camps and lived off garbage the GIs generated. Hundreds were scurrying throughout Camp Gorvad at any given time, and since the rats carried a number of diseases, including bubonic plague, rodent eradication was a standing priority for the units in the base camp. Rattraps were set out, and each morning they were checked and the number of rats reported to the first sergeant.

The company's mascot, a brown and black mongrel named Lurp, was used in the process of eradication in morning formations. Lurp had been brought back from the streets of Sin City, just outside Camp Radcliff in An Khe, by one of the original eighteen Lurp volunteers a year and a half earlier.

One of two Ranger mascots, Lurp had grown and thrived; Corporal, the second canine mascot, never made the move to Camp Evans when the division deployed north. While there was an official military policy forbidding pets and, specifically, dogs in the base camps, Lurp, officially, didn't exist. When the dogs were rounded up for extermination, the company reported that it had no pets in the unit let alone any dogs.

Lurp grew to forty or fifty pounds and his loyalty to the company was undeniable, and that loyalty was returned by everyone in the company. At morning formations, he stood near the company commander or first sergeant, eagerly waiting to please. His specialty was killing rats, and when the evening's catch was brought before the morning formation, Lurp would chase a fleeing rodent down and scoop it up in his powerful jaws. After shaking it viciously once or twice and snapping the rat's neck, he would proudly bound back to the company commander or first sergeant with the catch in his mouth, whereupon the entire Ranger formation would applaud.

Lurp also followed deploying teams to the edge of the company compound and was there to greet them upon their return. For a generation who grew up on Lassie and Rin Tin Tin, the Rangers saw Lurp as their canine protector and friend.

The newsletters also reminded the personnel of the advantage of using long whip antennas over the short whips and the need to use acetate map covers to protect the few maps the unit had available for the teams. They informed the Rangers of Bible services offered by one of the division chaplains; warned of the need for test-firing weapons before patrols went out; why it was important to take salt tablets in a tropical climate; why cigarettes or other tobacco products were taboo in the field; and why no reading material should be taken out on patrol (this came about after an enemy soldier nearly walked in on a team because one of its members was reading a book and not paying attention to security).

From advanced patrolling techniques to the finer points of rat catching, to everyday reminders, bits and pieces, and necessary odds and ends, the newsletters provided a valuable tool to the Rangers. The company commander's goal with the newsletters was to help improve the effectiveness of the teams, primarily for their sake but partially to show their critics that the Rangers were a viable asset to the division. First impressions die hard, and even at brigade level there was still some doubt about the Rangers' effectiveness.

In one case in the 2d Brigade area of operations, when one of Paccerelli's teams reported heavy enemy movement around them, killed two of the enemy soldiers when they had gotten a little too close, and then requested extraction, the brigade TOC didn't believe the patrol's report and was reluctant to extract the men.

When the Ranger radio-relay team reported the matter to Paccerelli, who was in Phuoc Vinh, Paccerelli contacted the 1st of the 9th Cav and requested that their people pull his team out. Then he ordered the team to bring out the two dead enemy soldiers with them and take them to the 2d Brigade TOC, and deposit the bodies of the Viet Cong soldiers at the TOC's front door, weapons and all, which they did.

Paccerelli knew he'd catch hell for that, but he also understood that it was the only way to make a lasting impact on those who questioned the patrol reports. Division had already slipped a CID officer into the company to spy on the teams, so the reluctance on the part of 2d Brigade was nothing new.

Captain Paccerelli was chewed out for the act of "insolence," but he took the matter in stride. His "insolent" action apparently achieved its purpose; the sighting reports of the teams were never questioned again.

By June 1969, the 1st of the 9th received a new squadron commander; Lt. Col. James W. "Pete" Booth replaced Lieutenant Colonel Peterson. Paccerelli was amazed at the high quality of the officers assigned to lead the squadron, figuring command of the squadron had to be a plum toward making general. Like his predecessors, Lieutenant Colonel Booth was an outstanding leader.

Booth was a forty-year-old pilot from Hartwell, Georgia, who preferred using a gunship as his command and control aircraft, rather than the more traditional Huey slick, which told Captain Paccerelli something about him. As Long Knife Six the new squadron commander could have easily let the gunship pilots under his command handle the ARA requests, including those from Hotel Company, but Colonel Booth preferred to lead by example. But, in combat, leading by example was always a dangerous proposition; it sometimes meant Booth had to charge into heavy machine-gun fire to provide critical gunship support for his own men. Booth was that kind of commander, and the Ranger patrols were discovering that early on.

Turning things around had taken many months, and the relationship that Hotel Company enjoyed with the 1st of the 9th as well as the three brigades and the general staff took a great deal of effort on everybody's part. While the commanders played an important role in guiding the transformation, it was the men of Company E (LRP) and then Company H (Ranger) and the 1st of the 9th who made it possible.

CHAPTER TWENTY-FIVE

Madam Pham Thi Loi was dead, shot and killed by a Ranger patrol leader from Hotel Company in the vicinity of the Suoi Bien Moc bridge in Binh Long Province on 23 June. Now Major Truong Van Phuc, the province chief, wanted to know how and why the innocent civilian had died.

The division began an immediate investigation so that Major General Roberts could offer the facts to the province chief. The company was ordered to provide a thorough chronology of the incident as well as of the events leading up to and following the death of Madam Pham.

The time line would show that it was an accidental shooting, while the facts would reveal much, much more.

On 13 June, the company received a mission to send a six-man patrol into an area in the neighborhood of the Suoi Bien Moc bridge to conduct reconnaissance and surveillance and to locate suspected enemy base camps. The emphasis was placed on enemy identification through the capture of a prisoner of war or the recovery of documents.

The following day, the operations sergeant and the patrol leader flew to the Minh Thanh Special Forces Camp to notify the detachment commander there of the patrol and to arrange for fire support if it was needed. The Special Forces commander agreed, noting that there were no friendly personnel in the team's recon area.

On the fifteenth, the six-man patrol was inserted into the area and discovered plenty of well-used trails and fighting positions. The following day, the Rangers got into a brief fire-fight with two enemy soldiers who were dressed in gray shirts, black trousers, and green hats. They were probably part of a Viet Cong unit, but which one was anybody's guess. They weren't wearing packs or carrying anything other than Soviet-style assault rifles.

When they finally broke contact and ran, the Viet Cong left behind only spent shell casings. The Rangers patrolled on and, four days later, discovered a fresh campsite three or four enemy soldiers had used within the previous forty-eight hours. Finding a trail that intersected with a tired dirt road, the patrol set up an observation post to monitor the area. On the map, the road was referred to as 242, just a crooked line through a jungle of green.

An hour later, they observed two enemy soldiers on the road seventy-five meters away. The men wore black clothing and green hats, and one had brush tied to him as camouflage. About thirty-five minutes later, the Rangers heard movement and talking by two to three people to their east, so the patrol leader requested a Pink team—a scout helicopter and gun-ship escort—to investigate. They were on their way when the patrol leader called the Minh Thanh camp to ask if any friendlies were in the patrol area. The answer was "No."

When the Pink team arrived on station, it quickly located the trail the enemy had used, reconned by fire on several sus-pect sites, and when they received no return fire, the Pink team departed. Within minutes after the helicopters broke station, one Vietnamese yelled out to another who quickly re-sponded. Before they could react, the Rangers distinctly heard five to six other voices coming from the northeast.

The team leader called in artillery on the location, and when they moved up to take a look at the results, they found fresh enemy sandal prints. When nothing more was discov-ered and no more movement or voices were detected, the team leader moved his people into a night defensive position.

The next day, the patrol observed two enemy soldiers cross

242. They, too, were wearing black clothing and green hats. This time, however, they were shouldering heavy packs, equipment, and weapons.

Later in the day, the Rangers heard six small-arms rounds fired at a Chinook helicopter as it lumbered toward Song Be. The enemy soldiers were taking potshots.

On the day the team was to have been extracted, Captain Paccerelli extended the mission for one day in the hopes of capturing a POW. The area was very lucrative, and because of the small size of the enemy patrols observed, the team was ordered to make every effort to take a prisoner.

The next morning, the Ranger team heard two Vietnamese voices to their west, and the Rangers worked their way through the jungle toward the sound. A short time later, the patrol found a bicycle hidden under a bush just off the road. The Rangers soon discovered a second bicycle hidden nearby and decided to set up to capture the bicycles' owners when they returned. To make sure that the bikes weren't decoys to draw the Rangers in, the team leader and one other patrol member conducted a brief reconnaissance of the immediate area.

As the patrol leader worked his way through the brush, he spotted movement twenty meters to his front and brought up his rifle. When a person in a khaki shirt and green bandanna suddenly jumped up from behind a bush, the Ranger fired a single shot that dropped the individual. The bush had covered the lower portion of the man's body when he stood up, nor could the team leader see his hands.

"*Chieu Hoi!*" the patrol leader yelled, still covering the area with his weapon. There was no answer.

Back at the team's position, two individuals in gray shirts and black trousers were spotted while trying to flee the area. The Rangers stepped out on the trail and captured them. Both were females.

When the patrol leader called for the team's medic to help

the man he had shot, the medic discovered that the man wasn't a man at all but a woman.

The patrol leader requested an immediate extraction and informed Phuoc Vinh that it had a wounded female prisoner.

"Roger, how bad is she hurt?" asked Phuoc Vinh, giving the Slashing Talon team call sign.

"She's hit in the side," the team leader immediately responded.

"Roger. Keep up a tight security and do everything you can to keep her alive. Slashing Talon Six. Out."

There wasn't much the Rangers could do for the dying woman, and twenty-five minutes before the extraction helicopter arrived, Pham Thi Loi died of her wounds.

The Ranger patrol and the two remaining detainees were then extracted and flown to Fire Support Base Buttons, where the prisoners were turned over to the MPs. At eight o'clock that evening, Captain Paccerelli was notified that the three women had been classified as "innocent civilians," and then was asked if there was any way for the Rangers to recover the body of Madam Pham.

The Ranger Commander offered that there was and called for volunteers, including the six men who had conducted the nine-day extended patrol. With the company commander serving as the recovery-patrol leader, he and five others made a combat assault back into the area, accompanied by a Cav Pink team.

The helicopter scout pilot reported numerous spider holes that showed signs of recent use along the edge of their landing zone. The recovery team wasted little time getting to the site where the previous patrol had left Madam Pham's body, and after setting four of the patrol members up to provide security, Captain Paccerelli and his lead scout moved directly to the body. Sandal tracks crisscrossed the previous patrol's boot tracks, and a thin covering of dirt coated the dead woman's body. Bells and whistles sounded for Paccerelli.

Whoever had tried to cover the body was most likely still around, and he was certain that it was the presence of the scout and gunship helicopters that kept them in hiding.

The captain loaded the dead woman into a body bag, then he and the lead scout carried it back to the patrol's defensive position. The recovery team was quickly extracted, and the Ranger company commander delivered the body to the 2d Brigade's S-5.

Officially, the woman's death was ruled an accident, which was what was reported to the province chief. Major General Roberts sent along his personal regrets and condolences. However, in the letter outlining the facts to Major Truong, the 1st Air Cavalry Division Commander also expressed his concern about what Madam Pham and her two companions were doing in that remote region.

Roberts wrote: "This unfortunate incident occurred when Madam Pham and her two companions were in the jungle off road 242. Madam Pham was to the east of the road approximately 35 meters while her two companions were to the west of the road approximately 20 meters. Their reason and purpose for being at that location, 15 kilometers from her village at Xa Minh Hoa, is not known."

Everybody had suspicions, but only the Viet Cong knew the truth, and they weren't talking. At least not about what Madam Pham had been doing in the region. It was easier to capitalize on her death at the hands of the Americans.

CHAPTER TWENTY-SIX

If it had all seemed like a bad dream before, then it was about to become a very real nightmare. Patrol 4-1 had been sent out to intercept the rocket teams that were targeting Phuoc Vinh, and while they had anticipated running into four or five Viet Cong artillerymen, they hadn't counted on this. The eighteen- or twenty-man file of enemy soldiers had stopped no more than twenty-five meters from McConnell's team, and the steady stream of bobbing flashlights the Viet Cong were using to find their way into the small bunker complex suddenly went out. Sappers usually led the enemy patrols to their bunker complexes and jungle base camps because they were specially trained to be quiet and extra cautious. For the Rangers, knowing that they were all sappers didn't help matters any. Whether it was just their normal degree of caution or the lead sapper had actually sensed something out of the ordinary, something had caused them to turn off the flashlights. However, the absence of artificial illumination had no effect on their forward progress; they were still coming on.

The Rangers had discovered the small but newly constructed jungle camp four days earlier, and in its largest bunker in the center of the base camp McConnell found medical supplies, a Viet Cong flag, and the company records including a complete unit roster and the names of others who assisted the sapper outfit. The enemy unit, which they had identified as the C504 Sapper Company of the SR-5 Battalion, were well-trained combat-support troops. Technically, sappers were engineers, but their primary specialty was infiltrating the perimeters of U.S. and Allied base camps with satchel charges strapped to their backs. Once they had carefully and quietly worked their way through the concertina and barbed-wire barriers, run the gauntlet of trip flares and other anti-intrusion devices, the sappers would plant explosives to blow holes in the perimeter wire large enough for the main assault force to rush through, destroy machine gun positions and mortar pits, take out communication and command bunkers, and destroy artillery pieces and aircraft.

Since sappers were usually local Viet Cong, i.e., who lived in the region, discovering the roster was an intelligence coup of the greatest magnitude, while the list of the names of the locals who supported them was a guarantee that the enemy unit would cease to exist for the next couple of months.

After calling in their find, McConnell's team had been airlifted out with the captured materials. But the very next day, the team was reinserted into the same area to see who might return, so after setting up their perimeter, the five-man patrol sat back to wait.

Staff Sergeant McConnell and Sgt. Craig Leerburg had daisy-chained five claymore antipersonnel mines across the front of their position and scattered five M14 toe poppers along a bend in the trail that led into the jungle base area. They had also set out a number of individual claymores on their flanks. The team had then set up in the standard wagonwheel defensive formation with PFC Roman Taijeron, Sp4. Michael Germany, and Sp4. Ken Burch in a shallow, bowl-shaped depression against the backside of a bunker. Burch was the team's tail gunner, Taijeron was the patrol medic, and Germany operated the team's PRC-25 radio.

The bunkers surrounding them had offered a two-foot-high earthen berm as protection for the team. It had provided a small but adequate perimeter and, more importantly, some cover to hide behind. The bunkers had been designed to protect those inside the small complex against sudden intruders. Anyone trying to attack the base had to get through the small ring of fortifications. The bunker provided good cover, and with the toe poppers and claymores spread out around them, the Rangers had plenty of surprises in their defense.

The handful of poorly constructed underground bunkers and fighting positions had told McConnell that they had been dug hastily, without the normal planning and consideration the enemy usually gave to his defenses. They had been only temporary positions, and judging from their size and number, they had been built for no more than platoon-size element.

When the rain began shortly after sunset, it started slowly and began to build with intensity. Soon the depression between the bunkers where the team had set up was rapidly becoming a wading pool. By midnight, the water was four inches deep, and the once hard earth that had formed the lip of the bunkers began to turn into soft mud. Staying warm and dry was becoming impossible, and during the next three hours the real battle for the Rangers was in keeping their weapons clean and their chattering teeth from giving their position away. Drenched camouflage uniforms clung to their bodies like a layer of cold, wrinkled skin.

When the rain had finally begun to ease, the night still hadn't become any more friendly. The cloud cover made for the kind of darkness that provoked fears that should have been left behind in childhood, the ones that made your heart race at anything that went *bump* in the night.

McConnell hadn't been able to see Leerburg or the others who were only a few feet away, and the small team was made to feel even more isolated by the total darkness. Fear was often easier to confront in light; in the dark it became difficult to define or voice.

Shortly after four o'clock in the morning, the Ranger on guard had spotted the flashlights snaking their way through the winding jungle trail that fed into the base camp, and he had awakened the rest of the team. The men had come up with their weapons ready. As the enemy moved closer, the Rangers were able to hear the rustle of their wet uniforms as they moved. It had not been a squad-size element. The fifteen to twenty individual shadows that could be seen behind the pale yellow flashlight beams had told them that the unit approaching had been much larger than the number of bunkers had originally indicated. How much larger was anybody's guess, but it had begun to look like Alamo odds to the Rangers inside the Viet Cong bunker complex.

Waiting for the command from McConnell, the Rangers had held their fire. In Basic and Advanced Individual Training, the closest pop-up target on the rifle range had been fifty meters away and had been referred to as a "gimme." If a soldier couldn't hit the pop-up target at fifty meters, he couldn't expect to nail the four hundred-meter silhouette easily. The silhouettes in the jungle in front of them had been less than twenty meters away. The element of surprise had been on their side, and McConnell had wanted to use it to the team's full advantage.

But the degree of surprise had suddenly seemed to diminish when the column of Viet Cong sappers had stopped and switched off the flashlights. If the Cav Lurps' adrenaline had been pumping before that, it had begun working overtime after the lights had gone out. Had they noticed something out of the ordinary? Had they smelled the Americans or spotted something that had given rise to their caution?

For one agonizing moment, the predawn jungle ten klicks outside Camp Gorvad was awkwardly silent. Then, as if on command, the lengthy column of enemy sappers began to move forward again.

McConnell and the others didn't know what was happening. All that they knew for certain was that they had a bunch of Viet Cong soldiers coming right at them, moving slowly in the darkness as they pushed through the vines and branches hanging over the trail. The enemy was being cautious, struggling to keep their steps quiet.

Watching and waiting in silence, the five Rangers eased below the lip of the bunker. To open fire too soon would only invite disaster, but waiting as the enemy walked deeper into the kill zone was horribly unnerving. But that would help reduce the odds against the Rangers even if the sappers had spread out. The claymore mines that the team had placed would cover a fan a full 180 degrees to their front and sides.

Suddenly, the Viet Cong column stopped once again. No audible command had been given. The silence was maddening. Then, the Americans heard faint footfalls. Someone just on the other side of the bunker was trying to be very quiet as he approached.

It was too dark for either side to see anything. Although McConnell couldn't make out the enemy's point man, he could hear him taking short steps just a few feet away from his own position, and he could hear the VC soldier breathing through his nose with each step. The Ranger team leader could also smell the pungent odor of fish and wild garlic mixed with the strong smell of sweat. McConnell fought back panic. He knew that the enemy soldier would soon be on the top of the bunker and then in among his teammates.

Slowly and carefully McConnell brought the barrel of his CAR-15 up in the darkness. It stopped gently against the enemy soldier's abdomen. The Ranger team leader pulled the trigger. The muffled report was still echoing in the night as the enemy soldier fell over backward screaming. The jungle erupted immediately with a heavy volume of small-arms fire, most of which came from the dozens of Viet Cong along the trail. Amazingly, the M-16 rifles of three of the Rangers jammed after the first magazine.

McConnell screamed for Leerburg to blow the claymores to clear the enemy from their immediate front and to buy them some time. With the thundering explosion of five claymores blasting simultaneously, the confusion that followed among the pulverized ranks of the enemy gave the Rangers a chance to clear their rifles and resume the fight.

Leaving their comrades in the kill zone to continue the fight head-on, half of the surviving Viet Cong tried to maneuver around the team. One of the Viet Cong was lying in front of the bunker, moaning and calling for help, but no one was coming to his aid. A few of the survivors were running blindly back through the jungle while others, too wounded to walk, were crawling away, firing back at the Americans as they moved.

The remaining Viet Cong tried throwing grenades, but in the dark, they couldn't see to get beyond the tree limbs and vines, and most of the small, wood-handled Chicom grenades pinballed in the dark right back at their owners. A few made it through the tangle and rained burning shrapnel down onto the Ranger patrol, wounding Sergeant Leerburg and Specialist Michael Germany, both of whom continued fighting.

McConnell felt a slight tug against his own rib cage after one of the Chicom grenades blew up at his feet. It didn't hurt, nor did it stop the war going on around them, so McConnell ignored the wound.

McConnell got on the radio and requested gunship support from nearby Phuoc Vinh. Within minutes the Cobras from Charlie Troop were on station and rolling in hot, and Specialist Kenneth "Red" Burch tossed out flares to mark the Rangers' position for the gunships. As he was doing so, a piece of shrapnel hit him under his armpit. Burch swore but continued throwing flares. The macabre glow of the burning flares gave sharp contrast to the shadows that were moving about and trying to kill them from less than twenty meters away. However, the Rangers weren't quite fish in a barrel, and with the gunships on station and McConnell directing them, the situation was about to quickly change for the better.

The Viet Cong sappers were no longer the real threat. The

rockets, minigun fire, and 40mm grenades of the Cobra gunships were rapidly becoming the new danger to the Rangers. Because of the enemy's close proximity to the Rangers' position, and the inexact art of firing close ground support on a cloudy night in the middle of a dense jungle, incoming friendly fire was a reality that had to be taken seriously. Once a bullet, or a rocket, or a grenade left the barrel of its weapon, it was no longer friendly ordnance. A tree limb, a ricochet, a simple error, anything could turn friendly fire into enemy fire.

As a group of VC tried to flank the Rangers, Leerburg ducked behind the back of the bunker and yelled, "Fire in the hole" as he squeezed the clacker on one of the flank claymores. There was a muffled "pop" as the blasting cap blew, but nothing from the antipersonnel mine. Unknown to the Ranger ATL, the claymore had been shot up in the dark, and the cap had been knocked from the mine. Leerburg swore and came up firing as Germany and McConnell quickly joined in. Taijeron and Burch had their hands full on the opposite side of the perimeter.

With each pass of the gunships, some of the fight seemed to fade from the enemy until, after a while, there was only the sound of the wounded or dying Viet Cong coming from across the short stretch of mangled jungle. An occasional burst of AK-47 fire indicated there were still some hard-core VC out there, but the battle seemed over.

The shout of "*Chieu Hoi*" suddenly came from somewhere out to their front, and one of the wounded enemy soldiers offered to surrender. But as the Rangers lifted their heads slowly above their earthen berm they were hiding behind, AK-47 fire raked the ground just in front of them. The Rangers returned fire immediately, and within minutes, the jungle was quiet again.

Low and disturbing moans began to replace the awkward silence, and they were soon joined by sobs and cries of those who'd been caught in the kill zone. One of the wounded Viet

Cong called out something in a labored voice. The Rangers weren't certain whether one of the wounded soldiers was still trying to surrender or if it was another ruse. There was the possibility, too, that maybe one of the wounded had wanted to surrender, while another had decided to stop him.

It didn't matter by then because the team wasn't going anywhere until daybreak when they could get a better look at the situation. One wounded enemy soldier was still moaning and asking to surrender, but when McConnell called for him to move forward, the soldier either couldn't or wouldn't move. The team leader talked to the soldier on and off through the night, but without success. And by dawn, the enemy soldier had died.

McConnell had taken inventory of the wounds received by his own teammates and was amazed when he discovered that four of the five Rangers had been wounded, none of them seriously.

As the soft morning light finally began to filter down through the foliage the full extent of their ambush was visible. The daisy-chain claymore blast had shattered the area in front of them and had even obliterated the markers McConnell had set up for the toe poppers.

In front of their position, three enemy soldiers lay dead, including the point man McConnell had killed at point-blank range. There were also ammunition, B-40 rockets, rocket launchers, and packs lying about that had been dropped in the panic and confusion caused by the eruption of the claymores. In the distance, the Ranger team could hear helicopters touching down in a small break in the jungle as the quick-reaction force moved in to assist the patrol.

After the Ranger patrol and the QRF linked up, the officer in charge, a young captain, began to move his people out to begin their search.

"Hold up!" McConnell shouted to the officer.

"There are mines on the trail," he said, pointing toward the mined area and bringing the QRF's lead squad to a sudden stop.

"I'll clear it first."

Using his utility knife and consulting his memory, the team leader dug out the mines one at a time, defused them, and loaded them into his rucksack. As a couple of the QRF's squads secured the area, another squad policed up the kill zone, picking up the dropped weapons and equipment. The Rangers, meanwhile, searched the bodies for maps and documents.

When it was learned that a blood trail led to a nearby tunnel in a little clearing, McConnell grabbed a pistol and started down the dark, narrow opening. After ten feet or so, the tunnel narrowed to the point where he could go no farther, so McConnell backed out. He hadn't slept all night, and he was exhausted. That wasn't the right state of mind or physical condition you wanted to be in to check out an enemy tunnel.

"Anything down there?" the young captain asked as the team leader crawled back out into the light.

"Probably," he said, "but it's too narrow, and judging from the amount of blood he's lost, he probably crawled in there to die."

The officer stared at the small tunnel opening and the thick, dark blood trail leading into it and nodded. There were enough enemy KIAs in and around the bunker complex to provide all the intelligence that division would need to assess who they were and what they had been up to.

An extraction helicopter was coming in for the Ranger team, and while he and Leerburg still had a debriefing to go through back at Phuoc Vinh, S.Sgt. Guy McConnell, Jr., knew the difficult part of the mission was over. Well, part of it anyway. The rest would happen when he stopped trembling.

* * *

A week or so later, McConnell awoke to the sounds of footsteps and watched as the flashlight beam came closer to him. He reached over, retrieved his rifle and brought it up, then pulled the trigger when the man stopped at the foot of his bunk.

Click! The CAR-15 wasn't loaded.

"Hey! What the fuck you doing?" demanded the company CQ.

"Nothing," whispered McConnell, just then realizing that he had been asleep in the platoon barracks and not out in the field.

Even when the trembling stopped, the symptoms still lingered.

CHAPTER TWENTY-SEVEN

The Ranger teams were becoming increasingly effective at stalking the enemy in the jungle, and they were also becoming adept at capturing enemy prisoners. Since taking prisoners always held a higher degree of risk than reconnaissance, Captain Paccerelli offered his men an incentive, a three day in-country R & R for any team that brought back a live prisoner. The captain cautioned the men that if they couldn't capture an enemy soldier within the bounds of safety, then they should "aim at his face and send him to God like a soldier."

The problem, of course, was when and how to snatch a prisoner. Most Viet Cong units operated in elements of three, and the small enemy patrols that had traveled alone between base camps until the Lurp/Rangers began ambushing them, now traveled in larger units. Travel in larger units made the Viet Cong and NVA targets of gunship and artillery fire directed by long-range patrols that seemed to be everywhere. So they were traveling more cautiously, sending tracking teams ahead on point to look for signs of American patrols in the area.

The only effect that had on the Rangers was to increase the degree of difficulty in capturing POWs; team leaders had to be more selective about the sites they chose for a snatch and more careful about how they performed the task. Snatches were never easy, but there were some who made the mission look that way.

Sp4. Daniel J. Roberts of Thousand Oaks, California, was

the assistant team leader on S.Sgt. Michael Carroll's Team 3-2. Joining their patrol was John Stein, Larry McEwen, and Keith Marquardt. Team 3-2 was assigned to monitor an old woodcutters' road that division believed was being used by the Viet Cong and the NVA to slip troops into the region. The areas the woodcutters worked were labeled "no fire zones," which permitted the VC and NVA to move through relatively unmolested. There were usually no American combat units operating in the area, and even when there were, the enemy soldiers knew that as long as they didn't initiate fire, the Americans would not be allowed to fire at them. The only real threat to the enemy came from passing helicopters that might not heed the rule if they saw an enemy soldier out in the open. However, the jungle surrounding the road was so thick the enemy could easily hide when they heard the noisy approach of an American aircraft. They only had to wait until it flew on before continuing their journey. The Viet Cong and the NVA were well aware of the rules of engagement that the Americans established for themselves.

Carroll's team had just set up in position to monitor the road. Sometime around 0930 hours, a single Viet Cong soldier walked down the dirt road. He seemed unconcerned about the dangers that might lurk in the thick jungle flanking the road, but he constantly scanned the bright Vietnamese sky for signs of helicopters. If he was worried at all about running into an American Ranger team hidden along the road, he didn't show it. Satisfied that the sky was clear of any danger, the Viet Cong soldier walked on.

The Rangers watched as the enemy soldier passed their position and turned off the road forty meters beyond. The Rangers slowly rose and followed the soldier and soon discovered two small footpaths leading into the jungle. Because there were fresh sandal prints on each path, there was no way to be certain which direction the VC had gone.

Knowing that if one soldier had used the road, then others would probably follow, Carroll decided to move the patrol back up the road 150 meters and set up for a prisoner snatch. He looked around the brush-covered area for a likely spot, then placed his people in different locations on each side of the dirt road a good distance apart. Only when he was satisfied that they were well hidden did he find a place for himself.

The five Rangers were in position to make a snatch without allowing their target any avenue of escape provided, of course, there was only one soldier to contend with; any more than one and the team would sit quietly, hoping they would keep going. But the enemy didn't always keep going, which was exactly what had happened to Roberts when he had served on S.Sgt. Tim Greenly's team.

The first day out on patrol, Greenly found a well-used trail and set up the team to monitor it. That night, the Rangers heard the noises of heavy contact coming from the distance, and Greenly brought the team up on alert. Less than fifteen minutes later, Dan Roberts and the others watched as over three hundred enemy soldiers came down the trail, carrying their wounded. Then the enemy battalion stopped for a night halt directly in front of them. The enemy soldiers pushed off the trail and set up all around the Rangers without discovering them hiding nearby. The Rangers remained on alert all night until the enemy soldiers regrouped and moved on just before dawn.

Roberts hoped that would never happen to him again, while Greenly appeared as though it was all just a matter of course. But then, for him, maybe it was. Later on, after his team had ambushed a group of enemy soldiers and one had turned to run, Staff Sergeant Greenly jumped up from his hiding place and chased after the soldier, leaving the rest of his team in place. About fifteen minutes later, the tall, lanky team leader walked back up the trail with his subdued prisoner in front of him, a little roughed up from being tackled, but in good enough shape to survive. At least, that's how Roberts had heard the story.

Not more than five minutes after Carroll had put his own team in place, a lone Viet Cong soldier turned a bend in the road and walked directly toward the patrol's snatch point. He was a small but hard looking Vietnamese with close-cropped black hair, green uniform pants, a white T-shirt, and sandals. Over his shoulder and chest, he carried an olive drab military pouch.

Carroll let the man walk past four of his teammates before stepping out on the road less than ten feet away from the approaching Vietnamese. He raised his rifle and called out, "*Chieu Hoi!*" the catch phrase for surrender.

The man's eyes grew wide with surprise but he turned to run while reaching deep inside the pouch.

"Put your hands up!" Carroll called after him as several of the other Rangers stepped out onto the road. There was no way out of the trap, and the Vietnamese knew it. Suddenly, the man stopped and slowly raised his hands over his head as the team leader directed the patrol to provide security for the area as well as their prisoner.

Inside the pouch, the Ranger team leader retrieved a Soviet Makarov pistol and a stack of documents. Only officers carried Makarov pistols, and the documents identified the man as a Viet Cong lieutenant. Roberts helped bind and tie the prisoner as Staff Sergeant Carroll called in the capture.

Captain Paccerelli requested an immediate extraction for the patrol and ordered them to move to a pickup zone two hundred meters away. Within twenty minutes, a helicopter had safely extracted the patrol. Back at Phuoc Vinh, Carroll's team had a small reception party waiting for them, with smiling faces all around.

Besides the three-day in-country R & Rs, the teams were allowed to keep pistols and bolt-action rifles as war trophies, with the company clerk handling the necessary paperwork.

Later in the summer the company commander and the first sergeant also came up with a green-stamp redemption program that rewarded the team members with something more immediate than an in-country vacation, a six-pack of beer or soda for every two stamps earned. They announced the new program in the company newsletter, and it was well received.

In keeping with the trend of today's Action Army, in an endeavor to bring a touch of home to Ranger operations and in lieu of Ma's apple pie and the girl next door, we announce that green stamps will be given with the purchase of all enemy equipment, personnel, and weapons, on the following basis:

Enemy Killed in Action	1 stamp
Individual Weapon Captured	1 stamp
Prisoner of War (EM)	3 stamps
Prisoner of War (Officer)	4 stamps
Crew Served Weapons Captured	2 stamps
Documents of Intelligence Value	1 stamp per inch

Other items will be judged on an individual basis.

The stamps could be redeemed at Otto's B&S Bar, a small shack between the orderly room and the training hootch, manned by the company mail clerk. "Otto" was Specialist Merle R. Otto, and his significance to the company was measured in more than just his job description. Otto ran a makeshift company store, selling unit patches, Lurp scrolls, and beer and soda, and as many Rangers soon discovered, he ran it exceptionally well and generously by extending credit between paydays or by simply forgetting how much beer money a Ranger had left in his account. The company had a policy of issuing a can of soda to each man on a team to drink before each mission, and another can of soda or beer when he returned. Otto handed them out and became one of the most well-thought-of men in the unit.

True to Captain Paccerelli's policy of "every man a Ranger," Otto had completed the training course, served in the field, and took over the full-time responsibilities when the need arose, which it inevitably did.

As the mail clerk, he was invaluable, since the only real link to the outside world—the World in the mind of a GI—came through the cards, letters, and packages that arrived to remind him that there was something beyond Vietnam.

Otto was responsible for the mail; receiving, sorting, dispensing, returning, and, when necessary, handling the mail of the company's dead and wounded. He dispensed the Christmas packages from home, and whenever the grade schools or church groups sent cookies or cards to soldiers at random, he managed to make sure they were always divvied out among the members of the company.

True comfort in a war zone is a luxury that few combat soldiers could find or afford, and all too often, the Rangers' only momentary solace came in the form of a letter handed to them by someone who understood its true value.

CHAPTER TWENTY-EIGHT

Ranger Team 4-3 was inserted into Binh Long province northwest of Doc Luan just prior to sunset. After lying dog for fifteen minutes, the team leader, S.Sgt. Stan Lento, moved the team out to find a safe night position to hole up in.

The terrain was a carpet of dense undergrowth, ferns, broadleaf plants, tangled vines, and bamboo thickets. It was covered by double-canopy trees where the thickest layers seemed to weave a green and brown mat high above them, at times blocking out the sky. Not that that was necessarily a bad thing since the weather was turning foul with gray-black clouds tumbling overhead. In brief downpours the thickly canopied treetops served reasonably well as natural umbrellas.

When they happened upon a trail junction with fresh boot-prints and sandal tracks, Lento set the team in an ambush position just far enough back in the cover to effectively monitor the intersection. When the team was in place and the clay-mores were set out, Lento moved thirty meters down the trail to their south to set up an unmanned ambush site.

He carefully planted half of his M14 antipersonnel mines and linked them together with det cord to a claymore mine nearby. With ATL Sgt. J. Walter Kraft covering, Lento then moved off to the team's exposed flank and planted his remaining mines. The Viet Cong were good at setting out booby traps and mines of their own in areas GIs considered safe, and Rangers went in for payback whenever they could.

The mines would offer an early warning system to the Ranger patrol if they were triggered by enemy troops; there was no way the Rangers could miss the explosions.

In the late afternoon of the following day, an hour or so before sunset, something or someone detonated several of the mines in the unmanned ambush site. In the wake of the explosions, piercing screams and cries from the site filtered back through the thick underbrush before suddenly dying out. The men of the Ranger patrol went on immediate alert, covering their sectors in the wagon-wheel formation.

Within minutes after the commotion at the unmanned ambush site had died out, Specialist Daniel Sheehan, the Ranger patrol's rear scout from Aurora, Colorado, detected movement to his front. Sheehan tapped his team leader on the leg and carefully pointed in the direction of the movement. Lento nodded and watched as several enemy soldiers searched the underbrush twenty feet away.

PFC Archie McDaniel, the patrol's medic, also spotted movement in front of his position and brought it to the attention of the team leader. The NVA were skirting the trail to avoid mines. They still weren't certain just whose mines they were, so they paralleled the jungle trail to make sure there were no other nasty surprises hiding in the bushes. Using hand signals Lento sent the team down on the ground to stay out of sight and remain quiet. They knew from their mission briefing and team meeting not to open up on the NVA until he did. The Maine native gestured for the radio handset from Specialist Gregory Chavez, the patrol's RTO. Pulling out his map, the team leader called for artillery and gunship support. The cannon fire would arrive almost immediately, but the gunships from Blue Max, the 2d of the 20th Aviation, and Bravo Troop, 1st of the 9th Cav, at Quan Loi, would take a little longer to reach them.

Whispering into the handset and giving the artillery battery's fire direction center the coordinates, Lento adjusted single-round cannon fire onto the NVA positions. The random artillery fire used to harass and interdict the enemy positions was better known as H & I fire, and after the 105mm howitzer high-explosive rounds pounded the suspected positions, Lento and his assistant team leader, Sgt. J. Walter Kraft, cautiously moved to the unmanned ambush site to check out the results.

Walking the first ten meters and crawling the final twenty, the two Rangers used the natural cover and concealment to their advantage, settling behind a shield of bamboo as they moved within view of the ambush kill zone. On the trail the body of one dead NVA soldier lay sprawled where he fell. There were also three clearly visible trough marks where someone had dragged several wounded enemy soldiers into the underbrush. By this time, a light rain was falling, and small pools began to form in the shallow drag marks.

Then Lento and Kraft saw movement at the same time and lobbed three hand grenades each into a cluster of enemy soldiers, letting the grenade spoons fall free before they threw them. They hoped to convince the NVA that they were being hit by mortar fire.

After the first few grenades exploded, the NVA began firing in every direction, but as more grenades rained down on them, the enemy small-arms fire suddenly ceased, and the jungle became deadly quiet.

When he was reasonably sure it was safe, Lento crawled out to the first dead NVA soldier and quickly stripped him of his equipment, documents, and weapon before rejoining Kraft.

Lento and Kraft could hear the gunships arriving on station high above them. As they hurried back to rejoin the rest of the team, enemy machine-gun fire tore into the jungle behind them. Lento directed the gunships to roll in on where he suspected the machine-gun fire was coming from. He also reported the events to Phuoc Vinh.

The NVA were moving through the jungle again, by this time certain that the mines, the mortarlike explosions, and the directed gunship runs were no random series of events. Their sweep was in earnest, and Private First Class McDaniels soon whispered that he had an NVA soldier standing less than ten feet away.

Lento ordered his team down again and motioned for them to hold fire as the gunships continued their runs over the jungle around them. Back at Phuoc Vinh, Captain Paccerelli ordered the team to prepare to be pulled out and requested an extraction ship to go after them. The patrol had accomplished its mission and much, much more. The NVA were in the area and Staff Sergeant Lento and his team had the documents and the equipment to prove it. With luck, division G-2 would be able to decipher which unit the enemy soldiers belonged to.

When the extraction helicopter arrived on the scene, it informed the Ranger team leader that the nearest pickup zone was 175 meters to his south, and due to the fact that the weather was closing in, the Lurps would have to hurry. Lento "Rogered" the transmission and then ordered two gunship runs to help clear their way.

Taking the point, Staff Sergeant Lento began to lead his team out toward the pickup zone. The five Rangers had only gone one hundred meters when Lento spotted two NVA soldiers thirty feet in front of him, one on each side of the trail, blocking their escape route. One of the enemy soldiers was cradling a light machine gun. He had already spotted the American and was bringing up his weapon. But Lento fired first and ordered his team down just as the NVA machine gunner began to walk scores of rounds up and down the trail where the Americans had been.

As the enemy soldier paused to reload, the Ranger team leader charged him and the second NVA soldier who, with eyes wide in terror, couldn't believe what was happening.

Firing as he ran, Lento killed the machine gunner first then turned his rifle on the second soldier and killed him. Since he couldn't take the Soviet machine gun with him, Lento used a grenade to destroy it, then continued on toward the pickup zone.

The patrol was still taking heavy small-arms fire, and Kraft had the others return fire. The team's RTO, Specialist Gregory Chavez, was on the radio, coordinating the gunship support while the ATL and the others concentrated on returning fire at the locations of the heaviest incoming small-arms fire.

After he jumped to his feet and lobbed grenades at the closest NVA positions, Sergeant Kraft became the focus of the enemy fire. NVA machine-gun fire chopped down the bamboo stalks just above him, but when they shifted their fire away from Kraft, he was quickly back up throwing more grenades.

The team's rear scout, Sheehan, spotted a squad of enemy soldiers coming up quickly behind the team, firing as they ran. Even as the rounds tore into his rucksack, Sheehan jumped up and opened fire on the group. The two NVA in the lead went down as the remaining enemy soldiers scattered, but not before one of their rounds hit Sheehan and knocked him down. The rear scout had been shot in the head.

"Sheehan's hit!" yelled McDaniels as Lento rushed back to help. Lento grabbed McDaniels's medical bag and ran to Sheehan's side. As enemy small-arms fire kicked dirt up around him, he tried to help the fallen Ranger.

Sergeant Kraft ran to the radio to direct the gunships again, this time having to bring rocket and minigun fire within ten meters of the team's position to keep the NVA back.

As the rain increased, the radio began losing power, and Specialist Chavez held it up over his shoulders to get better commo until he, too, was wounded, taking a round in the shoulders. But the gunships were finding their targets, and the NVA began to withdraw. The machine-gun fire died away and was replaced by enemy small-arms fire. As Sergeant

Kraft moved to help Chavez and protect the radio, an AK-47 burst shot off the long whip antenna at its base. The team was without commo until Kraft pulled out the short whip antenna and screwed it in to the radio. With the radio back up and operating Kraft again coordinated the helicopter support.

Meanwhile, at the other end of the patrol, an NVA soldier threw a grenade at Lento and the dying Sheehan. Lento shielded Sheehan from the explosion by curling up in a tight ball and placing himself between the grenade and the wounded man. After calling for a medevac to lift out the wounded Ranger, Lento lifted Sheehan over his shoulder and started toward the extraction point. "Let's go!" he yelled to the others.

It was already dusk, and the bad weather was closing in around them when the patrol finally reached a clearing where the medevac helicopter could recover Sheehan. As the medevac helicopter hovered over the small clearing and lowered the Stokes litter on a steel cable, Lento and McDaniels loaded Sheehan into the basket and secured the straps around him, then signaled the crew chief to take it up. Kraft and Chavez were busy covering the extraction, and once Sheehan was aboard, the pilot informed the RTO that the patrol had run out of time. Even if they pushed on to the pickup zone it wouldn't matter anymore; the NVA had already overrun it.

The medevac helicopter was taking fire as it hovered over the clearing, but the pilot radioed that he'd hold his position in order to take out the rest of the team. Then, one by one, each team member was pulled aboard on the aircraft's jungle penetrator.

On the way back to the rear, the Rangers realized that it didn't look good for Sheehan. Any sense of accomplishment they might have felt over the mission was overshadowed by the worsening condition of their teammate, who was bleeding on the floor of the helicopter.

Sheehan and Chavez were taken to the 15th Medical Battalion at Quan Loi, where Chavez would recover. Unfortunately, Sheehan's wound proved more serious.

For their actions during the patrol Lento, Kraft, and Sheehan received impact Silver Stars for gallantry in action, while Chavez and McDaniels received Bronze Stars with "V" device from the 1st Cav Division commander, Major General Roberts. Captain Paccerelli requested that Staff Sergeant Lento be awarded the Distinguished Service Cross, the nation's second highest award, for his actions during the mission, but to award a DSC, division would have to take time to investigate the matter, but the Silver Star, the next highest medal in line, was immediately approved, pending the outcome of the investigation of the higher award.

In a ceremony at the company area, General Roberts presented the medals to four of the team members before flying down to Long Binh to pin the Silver Star on Sheehan's pillow in the VSI ward of the 24th Evacuation Hospital.

Sp4. Daniel M. Sheehan later died as a result of his head wound. At the memorial service conducted in the company area two days later, Captain Paccerelli described Sheehan as "one of the finest soldiers I have ever met . . . and in spite of his small stature, he was a man to match the mountains of Colorado."

The ceremony followed by nine days the one for Sp4. Lon "Holly" Holupko, an assistant team leader, who was killed in Tay Ninh province after a group of NVA walked in on his team. The Rangers killed the NVA soldiers, but in the rapid exchange of fire, Holupko was shot and killed.

Holupko, like Sheehan, was well liked and well thought of by his comrades, and the two losses hung over the unit like a shroud. There was no way of knowing just how painful the month of July was going to be for Company H.

CHAPTER TWENTY-NINE

Two days after Holupko had been killed, Staff Sergeant McConnell led his patrol into the same area where the ATL had died. McConnell's mission was a scheduled three-day patrol to determine if the enemy was still in the region, and for most of the first two days the Rangers moved carefully through the patrol grids without encountering any new tracks, sign, or other indicators to make them think the NVA were still there.

However, late in the afternoon of the second day, McConnell's patrol came across a well-used jungle trail and set up an OP to monitor it. Sandal prints were fresh and plentiful; their edges sharp and overlapping, telling McConnell that a squad or more had marched by. The Rangers set up claymores, camouflaged their position, and waited.

During a rain storm that night, several NVA passed by the Rangers, but by the time the Ranger on guard had alerted the others, the NVA were long gone.

The following morning, the Rangers tracked the enemy unit through heavy vegetation to a junction with a much larger trail, guarded by a freshly built bunker. The larger trail had recently been cut through the brush and sap was still dripping from branches the NVA had hacked through.

McConnell opted to follow the new trail and walked on until he could smell food cooking and hear utensils being banged together. Those sounds, and the casual murmur of

Vietnamese voices farther away, told him that the NVA had a base camp just ahead of the Ranger team, so McConnell moved his patrol into the heavy brush, found good cover, and then radioed Tay Ninh requesting artillery and gunship support.

They could hear the Vietnamese going through their morning routine. McConnell was about to introduce a new element to their routine when the call came back that neither artillery nor gunship support would be forthcoming. The brigade boundaries were being shifted so all gunship and artillery fire was being halted until the shift was completed.

McConnell was told to move out his team immediately for extraction, which he did after rigging two claymore mines with trip wires at a brush-covered bend in the old trail.

As they moved toward the pickup zone, McConnell was angry and more than a little confused; the team had taken huge risks to move close to the enemy base camp only to find the gunships and artillery unavailable when they requested them. It would have been much worse if the Lurps had needed it. Their lives would have been forfeited because someone was playing with lines on a map. God help us, if we had needed it, he thought, and as the helicopter approached the pickup zone McConnell realized that God was a long way from the war zone.

In Song Be, the following evening, after a drawn-out firefight, Ranger team 4-3 was having a few problems of its own. The patrol had to be reinforced by the Aerorifle Blues Platoon from Charlie Troop, 1st of the 9th Cav, at 2030 hours in a move to sweep the battle area.

However, as the unit sent in a Pink team to cover the assault, a UH-1B gunship and a light observation helicopter had crashed along the Be River. Five minutes after the helicopters went down, a call went out to the Rangers at Phuoc Vinh requesting a platoon-size quick-reaction force be placed on standby. Within ten minutes, Captain Paccerelli reported to Lieutenant Colonel Booth that he had thirty-two volunteers ready and waiting to go.

At 2140 hours, the Charlie Troop commander requested a four-man Ranger team to rappel into the area where the UH-1B went down and search for survivors. Charlie Troop also requested that a second Ranger team be ready to reinforce the first team, if necessary.

Captain Paccerelli informed the Charlie Troop commander that he would lead the first patrol in and that the second patrol was to be inserted only on his orders. If the area proved too dangerous after the first team reached the ground, he wouldn't risk the lives of others. When he asked for volunteers for the two patrols, all thirty-two of the Rangers present said they'd go.

Paccerelli was deeply moved and proud of his Rangers as he made his selections. At 2217 hours Paccerelli, S.Sgt. David Mitchell, S.Sgt. Stephen C. Virostko, and Sp4. Ernest Squire boarded a Huey liftship for Song Be. Mitchell would act as the assistant team leader, Virostko the radioman, and Squire would carry an M-60 machine gun for extra firepower.

Back in the bush, the flames from the burning helicopter lit up the area of the crash site like a beacon. Captain Paccerelli went down first and, once on the ground, secured the area for the next Ranger in line. Once the team was on the ground, he deployed three men to the north, seven meters away, as a security screen in case the NVA or Viet Cong responded to the unfortunate opportunity.

After they were in place, the Ranger officer began the search for bodies and possible survivors, which, judging from the flames and the size of the crater at the crash site, seemed remote. The helicopter had broken up and exploded upon impact. The aircraft debris was scattered over a fairly large area.

As Paccerelli approached the first large piece of smoking

wreckage, he noticed a number of small objects on the ground, several of which were still burning. He had been warned that the gunship was carrying rockets, machine-gun ammunition, CS tear gas, and grenades, so his approach had been cautious. As his eyes adjusted to darkness illuminated by the flickering light from the burning fires, the Ranger captain suddenly recognized the small objects as human body parts.

The crater was six feet by six feet, and a small fire was still burning in its bowl. Next to the crater lay the severed tail section of the helicopter. Paccerelli walked a few more steps before abruptly coming to a stop. Just in front of him was the head, upper chest, and right upper arm of one of the crew members.

Paccerelli removed his flashlight and lowered the red filtered light to within inches of the head. The facial features were of a black man with full lips and a large flat nose. The head had been burned but the face was still intact. The crash victim's hair had been singed, and the eyes were either closed or gone. The man's ears were still intact, and the lips were tightly pursed together so that his teeth didn't show. The flesh on the rest of the body had been charred, and as Paccerelli pointed the light down to the exposed chest cavity, he saw that it was empty, the viscera were missing.

The sickening, sweet smell of charred flesh began to gag the Ranger CO, but he continued his search of the crash site, next walking over to the helicopter's transmission. It was there he found four fingers still attached to the knuckle section of a human hand. He walked in a spiral pattern another fifty meters, searching for more bodies or possible survivors.

"Hello! Is anyone here?" he yelled over the hissing and popping of the flames. "If you're hurt and can't talk, then make some noise."

There was no response, so Paccerelli walked on. The jungle surrounding the crash site was silent and still as he turned west. He pushed through the underbrush looking for signs of the remaining crewmen. B models usually carried four personnel—two pilots, a crew chief and a doorgunner. The body parts he had found totaled, perhaps, one man, at best, one man plus. He also located a few individual weapons, a machine gun and ammunition still in good working order, which told him that the Viet Cong or NVA had not yet discovered the crash site.

He continued walking for another thirty meters, using the fire from the central crash site as his radius vector, making spiral sweeps around the entire area. Just west of the small crater, he found the remaining section of the splintered aircraft. Because of the intensity of the flames, there was no way to move around the north side of the wreckage to what looked to be the forward section of the helicopter, so he circled around behind the fire, stopping again when he came upon two more bodies.

Both corpses were badly burned but still intact. They were lying facedown, side by side, with one curled up in a fetal position as though fast asleep. One still had its flight helmet in place, and neither airman was mutilated.

Because of their location in the crash site, he guessed that the two dead men were the aircraft's pilot and copilot. He stepped between the bodies to get a better look at them, but the fire was moving dangerously close. Paccerelli was reluctant to look at their faces anyway, realizing that they were men he had probably known or would recognize.

His search complete, the Ranger officer made his way back to Staff Sergeant Mitchell and the others, walking past the smoking pieces of flesh, reconfirming that there were indeed two shredded bodies in the mess.

When he reached the rest of his teammates, Paccerelli called in his findings, reporting that he had two bodies intact, the head and chest of a third, and what appeared to be the body parts of a fourth victim. There were no survivors. He had no way of knowing for sure how many men had been aboard the helicopter and told the squadron commander that he would immediately begin a second search just to be sure.

Paccerelli canvassed the crash site a second time covering a broader area in his sweep, but didn't find anything new to report. By the time he'd finished, the flames were creeping toward the gunship's rocket pods, threatening to explode them.

Returning once again to the patrol, he confirmed his earlier report to the squadron commander who told him that he and his Rangers would be extracted by jungle penetrator.

The Rangers returned to Phuoc Vinh shortly before midnight.

The following morning, Charlie Troop inserted their Blues rifle platoon into the crash site to recover the bodies, weapons, and equipment. But when they conducted their search, they reported finding three intact bodies but not the head and severed chest of the black soldier Paccerelli had reported. When Paccerelli heard this from squadron headquarters, he volunteered to go back in to look for the remains.

The third intact body had been burned beyond recognition and was located just north of the crater, where the fire had been the most intense, which explained why he hadn't found it on his own search. He had his suspicions about what had happened to the remains but held his opinion until he returned to the crash site and took a look around for himself.

At 1015, he was once again rappelling down to the site, and after being briefed by the Blues platoon leader, he began his investigation. He studied the ground around where the head and chest had been, and because of the bootprints from the infantry platoon members, he began his search a little farther out than was necessary. Twenty meters north-northwest of the crash site, he had his answer.

On a small footpath, he found the burned pancreas of the dead man and part of his light green Nomex flight suit. He moved two meters farther south, following the spoor, before calling the platoon leader over and asking him for a squad of soldiers.

"Yes, sir," said the confused first lieutenant, wondering what the senior captain had in mind as he called over one of his squad leaders and told him what he wanted.

As Paccerelli explained, the Blues watched and listened. "I want you to look for animal tracks or drag trails and pieces like this," he said, pointing to the seared pancreas and a chunk of burned human flesh where it had been dropped beside the track of a large animal. Because of the matted leaf cover on the ground, it was difficult to make out what had dragged or carried off the human remains. The smaller pieces could have been carried away by rats, a mongoose, or even by some of the larger lizards, but the larger remains would take something much stronger like a tiger or a wild boar.

Less than forty-five minutes later, the searchers located several more human bones, pieces of flesh parts, and shreds of the flight suit along with two distinct sets of paw prints made by a large tiger.

Paccerelli's own search, sometimes down on his hands and knees in the underbrush, led to the discovery of a partially burned U.S.-issue jungle boot with two severed toes inside. The remainder of the search yielded nothing.

The search party had its answer. The remains of the fourth crewman had been carried off and eaten by a tiger.

Three of the bodies had been positively identified as those of the three Caucasian crew members, while the fourth crew member, whose body parts had been those carried off by the tiger, was that of a black cavalryman, which squadron headquarters later confirmed.

CHAPTER THIRTY

Sgt. Craig Leerburg knew the team was in a good place to set up shop. The bootprints and bicycle tracks on the trail they had found running through the underbrush were fresh, their edges still crisp and cleanly defined. That told Leerburg that the NVA were close. Just how close was anybody's guess. They could have just been passing through and were long gone, or they could be sitting just around the next bend in the trail taking a rest break.

The team leader from Colorado Springs, Colorado, placed the Ranger patrol a dozen meters off the trail in a position that offered good protection, if it came to that, as well as a good view of anything or anyone who might come down the red-ball. He had his ATL, Sp4. Roman Taijeron, set out claymores as Leerburg dropped his heavy rucksack before going out to investigate the tracks.

He eyed the surrounding jungle cautiously, sniffing the air and listening for anything out of the ordinary before moving a little farther down the trail to see if anyone was there. He peered around the first bend and studied the underbrush closely. Well-used jungle trails like that one usually led to bunker complexes, and bunker complexes tended to wrap themselves back around the trail in a calculated defensive posture. A manned bunker or fighting position could be just off the trail, guarding its approach.

Some teams had discovered this after they had suddenly found themselves inside one of those occupied jungle bases.

They were fortunate enough to be able to extricate themselves by slowly and very cautiously backing out, unseen and unheard by the occupants.

Other teams had discovered the bunkers only after their point man had suddenly spotted enemy soldiers staring back at him from only a few feet away. The mad dashes and intense fighting that had ensued were both frenzied and terrifying. Using an immediate-action drill—"contact front"—the team would break contact by having the point man empty his magazine at the enemy before turning to run, and each succeeding Ranger in line following the point man's lead until every man had emptied a full magazine and peeled back to the rear. If they had been lucky, the team would have gained a good running start before the enemy charged after them. If they had been unlucky, then the VC and NVA would have spotted them first and waited until most or all of the team had moved closer to the waiting guns . . .

From his vantage point Leerburg didn't see any bunkers or fighting positions, and when he peered behind the foliage, he didn't find anyone staring back at him, so he immediately turned his attention back to the trail and went into a tracker mode. An avid hunter, Leerburg knew that if you were careful and quiet enough, you could damn near sneak up on any wild game.

He had gone nearly five hundred meters before he stopped suddenly. His hackles went up. He couldn't shake the feeling that he was being watched, and whether it was a sixth sense or the mind's way of dealing with those danger signals it had subconsciously registered, the twenty-one-year-old Noncommissioned Officer started to slowly back up the way he had come while bringing his CAR-15 to the ready position.

No unusual sights or sounds were coming from the jungle, just the routine bird calls in the distance, treetops rustling high above him, and the occasional grunt or croak from something unseen in the brush. But Leerburg could feel there was definitely something else out there, so he cautiously slipped back around the first bend in the trail then turned and bolted.

Once, after he had stopped to listen, he thought he heard someone hurrying after him, so he took off again, cursing himself for getting too far ahead of the others.

As soon as he made his way all the way back to the team, he warned them that he had company behind him and to get ready. No sooner had he picked up his rucksack than four North Vietnamese Army soldiers came running into view. The NVA spotted the team leader through the trees at the exact same time the Rangers spotted them. The NVA soldiers quickly began to back away while bringing up their AK-47 assault rifles to fire.

Spec Four Roman Taijeron was the first to open up on the enemy soldiers, then the rest of the team members quickly joined in. Two of the four NVA went down while the remaining two dropped behind some nearby cover and returned fire. Within minutes, more enemy soldiers were maneuvering in around the Rangers. Fortunately, the heavy fire from the enemy soldiers was having little or no effect.

The team had good natural cover, and the NVA couldn't rush them without taking heavy losses. The team's RTO was already on the radio calling for gunship support, and within twenty minutes, the Cobra attack helicopters were on station, pouring heavy fire into the enemy positions. But rather than breaking contact as they normally did when the American gunships arrived on the scene, the North Vietnamese elected to stay and fight. Because of the thick jungle they, too, had some protection against the attack helicopter.

Suddenly an RPG round flashed in out of the forest in front of the Rangers and whooshed toward their perimeter, then exploded in the trees directly behind them. Hot shrapnel injured four of the five patrol members, including Henry Morris, John LeBrun, and the new guy, who suffered a very serious head wound.

Leerburg called in the team's situation and requested a

medevac helicopter for the new man. When it arrived a few minutes later, the crew chief on board lowered a jungle penetrator at the end of a long cable down through the trees. Leerburg helped his badly wounded teammate onto the jungle penetrator and signaled for the crew chief to hoist him up. To the team leader's surprise, the medevac crew drew no enemy fire, at least not enough to bring down the helicopter or injure its crew.

The lull in the battle didn't last, however, as the NVA once again moved in to attack. A second RPG thundered toward the team, but that one continued through the trees before finally detonating too far away to harm the Rangers. Leerburg's team still had a good defensive position, and the gunships were continuing to rip the NVA apart. So as long as the Rangers remained in place, they could likely hold out until a second helicopter could be sent in to pull them out.

When the call came from the company commander to secure the dead enemy bodies if they were able, then strip them of their uniforms, weapons, and anything else they were carrying, Leerburg gave a "Roger" into the radio. At the first opportunity, the towheaded team leader scrambled out to the trail and ran to the two slain NVA.

Both of the enemy soldiers were quite dead, and because they had already been there for a while, their bodies had begun to bloat under the scorching Vietnamese heat. The putrefying gasses that escaped from their perforated bodies mixed with the smell of cordite and the coppery aroma of the blood that had pooled beneath the two corpses. The stench was horrible. As Leerburg began stripping the bodies, the tree line in front of him opened up and enemy small-arms fire raked the trail.

Leaping behind the dead NVA soldiers and using their bodies for cover, the young Ranger NCO returned fire. Leerburg felt the machine-gun rounds thumping into the bodies in front of him. He had to get back to the protection of the team before the NVA got smart and overran his position.

Taijeron was up on one knee firing over Leerburg, and the others hurriedly followed his lead. Since the team leader had recovered most of what he had come for, he scrambled back to the others, firing over his shoulder as he ran.

Leerburg radioed back to Phuoc Vinh that he had stripped the bodies as best he could. Captain Paccerelli ordered the team's extraction, but because the gunships overhead were still taking fire and two had been hit, there would be no extraction for a while. The NVA still controlled the surrounding jungle, and it was beginning to appear that the only way out would be by McGuire rig or jungle penetrator, and either method required a helicopter to hover over the Rangers' position, which meant it would be a sitting duck. The patrol wouldn't be extracted until the enemy fire had been suppressed.

The remaining four Rangers were still taking sporadic small-arms fire, but none of it appeared to be well aimed. The gunships' rockets, minigun fire and 40mm grenade launchers were beginning to take effect. Taijeron, LeBrun, and Morris covered the small perimeter while Leerburg threw a bandage on a shrapnel wound in his neck. Once he had taken care of the wound, he turned to a more pressing concern. His stomach was growling and he realized he was starving. The Rangers hadn't eaten in quite a while. Sizing up the situation, Leerburg reached for his rucksack. The enemy seemed to be retiring back into their bunkers and fighting positions. The gunships would keep them contained there. The NVA would likely bide their time, snipe at the trapped Americans occasionally, and wait for darkness to finish the job.

As Leerburg pulled out his C rations, several of his teammates looked at him like he was crazy, especially LeBrun. LeBrun was a Canadian who had joined the U.S. Army and had come to Vietnam as a volunteer. Eventually, he had volunteered for the Rangers. It was his first long-range patrol, and probably the last thing he expected to see was someone taking a chow break in the middle of a battle.

Sergeant Leerburg smiled when he saw the look on Le-Brun's face, then continued eating. When the team leader had finished, he ran his tongue over his teeth, then eased back up into position, studying the jungle around them. "Anything new?" he asked, wiping his face on his sleeve. The others only shook their heads.

The gunships were still taking fire, and because of the risk involved in pulling out the team, the squadron commander for the 1st of the 9th radioed the Rangers that he would personally bring in his ship to pull them out.

"Roger, Long Knife Six," Leerburg said and popped a smoke grenade to guide the helicopter to its hover position over the team. One by one, each of the four Rangers was pulled up through the jungle and into the helicopter. The squadron commander held the aircraft steady during the entire extraction even though NVA small-arms fire was directed at his helicopter the entire time.

As Long Knife Six brought the ship up and away from the contact site, Sergeant Leerburg took one final look down at the jungle. They had killed several NVA, captured some enemy weapons and documents, been attacked by a far larger force, yet they had only one man wounded. They had used up a lot of good luck.

CHAPTER THIRTY-ONE

S.Sgt. Guy McConnell had been up all night pulling company CQ duty. CQ, or charge of quarters, meant that he was the baby-sitter for the company orderly room until he was relieved at 0600.

E-5s and E-6s pulled CQ duty, and it involved little more than manning a desk in the orderly room and just being there in the event that something happened, in which case, the CQ was to awaken the first sergeant or the company commander and inform him of the situation, then remain on hand to coordinate whatever needed to be done.

There was always more to it than that, but the routine allowed for plenty of time to write letters home, read a book, play solitaire, or hum to yourself while trying to remain awake.

Vietnamese nights always worked against a CQ in a base camp because the heat, the tedious drone of generators, and the utter boredom of the duty struggled to push the eyelids closed. Only a sense of duty and the fear of getting chewed out by a first sergeant who had been allowed to oversleep prevented the hapless CQ from giving in to the tender mercies of blessed sleep.

Anyway, duty and fear definitely won out with McConnell. And after he had been relieved as CQ, the exhausted Ranger trudged back to his barracks on automatic pilot, crawled into his cot, and immediately fell asleep.

At 1100 hours, he awakened to the sounds of Stan Lento

barking commands as he ran his team through some sort of drill down the center aisle of the barracks. It was obviously a routine of some sorts, and from the looks of it, it was being done by the book.

McConnell sat up and rubbed his eyes, then stared angrily at his fellow team leader. "What's going on?" he asked, checking his watch.

"Demonstration tonight at headquarters for some VIPs," Lento answered as several of his team members grinned with satisfaction. The Rangers were decked out in full field uniform and gear, complete with rucksacks and everything else they would typically carry for a five-to-seven day mission in the jungle. The team was supposed to walk out on a stage in patrol formation and, with the help of hand-printed training aids, demonstrate to the audience their position on the team and the equipment they used in the field.

"With the appropriate amount of awe and wonder, right?" someone asked a few feet away while another team member responded, "You got it!"

McConnell nodded in understanding, then got up and went to take a shower. He returned to the barracks a short time afterward. Then, dressed only in uniform trousers and thongs, he sat back in an old lawn chair to relax. The demonstration team was just winding up its practice routine.

McConnell was sitting with his back to the aisle when he heard Lento tell the demonstration team to line up their rucksacks. The sudden explosion sent him tumbling head over heels, but he couldn't remember hearing anything other than a small harmless-sounding *pop*. The barracks was rapidly filling with smoke and fire trails from a white phosphorus grenade that had accidentally detonated, sending its burning contents spewing out in a myriad of directions. The barracks was soon on fire, and the flames were racing up the wooden walls.

McConnell's ears were ringing, and he was still disoriented, but he didn't feel he was all that hurt. Several Rangers were racing for the door thinking the explosion was from in-coming rockets. McConnell followed their lead. He had nearly reached the screened door at the end of the barracks when he realized that he had been hit in the back, neck, and head by flying shrapnel, and judging by the burning sensa-tion spreading across his back, he had most likely caught some of the white phosphorus, too. He was bleeding badly and in a state of mild shock as he came out of the door but hearing the cries and screams of pain from the others, McConnell ignored his own wounds and turned back into the burning barracks to help.

Black, acrid smoke from the chemical fire was billowing up into the open rafters where it was confined by the sheet-metal roof and curled back down the interior walls of the building.

Staff Sergeant McConnell quickly helped one wounded Ranger out of the barracks and then went back in for another. The first man had a wound to his side while the second had lost part of his nose. Going back into the barracks a third time, McConnell helped carry the badly mangled body of a third Ranger to an ambulance that had just pulled up.

"Is that all? Is that it?" a frantic medic asked McConnell, who could only nod at the question.

"Yeah, I think so," he finally said. Since the injured Rangers needed more immediate attention than the medic could provide, he hurriedly jumped into the vehicle and drove off. The medic had not realized that McConnell had also been wounded because the Ranger NCO had kept his back away from him. There was no way the medic could see the full extent of McConnell's own wounds, let alone realize that the surprisingly calm NCO had even been wounded.

McConnell watched the ambulance drive off in a trail of dust, and in the ensuing confusion of the explosion and fire no one noticed the injured Ranger as he followed the ambu-lance to the aid station on foot, wearing only a pair of jungle fatigue trousers and a sandal on one foot. He could tell he was on the verge of going into shock, and he had to get to the aid station. He was also acutely aware of the burning white phosphorus fizzing into his back. A few minutes later when a jeep came down the road behind him, McConnell turned and put his thumb out to hitch a ride.

"Where . . . where are you going?" asked the bewildered NCO who had stopped for the strangely dressed soldier. Then seeing his wounds for the first time, he wondered what in the hell had happened to the man.

"Can you give me a lift to the hospital?" McConnell asked calmly. The confused NCO nodded slowly, still eyeing the hitchhiker's painful looking wounds.

"The barracks blew up," McConnell added, almost as an afterthought.

Because of the blood flowing down his back, the injured Ranger couldn't lean back against the canvas seat of the jeep. He still hadn't fully processed what had happened, nor did he even want to accept it.

At the hospital, after being treated for his injuries and assigned a bed, he finally learned that Stan Lento, Archie McDaniel, and Paul Salminen were dead. Besides himself, among the wounded were Sergeants James W. Kraft and Charles Steele, and Spec Four Fred Doriot. While McConnell's physical injuries were not life threatening, his real pain went much deeper.

Stan Lento and he had been good friends, and they had often shared stories of families, friends, and personal woes. Vietnam had never been a good medium for personal relationships, and the two Ranger NCOs had frequently talked about their frustrations and fears. They had gone through the company's in-country LRP training together and, over time, had genuinely come to admire and appreciate each other.

Someone later told him that when the rucksack exploded, Lento's first reaction had been to push the man in front of him down and away from the full impact of the blast. McConnell could only agree that it sounded like something Lento would do.

The loss devastated many in the company and back home in the States, but for McConnell, the pain would remain deep and very personal.

An investigation failed to reveal the cause of the explosion, but the best guess was that a pin must have worked loose from a grenade in one of the rucksacks and exploded, setting off the two claymore mines that were packed inside, which in turn caused a sympathetic chain reaction in two other rucksacks.

Hotel Company had lost four Rangers in less than two weeks, and the accident would have an even greater impact on the 115-man Ranger company. In a six month period, they had lost six killed and forty-two wounded, and during the following year those numbers would climb even higher. Measured against the seventy-two to eighty Rangers who made up the two platoons of field Lurps, the numbers were staggering. The Rangers were taking exceptional risks, but they were achieving results.

In the previous six months, they had deployed 328 patrols accounting for 143 enemy sightings, most of which had resulted in contacts—the sudden deadly firefights that usually pitted the small recon teams against superior enemy forces. The Rangers had accounted for 128 confirmed enemy KIAs, 56 possible KIAs, and 16 POWs. They had brought back a pile of enemy documents over twenty-eight inches thick and had discovered four major enemy base camps. But the price of their success was too often measured in Purple Hearts and body bags.

Condolences over the recent loss poured into the company from the cavalry squadron and the three brigades, and if there had been any doubt where the Rangers stood in the eyes of the division it quickly disappeared beneath the flood.

Less than a week before the barracks incident, S.Sgt. Stan

Lento and two of the other members of Ranger Team 4-3 who had just died had conducted a briefing for the division chief of staff, Col. R. M. Shoemaker, who was deeply and sincerely impressed by Lento and his team. The colonel had passed on his personal compliments and those of the division commander, Major General Roberts, to both Ranger Team 4-3 and to the Ranger company for a job well done.

Shoemaker later told Captain Paccerelli that he hadn't realized how young the members of the Ranger company were. Judging by their excellent past accomplishments and their professionalism, the chief of staff had expected much older men.

Many of the Rangers were nineteen to twenty-one years old, and some like Griffin, Bell, Durham, Largent, Arnold, Sheehan, Salminen, McDaniel, and Lento would never get any older.

CHAPTER THIRTY-TWO

It was a long flight, made even longer by the shelling of Cam Ranh Bay, which meant that the planeload of new arrivals couldn't land until the barrage of rockets and mortars had stopped. So the pilot circled the South China Sea for a while before finally receiving the word that it was safe to land.

Lt. Mike Brennan stepped from the aircraft to begin his tour of duty with the Cav. The short, well-built West Point graduate had spent six months with the 82d Airborne at Fort Bragg, North Carolina, before coming to Vietnam. He was actually looking forward to his assignment to the 1st of the 7th Cav of the 1st Cavalry Division. It was the "Garry Owen" Cav, and what American of Boston Irish ancestry in his right mind would serve anywhere else? The 7th Cav was the stuff of folklore and legend, and even a John Wayne movie or two managed to celebrate the unit. Damn near most civilians Brennan knew could recognize its theme song, even if they couldn't tell you anything else about the outfit.

But just then, he was simply satisfied to troop off the plane and shuttle into the replacement center to wait for his new assignment with the Cav. Brennan was Airborne and Ranger qualified but the two officers who arrived with him were Ranger and Airborne qualified as well as Pathfinder trained. The Pathfinder school, like the Airborne school, was three weeks in duration; the extraordinarily grueling Ranger school consisted of eight weeks of advanced patrolling. The young officers had been told that the Ranger course was the best form of life insurance they could obtain. They would soon learn why.

While each man was proud of his Airborne wings, and Brennan's two friends were proud of the winged-torch insignia on the pocket of their jungle fatigues, it was the Ranger tab they wore on their left shoulder that they were proudest of. Each was looking forward to a combat assignment with the 1st Cavalry Division, but none of them had expected to find the war as quickly as they did. Their first night in country, the Viet Cong attacked Cam Ranh Bay from the seaward side of the base, infiltrating into the large rear area and wreaking havoc on the airmen, sailors, and soldiers who lived and worked there.

The newly arrived officers could hear the enemy small-arms fire near their holding barracks and wondered what was going on. Then, when VC satchel charges started exploding in the vicinity of the 6th Convalescent Center, they recognized the noise for the attack it was. Someone was yelling, "Incoming! Out of the barracks! Out of the barracks!" The three officers quickly followed the stream of new arrivals as they emptied out of the holding barracks and into the dark night searching for a place to hide. They hadn't even been issued weapons yet. That was always taken care of only when the new men arrived at their units; no one saw the need for weapons in rear-area bases. That's why there were MPs and armed perimeter guards. Cam Ranh Bay was supposed to be one of the safest places in Vietnam, which is exactly why the Viet Cong had targeted it for a raid.

Brennan and his two companions found a small bunker built over a metal culvert and dove inside. Brennan was the middle man in the temporary shelter, but all three men were partially exposed to anyone passing by, which offered little comfort to any of them. At least the culvertlike bunker would deflect shrapnel or concussion from a mortar round or a grenade exploding on the surface above them. But a satchel charge tossed into the culvert itself would surely kill them all.

They could hear the swell of the small battle rise and fall over them as excited voices shouting in Vietnamese came very close. They heard the distinctive sound of AK-47s firing nearby, then listened as the base defenders returned their fire and drove them back. It wasn't the M-16s that gave them some degree of comfort as much as it was sounds of voices speaking in English.

When the Viet Cong came dangerously close to their position, the three American officers pressed tighter together and remained as still as possible. Then, after the tide of the battle had turned in favor of the Americans, they came out cautiously to have a look around. Although it had seemed like hours, probably no more than five to ten minutes passed before the Viet Cong had been forced to retreat.

Brennan decided then and there that he would never be caught without a weapon again. After he had reported in to division at Bien Hoa and received his .45 automatic and a rifle, he'd always make sure to take one of them with him wherever he went.

When he reported in to the 1st Cavalry Division Replacement Center in Bien Hoa, he quickly discovered that he wasn't being assigned to the 1st of the 7th Cav as he had thought. His two comrades received orders assigning them to the Cav's Pathfinder detachment as they had expected. Since Brennan hadn't gotten orders assigning him to the 1st of the 7th, and since he was Ranger qualified, and since the Ranger Company was reportedly looking for a new junior officer, he rightly assumed that he would be assigned to Company H (Ranger). End of story. He knew that the job would be a staff position, which meant rear area support, and he didn't like that a bit.

The feisty Irishman formally protested the decision. He wanted to go to a line unit, an infantry company, and fight a war, damn it! Wasn't that what he had been trained to do?

"Report to Hotel Company, Lieutenant," the unsympathetic assignments officer said as he handed Brennan his orders. The West Point graduate trudged out of the office and down toward the flight line but he vowed to himself that he would find a way to get to a line company.

When he arrived at Phuoc Vinh, the lieutenant decided to go and see the G-1, division's personnel officer, to try a more direct approach. He took it as a good sign when he was immediately granted an interview. The G-1, a crusty old infantry colonel on his second or third tour of duty, listened to Brennan's explanation, then offered him a simple choice: either he could go to the Ranger company as ordered, or he could be court-martialed.

"Your call, Lieutenant."

Brennan reported in to the Ranger company a short time later, but once he spotted the sign hanging in the orderly room that read something to the effect that ". . . every man a volunteer," the lieutenant quickly informed the company first sergeant that he wasn't a volunteer and he didn't want to be there.

First Sergeant Jerry Price nodded at the young officer and then walked into the CO's office and informed him that his new lieutenant had just arrived, only he didn't want to be in the company.

"Is that right?" Captain Paccerelli smirked at the senior NCO, who nodded and smiled.

The CO's mood suddenly darkened. "Send him in," the captain said.

Lieutenant Brennan entered the CO's office and saluted. Paccerelli returned the salute, gave him an "At ease," and then said, "So you don't want to be here! Is that right, Lieutenant?"

Brennan swallowed and answered, "Yes, sir," and then told Captain Paccerelli that he didn't want to be there because he had been slated to go to a line unit, and he very much wanted to be assigned to the 7th Cav. Paccerelli leafed through Brennan's file, and when the twenty-three-year-old lieutenant had finished explaining his predicament, Paccerelli closed the file, stiffened noticeably, and sneered. "Fine," agreed Paccerelli. "If you don't want to be here, then we don't want you here." Nothing else was said and he dismissed the surprised lieutenant.

But as Brennan turned to go, the captain bellowed after him, "Lieutenant, get back in here!" The young officer stopped dead in his tracks, turned on his heels, and marched back into the company commander's office.

"The job—your job—is not exactly a staff position," Paccerelli offered, outlining the responsibilities of the position, and he painted an accurate picture. The extent of the job description surprised even Brennan. The job, as Paccerelli explained it, would be to serve the troops, doing everything possible to protect them both in the rear and in the field, and being ready at a minute's notice to go to their aid if they got into trouble.

"I suggest you give the company five to six months and see for yourself what it's all about. If you don't think it offers its share of risks, then I'll be more than happy to honor your request to transfer to a line unit."

The Ranger captain then went on to tell him more about the unit, its history, and more specifically about the other two lieutenants—Robert McKenzie and Clark Surber. McKenzie, a former enlisted man, was getting ready to rotate home within a few weeks. Surber, who had been brought in after Lieutenant Bell had been shot down and killed, would still be around for a few weeks more. It was clear to Brennan that he would soon be the only lieutenant left in the unit, and that both Captain Paccerelli and the company needed him. He would have to be a fast learner.

He knew he wasn't going anywhere, not for a while anyway. Captain Paccerelli had made that clear. On the orderly room wall was an enlarged shield-shaped crest of the 75th Infantry with the Latin motto underneath: *SUA SPONTE*, "Of

Their Own Accord." The Rangers had adopted that motto because their units were made up strictly of volunteers. Like it or not, he had just "volunteered"—almost of his own accord.

"Welcome to Hotel Company, Lieutenant," Paccerelli finally said, smiling and offering his hand. "Let me show you around."

CHAPTER THIRTY-THREE

PFC James F. McIntyre didn't get accepted into H Company's Lurp training program on his first attempt simply because he had the wrong MOS, the wrong military occupational specialty. The nineteen-year-old soldier from Watertown, New York, had been trained in the field of communications. He was a radioman, and H Company didn't want any more radiomen, thank you.

They wanted Airborne infantrymen. Second-tour veterans, if they could find them, and if not, then they wanted some motivated grunts they could turn into Lurp/Rangers. McIntyre had been told as much by Captain Paccerelli himself, and he was warned that if and when he tried again, then he had better come back with the proper haircut.

The captain dismissed the private first class, but when the determined radioman showed up again one week later with a close-cropped haircut and spit-polished jungle boots asking if he could be accepted into the training program, the company commander could only smile at the new volunteer.

"You think you can make it?" Paccerelli asked.

"Yes, sir!" said McIntyre.

"We'll see," the captain replied, ordering the young private first class to see the company first sergeant on his way out.

Upon graduation from the twelve-day Ranger training program, McIntyre was assigned to a team for his first mission. As the team medic. All new team members served as a patrol's medic during their cherry mission simply because the team aid bag added more weight to an already heavy rucksack. It was a Lurp/Ranger rite of passage, and he accepted the aid bag without complaining.

After five days in the field without sighting the enemy, the team was extracted. McIntyre felt relieved. He had pulled his first Lurp mission and had done well. As the helicopter roared into the pickup zone and the Rangers jumped aboard, he was looking forward to getting back to the company area to take a shower and put on a dry pair of anything! In the field, you wore the same uniform for the duration of the mission. It got wet and filthy, and after the second day, it began to smell. Early mornings were the worst time since there were no fires, and until the chilled fog burned off, there was no way to keep from trembling with the cold. But by midafternoon, in the searing heat, there was no way to keep from sweating under the staggering weight of a seventy-five-pound rucksack. The sweat mixed with the dirt and grime, camouflage paint, and doses of oily bug spray to combine for an all-around physically uncomfortable outing.

It was finally over, at least for that mission. But as the helicopter fought to lift out of the pickup zone and clear the trees, the pilot realized that the transitional lift he needed wasn't there.

"Hold on! We're going down! Mayday! Mayday! Going down!" the pilot shouted into his radio mouthpiece just before the aircraft's underbelly and skids caught in the treetops, causing the ship to cartwheel. The ship flipped end over end then bounced off the tree limbs as the main rotor blades sliced through the thick vegetation before shearing off. The tumbling aircraft bucked and twisted before crashing hard into the jungle floor below.

McIntyre remembered the terrified looks on the faces of several of his teammates as the helicopter rolled to a stop, but then he was slammed into the bulkhead and knocked unconscious. When he came to, he sat up slowly, holding his pounding head in his hands. Someone was moaning nearby, but when he turned to see who it was, he was shocked to discover the extent of the damage received by the aircraft and everyone aboard.

A few of the Rangers who could still function crawled out of the wreckage and formed a hasty defensive perimeter around the crash site as other helicopters circled somewhere overhead. Unknown to the men on the ground, one of the pilots in the orbiting aircraft was already on the radio, guiding in the medevac helicopter for those injured in the crash. However, there were more than just injuries involved. Some of the passengers and crew were already dead, among them Rangers Kenneth Burch and John Williams, veteran Rangers who had even congratulated McIntyre on completing his first mission while the extraction helicopter was just beginning its short final run to pick them up. He hadn't known them well, and now he never would.

The medevac helicopter took out the more seriously wounded and the dead. McIntyre was helped aboard in the first lift, but was dropped off to be treated at an aid station on a nearby fire support base because the aircraft was overloaded.

McIntyre didn't mind. His head was still pounding from the concussion he had received in the crash. After being treated at the aid station, the young Ranger was told to go find someplace to take it easy until another aircraft came for him. The sun had set before his ride showed up, so he was stuck on the firebase until the next day, when a 1st of the 9th slick would arrive to pick him up.

Finding a place to relax away from the noise of the base's artillery battery, McIntyre sat back against the sandbagged wall of the base TOC and reflected on his good fortune at having survived the crash. He was about to find out that his luck was only fleeting.

The enemy attack began with a shower of 82mm mortar rounds raining down on the small firebase perimeter, punctuated by the distinct echoing blasts from an enemy 75mm re-

coilless rifle. The rain of mortars and the recoilless rifle fire
came from the heavy weapons element supporting a large
NVA force zeroing in on the jungle outpost.

McIntyre grabbed his rifle and LBE and leaped behind a
sandbag wall as the rockets and mortars found their targets.

The barrage seemed to go on forever. Then small-arms fire
and secondary explosions began erupting all over the outpost. GIs were running for cover, but not all of them made it.
Horrible cries and screams came from a nearby artillery position right after an incoming mortar round scored a direct hit
on it. Through the thick acrid smoke illuminated by the pul-
sating glow of the fires, McIntyre could make out a human
torso hanging from the barrel of the destroyed howitzer.

When the ground assault began, McIntyre moved up to
join in the defense of the base's perimeter, firing at groups of
enemy soldiers coming through the wire. Grenades, claymores, RPGs, mortars, shoulder-fired rockets, and cannons
exploded in a mind-bending chorus of massed pyrotechnics.
The long throaty rattle of heavy machine guns and the
crackle and pop of small-arms fire punctuated the dark and
deadly song.

The battle raged all through the night, and by first light, the
extent of the damage could be seen. But in the early morning
light, there was no new promise of hope and salvation as the
fight continued unabated. Dozens of dead American infantrymen and scores of wounded were scattered around the
firebase. The sky overhead was thick with gunships, and
fighter/bombers were rolling in on the enemy positions in the
surrounding jungle. Hundreds of enemy bodies littered the
no-man's-land between the jungle and the outer perimeter
wire, and not all of them were dead. Some of the Viet Cong
and NVA were trapped behind cover breaks and in shell
craters, still firing at the Americans defending the base while
others, too wounded to continue fighting, dragged themselves back to the jungle or bled to death in the attempt.

McIntyre's heart sank when he realized he was stuck on

the fire support base until the fight was over. There was no way that anyone was leaving soon, as the enemy continued to press home their attack.

All through the day and long into the next night, the battle raged as the enemy pushed to overrun the small fire support base. On both sides wounded soldiers too injured to withdraw sniped away at nearby targets until they were either cut down in the changing tide of battle or ran out of ammunition. The Communist mortars and rockets were still hitting with deadly accuracy, hammering at the base tactical operations center and the remaining artillery pieces. The surviving grunts continued to repulse the repeated human-wave assaults, shifting positions to cope with each push.

McIntyre joined them in each effort, himself unsure of what to do but following the lead of nearby grunts. His head still hurt, he was dead on his feet, and he was hungry and thirsty, but none of that mattered. Human demands had to be ignored until the battle was won by one side or the other. Each time McIntyre expended his ammunition and grenades, he found more, and finally he grabbed rifles and grenades from the cold hands of the dead and continued the fight. Throughout the second night, the battle raged. Finally, at first light, the fighting had begun to die out, and for the first time the full extent of the catastrophe could be fully measured.

Enemy bodies littered the perimeter wire and choked the open area surrounding the small outpost. Some of the NVA who had made it inside the camp still lay where they had fallen. The U.S. dead were loaded into body bags or covered with ponchos that fluttered in the strengthening breeze, slapping against the cold flesh of soldiers who no longer could feel their sting. The wounded were treated by overworked medics and the debris of the battle lay scattered across the fire support base.

The soldiers who lived on the fire support base had paid an enormous price for its defense, and after the cleanup, it would be ordered closed. As wave after wave of helicopters flew in to retrieve its defenders and their wounded and dead, Private First Class McIntyre finally got his chance to relax.

"This place have a name?" he asked one of the grunts who had just offered him a can of C rations.

"Becky," the grunt said as he slowly surveyed the wreckage. "It used to be Fire Support Base Becky."

The grunt, Spec Four Frank Duggan of Boston, Massachusetts, had had his share of being a target. He had convinced himself there had to be a better way of fighting the war. He had just about decided to apply for a transfer to the Rangers. It had to be better to catch the enemy off guard in their own camps than to sit and wait for another Becky.

"You like being a Ranger?"

Surprised at the grunt's question, McIntyre nodded. "Better than this."

When McIntyre finally reached Phuoc Vinh, Captain Paccerelli called the young Ranger into his office and asked him if he wanted a transfer out of the company. After all he had been through during the past three days, Paccerelli felt that McIntyre might want to go back to his old unit. Private First Class McIntyre took the officer's invitation the wrong way.

"Did . . . did I do something wrong, sir?"

Paccerelli sat back and stared hard at the young Ranger. "No," he said. "I just figured that after what you have been through, you might have had a change of heart about becoming a Ranger."

"No, sir," McIntyre answered. "I'd like to stay, sir."

Paccerelli nodded and dismissed him, and as McIntyre walked out the door, the captain marveled at the kind of people he had in his company. They weren't just good soldiers; they were remarkable soldiers. Although an occasional MP report might dispute that claim, it didn't matter to George Paccerelli. His Rangers were hardly saints, but every so often they could still pull off miracles.

CHAPTER THIRTY-FOUR

"One of our teams has a visual on an enemy patrol, Captain," the operations NCO said to the company commander over his shoulder as he monitored the team's latest radio transmission.

The team was working the border along Cambodia, a five-day mission to monitor the major trails leading into South Vietnam. Everyone knew that COSVN—the Viet Cong's field headquarters—lay just over the Cambodian border, and that the Viet Cong and North Vietnamese Army operated openly from large base areas and used those sites to launch their attacks into South Vietnam.

"A six-man enemy patrol. And are you ready for this . . . one of them is Caucasian!"

"Caucasian!" echoed an open-mouthed Paccerelli as the operations NCO nodded.

"Carrying an AK, pack, and dressed like the others," added the NCO.

"Did they get him?"

The NCO shook his head. "Just a visual."

"Any chance of tracking them?"

"No, they went back across the border."

"What do you think? A salt-and-pepper team?"

"Maybe," said Paccerelli. "But we won't know for sure until we get one." There had been a number of reports of "salt-and-pepper teams" consisting of a Caucasian and a Negro leading enemy patrols against American forces.

Rumor and informed speculation had it that the black and white members of the enemy patrols were either former GIs working with the Viet Cong or Soviet Bloc advisers. But until a salt-and-pepper team was captured, killed, or otherwise positively identified, it was all just talk.

On extraction, the team would be debriefed, and more than likely, the Military Intelligence people would be on hand with the book of photos, asking the team leader and assistant team leader if they could match the man they saw with any of the faces from the photographs in front of them.

The idea of American turncoats frosted Paccerelli, and he preferred to think the sightings were the result of Soviet Bloc soldiers assisting the Viet Cong and North Vietnamese. It certainly wouldn't have surprised him if Soviet advisers were across the border. The Viet Cong and North Vietnamese had tens of thousands of soldiers and a number of bases just across the border in Cambodia. They used the bases to launch attacks in the province and rearm and equip units operating in the region. Cambodia was the Viet Cong's sanctuary, and until it was attacked, the surprise storm was never really all that far away.

The next brush with Cambodia and the frustrations it presented was a request from division to put together a quick rescue force to go after American and South Vietnamese POWs being held in Cambodia.

After receiving the mission request, Captain Paccerelli personally selected four five-man teams for the rescue operation. He spent long hours poring over the details of the mission, analyzing and weighing his options before laying out his plan. After studying the maps and the intelligence information, he was certain it could be done. They'd have the element of surprise going in, not to mention the massive firepower available. His people could carry off the raid and the recovery down to the last detail.

Paccerelli oversaw the training and ran a number of dress rehearsals and drills with his men to effectively work out the details of any eventuality they might face. Getting in might be the easy part; getting out might take some doing

The mission was simple enough. They would swoop in on the suspected jungle prison site just over the border, swiftly secure the camp before the prisoners could be moved or executed by their captors, then quickly bring the POWs out before enemy reinforcements could arrive. Since the Viet Cong and North Vietnamese Army knew the Americans would never openly send forces across the border after them, especially a major operation complete with helicopter, jet aircraft, and artillery support, they would never expect a raid such as the one Paccerelli planned, and would not be prepared to counter it.

The Rangers from Hotel Company were well into the training phase of the operation when the POW recovery mission was suddenly canceled. Few reasons were ever offered, and the Ranger CO's frustration was evident to all around him; he didn't like the idea of leaving American soldiers in a prison camp. But the matter was out of his hands. Someone, somewhere had scrubbed the mission. The summer months were proving to be difficult in ways he hadn't imagined, and it was more than the sweltering heat that was sapping away his strength.

CHAPTER THIRTY-FIVE

The Huey liftship with Team 4-1 aboard rose from the flight line, dipped its nose to pick up airspeed, and flew out over the Phuoc Binh base camp perimeter, climbing for altitude over the surrounding rice paddies. It veered west-north-west away from the nearby White Virgin Mountain as it continued on toward the mission site northwest of Fire Support Base Buttons. Sgt. Cal Renfro, the patrol's assistant team leader, stared out the opened helicopter bay doors and watched the show unfold.

Nearly three thousand feet below, the hard-packed dirt road that was Highway 14 cut through the green-and-brown jungle that covered most of the region. Highway 14 veered northeast back toward Vietnam and soon disappeared as the helicopter flew on toward its final destination south of Bu Dop. The magnificent trees were old growth, wrapped tightly in thick vines and dense jungle foliage.

Because it was a living thing, the jungle spread and grew with no real pattern or form, often leaving thick growths of vegetation around light brown grass fields, swampy sumps, and the decades-old craters left by Japanese, French, and allied artillery and bombs.

Shortly after insertion, Team 4-1 found a concrete road hidden beneath the jungle. It was no wider than an ordinary driveway, and its length was anyone's guess. After they had reported it to the radio-relay site at Phuoc Binh, Captain Paccerelli ordered the patrol to set up an ambush on the road and wait to see who showed up to use it.

As Sergeant Renfro and the rear scout were setting out their claymores, they suddenly froze in place as three NVA crossed the road forty meters from their position. The three enemy soldiers hadn't bothered to scan the road before they crossed, or they might have been attracted to the two "trees" holding weapons just up the way a bit. Taking no notice of the two Rangers, the three NVA casually left the red clay trail, crossed the road, and reentered the jungle on another footpath on the opposite side.

After his heart had finally settled down, Renfro and the rear scout finished placing antipersonnel mines and moved back to the team to report what had just happened. As the team leader called in the situation, he decided to shift the ambush site to the trail since it seemed to offer a better opportunity to score. Renfro offered to move up to check it out first, and the team leader agreed, sending the rear scout with him, just in case.

Renfro decided to use the concrete road to get to the trail because the NVA were not likely using it, and because it would certainly be more quiet than sneaking up on the trail through the underbrush, especially since there still might be other enemy soldiers around.

There was a risk that the NVA might have booby-trapped the road, but he suspected they hadn't since the area hadn't seen any American or South Vietnamese operations. So, CAR-15 pointing the way, he eased out onto the road and slowly made his way down its center toward the trail as the rear scout followed five meters back. He kept his eyes riveted on the spot where the NVA had left the jungle.

He had gone thirty yards when he heard the clink of metal against metal in the jungle to his left. He also heard hushed conversation in Vietnamese. As he turned to see who it was, he spotted a platoon or more of NVA soldiers sitting just in-

side the jungle, resting and eating. The nearest enemy soldier
had his back turned to the road.

Not taking his eyes from the NVA, Renfo raised his hand
signaling the rear scout to halt. But the rear scout couldn't
see the signal since he was walking backwards, covering
their rear. Renfro heard the rear scout's footsteps and
watched in horror as the nearest enemy soldier heard them,
too, and turned to see why one of his people was out on the
road.

When he saw the tall Ranger's camouflaged face he
quickly dropped his food and reached for his AK-47. He
never had a chance to bring up the assault rifle; Sergeant
Renfro shot him in the face and chest. Renfro then finished
off the rest of the magazine spraying the NVA soldiers before
turning and yelling for the rear scout to run as he himself
leaped for a nearby ditch. Once under cover, he quickly
dropped another magazine in his rifle and prepared to defend
himself. When a massive volume of return fire sprayed the
spot where he had just been standing, Renfro began tossing
grenades into the underbrush where the NVA had been having their picnic.

"Stay down; we're gonna blow the claymores!" someone
yelled from back where the team was hidden as the NVA
were beginning to come out on the road. When the team
leader set off the antipersonnel mines, there was a tremendous explosion and a deadly hurricane of steel ball bearings
swept the road. Following the detonation, Renfro fired up
several more magazines, then hurriedly low-crawled back to
the team.

Covering his retreat until the missing Ranger could rejoin
the patrol, the team leader then ordered them to move out
running as the RTO called for gunship support. The thoroughly confused NVA were still struggling with their dead
and wounded, trying to figure out just what had happened,
but it wouldn't take long for any confusion to soon disappear.

"Go!" the team leader yelled as the RTO called in the contact and reported their precarious situation. The team leader pulled his map out and was calling in fire support to keep the NVA from pursuing too closely, which they did anyway despite his efforts. Renfro followed behind the rest of the team as the rear scout, stopping every once in a while to fire at the pursuing enemy troops who were coming on with vengeance on their minds. As the team continued to escape and evade, Renfro tossed a smoke grenade over his shoulder and told the RTO to radio the gunships just arriving on station to fire on and around the smoke.

During the running battle several of the Rangers had been slightly wounded, but before it was over, all five would be hit.

Any chance of pulling the team out in a nearby clearing disappeared as the NVA began to close the gap in their pursuit. When it was finally decided to pull Team 4-1 out by McGuire rig, the team quickly set up in a circular defensive position and began putting down a heavy volume of fire at the determined NVA.

The first Huey liftship that approached the trapped team could only take out three of the five Rangers so the team leader and Renfro stayed behind to cover the extraction as the helicopter hovered over the trees and kicked out the three McGuire rigs. The Rangers snap-linked themselves onto the extraction ropes and signaled for the aircraft to lift them out. By then the helicopter was taking hits, and the door gunners were returning fire as the aircraft quickly rose, pulling the three men up and over the trees.

The second aircraft moved in over Renfro and the team leader and dropped two more McGuire rigs; the first was ninety feet long while the second was a little over one hundred feet in length. As the gunships covered the second extraction, the team leader and assistant team leader were lifted out of the jungle and into the sky, dangling like helpless puppets beneath the aircraft.

Both Rangers were firing and taking fire as they were pulled out. Renfro discovered he was bleeding but knew he'd have to wait until they landed to find out how badly he was hit because his rope had twisted, and he was spinning like a top, several thousand feet in the air. When things finally settled down, he looked below and saw the team leader hanging on literally by a thread. An enemy round had hit the Ranger's snap link, breaking the locking device that held the jury-rigged extraction harness in place. Worse, the team leader's pack had somehow flipped over his shoulders forcing him to struggle desperately to hold on to the harness and the pack at the same time.

Renfro tried yelling up to the helicopter with no success before turning to scream for the team leader to drop the pack. If the man had heard him, he wasn't taking Renfro's advice. Finally, the crew chief leaned out of the helicopter bay well, saw the Ranger TL's predicament, and within an instant the helicopter was heading down to land in an open field.

Once on the ground Renfro unhooked himself and raced over to help the team leader.

"Why didn't you drop the ruck?" he asked as the Ranger massaged his aching arms and back. Renfro was checking his own injuries and quickly discovered that his wounds were minor.

"I think the weight of the pack was the only thing that kept me from falling," the Ranger TL answered.

When they jumped on the helicopter, Renfro was mentally kicking himself for walking down the center of the road. It was not only dangerous but a stupid thing to do. He was certain that at the team's debriefing, Captain Paccerelli would point that out before jumping all over him for it. In one of the company newsletters, Captain Paccerelli had warned the Rangers that they should never think that the Standing Orders for Rogers' Rangers were out of date, and at that moment Renfro could think of at least one of them that applied in his case: "Don't never take a chance you don't have to." It wasn't important that the grammar was incorrect; the basic rule still applied. The Standing Orders had been a mainstay of Ranger and Scout activities since 1756, and the nineteen that were featured on Ranger posters everywhere easily applied to this latest war.

Back at Phuoc Vinh Captain Paccerelli did chew him out for using the road, and then submitted a request for a Bronze Star for valor, to be awarded to the assistant team leader, who bore the brunt of the enemy's assault.

In a newsletter following the mission, Paccerelli also had an opportunity to remark on the mission while pointing out the obvious problems of taking on a superior enemy force.

"Marksmanship has improved during the past week," he wrote. "Sergeant Renfro of Patrol 4-1 north of Phuoc Binh displayed excellent form in bringing down his adversary. However, the fifty uninvited northern pallbearers did give the patrol and its support ample training aids."

CHAPTER THIRTY-SIX

McIntyre's team found the well-used trail and began paralleling it to find a place to set up an ambush. Something glistened on the dirt stretch, catching his eye and immediate attention. Spit. McIntyre immediately brought up his CAR-15 as Specialist Dick Cramer, the ATL, quickly followed his lead just as the Viet Cong soldier turned back around and saw the Americans coming through the underbrush. But before he could bring up his AK-47, McIntyre and Cramer killed him.

There was no time to take inventory though; the Viet Cong who were huddled in the bunkers and fighting positions behind the dead man returned fire. The Rangers dove to the ground as the small-arms fire picked at the jungle above them. In their tight perimeter and minimum cover, the Rangers had a reasonable field of fire for 360 degrees, not that they needed it just then; the fire was coming at them straight on. Soon, though, the Viet Cong would try to flank them unless the gunships McIntyre was requesting arrived in time to drive them off. The team's radioman was relaying the request above the din of gunfire.

The baseball grenade fell in the midst of the team, and Rick Arden knew what it was when it made a sickening *thump*. A quick glance over his shoulder confirmed his guess, and before the soldier from Columbus, Ohio, could say anything, someone else yelled, "Grenade!" Like the others, Arden scrambled to get away. They low-crawled as fast as they could for any immediate cover knowing that the explosion was only seconds away. The grenade had a five-to-six second fuse, and several of them were already gone. But slow, deliberate motion back at the live grenade caused Arden to stop and stare in disbelief. In the midst of the action, oblivious to the firefight, Jim McIntyre was standing over the grenade. The New Yorker lifted his heavy rucksack by its shoulder straps and carefully placed it on the live grenade, then he used his weight to buffer and deflect the blast away from the team.

Time didn't slow down on such occasions; they just accelerated your fear, and the quiet Ranger sergeant discovered that there was just enough time to become more frightened than he had ever been before in his life. Later, McIntyre would say that his mind raced through a hundred possible scenarios and most of them weren't pleasant.

The violence of the explosion hurled McIntyre back up and tumbling as the large pack absorbed the brunt of the concussion and shrapnel, and only minor shrapnel wounds resulted. For a moment, the small battle ceased. Even the Viet Cong were momentarily confused. Through the dust and debris Arden could see that McIntyre was dazed and on all fours and Cramer was yelling at him.

For a long moment, McIntyre tried to catch his breath. He felt like somebody had just run over him with a truck. The Ranger tried to shake it off before getting back down and returning fire on the Viet Cong positions. His quick thinking had possibly saved the entire patrol. Arden thought McIntyre's feat was the most amazing thing he had ever seen and later said as much. As did the rest of the team. The company commander was equally impressed when he learned of McIntyre's selfless and smart act.

The quiet New Yorker played it down, but Paccerelli wouldn't allow it to go away. He requested an impact award of the Silver Star for gallantry and an impact promotion to sergeant E-6, both of which were approved by the 1st of the 9th Cav.

Discovering that impact medals and promotions weren't easy things to get approved, First Sergeant Price had to politic fast and furious to find an allocation somewhere in the division. Each impact promotion had to be within the division's allocation, and although on paper a Lurp/Ranger company's rank structure for enlisted personnel looked good, Captain Paccerelli discovered that as a separate company, going the normal route and waiting for rank allocations was time consuming and frustrating. Captain Paccerelli spent countless hours at the G-1 and adjutant general's offices begging, borrowing, and stealing promotions.

As an officer he could understand the division headquarter's company commander and staff wanting to promote their people first. But, as a former enlisted man for ten years, he had watched NCO promotions go to clerks and jocks while the rifle squads were still led by corporals or spec fours and platoons were led by sergeant E-5s and staff sergeants.

He wouldn't let that happen to his men if at all possible, and between his efforts and those of First Sergeant Price, they managed to pull it off. Of course, no matter how hard they tried, the army kept E-7-and-above locked up with the key nowhere to be found. Had they managed to find it, Paccerelli had a documented list of four E-6s he wanted immediately promoted to E-7, foremost among them staff sergeants Barnes and Torres.

In Major General Roberts's address to the company during the awards ceremony, he remarked that McIntyre's deed was brave and smart, noting that McIntyre had managed to think quickly enough to throw his rucksack on the grenade instead of himself.

Captain Paccerelli suspected that the general enjoyed pinning medals on real heroes. The division commander seldom, if ever, refused to attend an awards ceremony. In fact, lately he seemed to be on hand even for the graduation of new Rangers through the company's training program, shaking the hand of each new graduate while congratulating him as he awarded the first company scroll. A proud infantryman himself, Elvy Roberts knew soldiers and soldiering. He was proud of his Rangers, and Lieutenant Brennan had even heard him refer to them as "the best soldiers in my division." Major General Roberts seemed genuinely pleased at presenting the scrolls to the division's only all-volunteer force, a fact not lost on Lieutenant Brennan who had helped oversee their training.

Brennan had to admit that he liked it at the Ranger company and liked *being* a Hotel Company Ranger. He had pulled one mission as an "observer," which the captain had said was a way for the platoon leaders "to check out their team leaders." Brennan suspected that it was also the CO's way of offering the junior officers a firsthand chance to learn to appreciate the men and the job the men performed in the field, where even "good" missions were difficult. There was always sweltering heat, humping through the bush, chilling cold rain at night during the monsoons, mud, swarms of mosquitoes, leeches, poisonous centipedes and other exotic insects, snakes, and God knows what else lurking in the jungles. Never mind the Viet Cong and NVA who were never all that far away!

Brennan had already played a role in several hot extractions, pulling out teams that were being chased by enemy they had ambushed.

Mike Brennan had no way of knowing the hardships he would face in the coming months and how several Rangers in his platoon would be killed in action, or how he would struggle to try to keep a dying Ranger alive on a helicopter heading back to Phuoc Binh, only to have the soldier die in his arms. But that was still weeks away and still something those who survived the ordeal would come to know and respect about the young lieutenant. Just then, though, the Ranger Company was still the best place to be.

Captain Paccerelli, too, was proving to be something more than he had first appeared. The lieutenant came to see that, in many ways, the captain was like the Roman centurion who had worked his way up through the ranks in combat and had arrived at the position of leadership because he had earned the right to be there. He was tough, loyal, and instilled confidence in his people by helping them become the best soldiers that they could be. At West Point words like "Duty, Honor, Country" were held in high esteem but it was in combat that officers like Captain Paccerelli gave those words value and meaning. For Brennan, although he would serve with many fine officers in the next twenty-eight years, including many general officers, George Paccerelli would always be his ideal of the true combat soldier.

Paccerelli took good care of his people but he also looked after those who helped his people, and Brennan noted how the captain always made a point of writing up air crews for awards while offering their commanders something in return for their support as well. On occasion, the Ranger company commander presented SKS rifles—with permission from the teams that had captured the weapons—to those commanders whose air crews provided the team with gunship or liftship support.

The gifts not only ingratiated them to these commanders, but they provided something more than a mere "thank you" for the much-needed support. The lieutenant had seen the letter that the 1st Aviation Brigade's commander had sent to the captain, and had read how Captain Paccerelli had focused all of the attention on the enlisted men who had captured the weapon.

Dear Captain Paccerelli,

Please accept sincerest thanks for the SKS which you sent me. I am especially pleased to have the story behind its capture. Sp4s Talbot, Storm, Edwards, Lennon, and Gray are obviously very brave men. I would appreciate your conveying to them my gratitude for the job they did and for the weapon they captured.

With all my best wishes to you and your wonderful people.

> Most sincerely,
> Allen M. Burdett Jr.
> Brigadier General, USA
> Commanding

It was gratitude and thanks, the right thing to do, and it was a little politicking, too. For Lieutenant Brennan, the tutelage provided by Captain Paccerelli was a true infantry leader's finishing school.

CHAPTER THIRTY-SEVEN

Orders had come down for Captain Paccerelli, requesting him to report to Fort Benning, Georgia, to attend the Infantry Officer's Advanced Course. This not only surprised him but left him with a permanent grin. In spite of all the toes he had stepped on, his career was not over, not yet anyway.

He would officially turn over command on 1 September 1969. A new company commander had already been selected and until he arrived, Lt. Clark Surber would fill in. This tour of duty, Paccerelli's third, was complete, and he was looking forward to going home. He missed Barbara and the kids and couldn't wait to see them again.

Hotel Company was going strong, although Paccerelli could think of a million things he still needed to do before he left.

Company E and Company H had come a long way. The early days had been rough, and he had indeed stepped on a great many toes . . . oh hell, he had even stomped on a few at times, especially on those of the critics who couldn't comprehend the job let alone what kind of men it took to do it.

The Rangers—his Lurps—gave everything they had and then some, and received so little in return. They asked only to be part of the "best," and then defined the term with their actions. Now their work was appreciated; the criticism largely gone, the respect renewed. The squadron and the division now backed both the commander and the unit one hundred per cent, and the black beret and the red, white, and black 75th Infantry Ranger scrolls had become well-earned badges of honor.

His next rung up the ladder had been guaranteed by the accomplishments of the company, and any success he personally enjoyed, he attributed to the men in the company. With that thought in mind, Paccerelli sat down and struggled to find the right words to show his pride and gratitude.

Ten months ago I assumed command of what was then, Company E (Long Range Patrol) 52d Infantry. Those few of you who were at Camp Evans last October will recall that in addition to a change of company commanders, the company was attached and placed under the operational control of the 1st Squadron, 9th Cavalry. This transition, from direct G-2 control to the squadron, was not in its initial stages a smooth operation. Due to an apparent inability to comprehend our mission, it restricted our employment; the relationship was often strained between the two general-support reconnaissance elements of the division.

It was there at Camp Evans, as we prepared for the move to our present location, that I first bore witness to your invincible esprit de corps, your perseverance and professionalism. I can readily say that, because of you and those who have gone before you, the basics were quickly and effectively ironed out. You met a new enemy in III Corps; he also met a new enemy. You took your bumps and did not waver. You carried your pride with dignity as a member of the Long Range Patrol company. You carried the laurel wreaths of honor won into the Ranger Company.

You have no equals. You do not need banner headlines to proclaim your achievements. Your deeds are known throughout the division; it is by those deeds that you are revered. You have demonstrated your personal courage and knowledge on the Serges Highway, the Adams Road, the Fishhook, the Dog Face, and every enemy base area in the division's operational area. You have met the enemy on his rivers: the Saigon, Song Be, and the Dong Nai.

You have met and fought the best the enemy has; his line divisions, the 1st and 7th North Vietnamese and the 5th and 9th Viet Cong. You have harassed his Rear Service Groups, upset the firing timetable of his 69th Artillery Command. In teams of five and six men you have met the enemy. You have danced to the tunes the AKs played, and you have won. You have proven that the trained American soldier can master the terrain which the enemy and several other misguided souls repeatedly state are his, and his alone.

You have monitored his infantry on the move; his rocket battalions; his supply elements and have rained artillery and helicopter fires on them. You have repeatedly held numerically superior enemy forces at bay for extended periods of time. It was at these times that you demonstrated your training, military discipline, teamwork, and expertise with your organic and supporting weapons.

It was you who captured documents stating the 9th Viet Cong Division was moving north into Tay Ninh Province. It was you who captured documents stating the 88th Regiment of SR5 had been reassigned to the 9th, and the 275th Regiment had been moved. It was you who lay five meters off the trail on that moonlit night, as the 141st Regiment, stumbling over your claymore wires, withdrew north out of the Michelin Plantation. Then you heard the "Doubting Thomases" question the truth of your reports, until the 141st aggressively made their new location known.

Your ranks have been thinned by battle, illness, and DEROS. But you tightened your belts and doubled your efforts and never failed to accomplish your mission. When replacements arrived, you taught them the skills of the long range patrol and the art of reconnaissance.

You did not complain when, due to necessity of increased enemy movement, you returned from a four- or five-day patrol, or a firefight, and found that you would be going out again the next night. The brigades always wanted more patrols than we had. That alone is a mark of the esteem in which you are held. You have proven the current concept of the Ranger companies in Vietnam. The armchair strategist may argue the necessity and expense of your existence, but the combat commander no longer questions the need for the Rangers. Theirs is a demand for more Rangers.

You are professionals; you for the most part are draftees. Your reasons for volunteering for the Rangers are as many as there are of you. You chose the best, to be the best, to do the most, during your tour in Vietnam.

On the morning of 4 September 1969, I turn the command of the finest company of men with whom I, in my sixteen years in the Army, have served, over to your new commander. I know that you will serve him as magnificently as you have served me. I am off to Fort Benning, Georgia, to attend the career course. I will not deny that I am looking forward to the course. After all, it is a stepping stone to the Command and General Staff College, etc. etc. I will never forget the company, and the men who made the company what it is today, and will be tomorrow. If I can ever assist you in any way, I am at your service. Always remember your regiment, your company, and your comradeship. "You haven't lived, until you've almost died; for life has a special flavor, that only a recon man will ever know."

Keep alert. See what you see. Hear what you hear. Think before you act.

Until we meet again, God be with you.

George A. Paccerelli
Captain, Infantry
Commanding

The captain read and reread what he had written and began the slow, arduous task of editing, finally deciding an hour later that his latest draft would have to do. There was much more he had wanted to say, but in the late evening, tiredly slapping at circling mosquitoes, he settled on that final draft. He posted the letter, wanting to be sure that everyone saw it so that if he fumbled to find the right words in his going away speech, then the letter would make it all clear.

Then, with new energy that came from knowing he was going home, he began packing. After three one-year tours of duty, he was finally going home. He knew there was the possibility that he might have to come back to the war after his next school and assignment, and he accepted that. He was a professional soldier, and he would do his duty. But even as he pondered the remote possibility, one thing was certain— he would never serve with finer combat soldiers than those he had just commanded. In behind-the-lines operations, the unit held a forty-to-one kill ratio, and in terms of accomplishment for the division, the Lurp/Rangers had done everything that was required of them and more.

That ten of his Lurp/Rangers had died under his command and at least half of those in the company had received Purple Hearts for combat-related wounds haunted him. And he wanted to ask his men for their forgiveness, for what he perceived as his sometime lack of tact, poor judgment, and hardheadedness in command.

The job of the Lurp/Ranger held more than its share of dangers, but the men had shown incredible acts of heroism and a professionalism the likes of which he had never seen before and perhaps would never see again! Even the intelligence officer who had been brought in to spy on the company had opted to stay and remain a Ranger when his official job was done!

No, he would never forget their personal sacrifice or service, nor would he let others forget it or take it for granted. He had said as much during his good-byes, making sure his junior officers and NCOs well understood what he was saying.

Later, with little fanfare, Capt. George A. Paccerelli left the company as new patrols readied for their missions, practicing immediate-action drills or checking equipment while Lurp, the company mascot, watched over his Rangers. And as a slight breeze wafted through the company area, the brown-and-black dog's ears shot up, and he cautiously sniffed the air. His tufted hackles rose for the unseen threat he sensed but couldn't see, keenly aware of the dragon's whisper.

CHAPTER THIRTY-EIGHT

It was a running firefight. The team on the ground was in trouble and Lieutenant Brennan was on the radio in the TOC trying to get the patrol's RTO to settle down so he could get a better idea of what exactly was going on and what the TOC could do to help the team.

After the patrol had sprung its ambush and killed three enemy soldiers, the team leader and rear scout raced out to retrieve their weapons, equipment, any documents they could find. The trouble was that the three soldiers they ambushed turned out to be the point element of a larger NVA force, which was moving to box in the Rangers. The patrol leader executed an immediate-action drill that allowed the team to peel away from the advancing enemy soldiers, but while the drill slowed the enemy down, it didn't end their pursuit.

The five Rangers were running for their lives and calling for assistance with each situation report they gave, but when Brennan tried to find out exactly what they needed and where, "Somebody Six" broke in on the Ranger's radio frequency offering his own suggestions and advice.

The Ranger lieutenant didn't like that one bit and tried a less than diplomatic approach to keep whoever it was off their net. "Get the fuck off my net!" Brennan shouted, staring into the radio handset. There was an immediate pause on the other end of the radio followed by a cautious, "Say again?"

"You heard me. I said get the fuck off my net. I have a team in contact, and I need to communicate with them. Over."

This was followed by another momentary pause. "What's your call sign, Slashing Talon element?" came the request. Brennan quickly provided it, adding "Break," then turned his full attention back to the team that was in trouble. The contact was broken as the gunships arrived on station and gave the patrol enough breathing room to make good its escape. The lieutenant coordinated the E & E, and when the liftship had finally extracted the team, he breathed a sigh of relief. However, it didn't last very long as a request came over the radio for the Ranger lieutenant to report to the brigade commander at the 2d Brigade base camp at Song Be as soon as the extraction helicopter touched down.

This was a big "Oh-oh," and like a good West Point graduate—especially a good West Point graduate of Irish ancestry—Mike Brennan responded with a sullen "Yes, sir!" and marched toward the proverbial sound of the guns.

At brigade headquarters, he expected to receive both barrels. When he walked into the command center and identified himself, he noticed that officers and enlisted men in the immediate area gave him a look that could only be described as "the poor bastard!"

"The Ranger lieutenant is here, sir," an aide to the brigade commander announced to the full bird colonel sitting in the next room. Brennan knew that this "Somebody Six" was the unknown voice that he had told off over the air.

When the Ranger lieutenant was told, "The colonel will see you now," Brennan swallowed hard, marched into the colonel's office, saluted, and stood at attention until the officer gave him a curt, "At ease."

There was another long period of silence as the colonel sized up Brennan. When the senior officer finally spoke up, it was to apologize for his error in judgment out in the field. The Ranger officer was shocked, and missed some of what the colonel was saying, but the gist of it had been that the officer was sorry and that Brennan had every right to do and say what he did. He had been the officer in charge of the situation, and it had been his call.

The lieutenant graciously accepted the brigade commander's apology, and when he was dismissed, snapped his best salute. He then executed an about-face and marched out of the colonel's office slightly taller than when he had walked in. He overcame a strong desire to yell over his shoulder, "Yeah, and don't ever let that happen again!" just to get the full effect from the stunned onlookers. Instead he smiled and left the brigade headquarters with a decidedly proud gait.

In the relatively short time Brennan had been with the Ranger company, he had reluctantly come to understand that Captain Paccerelli had been right; there was enough to the job to make it considerably more than a staff position, and while he still wanted the assignment to the 7th Cav, he was very proud to wear the 75th Infantry Ranger scroll and the black Ranger beret.

H Company's scroll took on some personal meaning for Brennan too, since he was one of the primary reasons the word "RANGER" had been placed over the word "AIRBORNE." He had argued that not everyone in the company was parachute qualified, but after the company training, they would be Ranger trained. The line of reasoning made sense, and so the unit scroll was altered to reflect it.

Of course, not everything had gone well during his time in Hotel Company, and he had been chewed out by the CO a time or two, specifically after one of his teams had been through a particularly rough mission and the captain had asked him where the awards recommendations were.

"What awards recommendations, sir?" the confused lieutenant asked.

"For the patrol members," the captain replied.

Lieutenant Brennan merely shrugged it off. "Oh no, sir. They were just doing their jobs."

In spite of the warm afternoon heat hovering somewhere in the low nineties, a sudden cold seemed to settle over the room. "Excuse me, Lieutenant?"

"Sir?"

"And what do you think their jobs are exactly? I mean, besides going behind enemy lines with only a handful of men to gather much needed intelligence for the division! That job, Lieutenant?"

Lieutenant Brennan tried to reply, only to be cut off at the larynx by his commanding officer. "Or say capturing enemy officers or ambushing hard-core NVA recon men who are hunting them, and then hightailing it out of there while the enemy all around them try to chase them down? Just that job, Lieutenant?"

Brennan suddenly got the message, and afterward when he had pulled a patrol or two, he had come to understand better the nature of the tasks the teams performed and the risks that went along with them. What the lieutenant hadn't understood until that day was how Captain Paccerelli really felt about his men. He wouldn't understand until later that the Ranger commanding officer also had a lot of respect and admiration for him and knew that he was turning out to be a damn fine Ranger officer.

A little over a month after he had reported to the 2d Brigade commander over the radio incident, another one of his teams was in contact and another "Somebody Six" came up on the Ranger net trying to put in his two cents worth, cutting into the transmissions between Brennan and the harried team leader.

It worked once, it should work again, thought Brennan. "Get the fuck off of my net!" he said forcefully into the handset.

"Say again. Over?"

"I said, Get the fuck off my net!" replied the Ranger officer, going into the litany of good reasons why he, as the officer on the scene, had final authority.

"What is your call sign? Over," came the request, Brennan once again gave the answer and "Somebody Six" signed off, leaving the young lieutenant to deal with his people. After he had pulled the team out during a hot extraction, and after his adrenaline level had dropped a bit from the usual surge caused by incoming enemy small-arms fire, the lieutenant breathed a sigh of relief. The team was safe, and so was the extraction helicopter.

When it touched down, he once again received word that the brigade commander wanted to see him. While he was glad that the brigade commander was an understanding sort of guy, he wondered if maybe the word "fuck" might be omitted the next time around or at least offered as "Foxtrot Uniform Charlie Kilo." It might have been a bit too strong in its present vernacular.

When he arrived at brigade headquarters, he received the usual sidelong glances from the collection of rear echelon officers and enlisted men in the room.

"The colonel will see you now, Lieutenant," an aide said to the Ranger platoon leader after a short wait. As Brennan marched into the brigade CO's office to report, he noticed that it wasn't the same brigade commander who had apologized to him previously. This colonel was new and he certainly didn't look apologetic. The scowl of his face was indeed a bad omen.

Although the new colonel chewed him unmercifully, he never used one word of profanity. But he did have a certain degree of intensity about him that left the young officer reaching back to see if there was enough muscle left for him to sit down again. He didn't appreciate the colonel's rebuke, and the muscles in his jaws were in a spasm over his tightly clenched teeth.

When the colonel had finally finished tongue-lashing the Ranger lieutenant, he curtly dismissed him as if he had only been a fly on his sandwich. This time when Brennan left the

brigade headquarters his step seemed hamstrung. The lieutenant knew he had been right and the colonel wrong, but
even that didn't leave him with much in the way of solace.
Battles were where you found them; ambushes came where
you least expected them.

CHAPTER THIRTY-NINE

The distinctive but barely audible clicks from the radio speaker brought the Ranger sergeant out of his daydream. He quickly grabbed the radio handset and held it to his ear. Outside Nui Ba Ra, the U.S. Army radio-relay station had been quiet. The early evening along the Phuoc Binh River had been beautiful as the sky opened up to reveal a blanket of stars. But tranquillity in Vietnam was only temporary.

Calling the team's call sign, the Ranger relay operator asked if the five-man patrol had the enemy in sight. It was a prearranged squelch code the Ranger patrols used when the enemy was too close to transmit audibly. One squelch-break meant "yes," two squelch-breaks indicated "no." The Ranger long-range patrol responded with a single click.

"Roger. Understand you have the enemy in sight. Using single clicks for every five enemy soldiers break squelch for their number."

The first click was expected because the NVA and Viet Cong usually moved at night and enemy sightings of seven to ten soldiers moving through a patrol area was pretty common. What was uncommon was the number of clicks the Ranger team was making every few seconds. The radio station's NCO began tallying the numbers in lines of four with the fifth line crossing the other four diagonally. The tally was forty-five and climbing.

"What's up?" asked another Ranger who'd been attracted by the activity.

"Dinks walking by a team," he said and turned his attention back to the radio speaker. It was still clicking away. By then the number was well over a hundred.

"I'm contacting Phuoc Vinh," said the second Ranger as the brigade TOC personnel moved in around the Rangers.

Maj. Gen. Elvy Benton Roberts was holding a tactical meeting with his brigade commanders in Tay Ninh, the purpose of which was to try to figure out where the next large scale Viet Cong and North Vietnamese Army attack would show up in the Cav's area of operations. When news came in that a division long-range patrol had a battalion-to-regimental size unit moving past its location, Major General Roberts had his answer.

Roberts ordered the assembled officers to make the necessary preparations. Not everyone was as convinced, and one officer even said as much. "Do you really think you can trust the Lurps' report?"

Roberts nodded to the senior officer. "I'd trust my life on their reports."

The Cav's LRP/Rangers had come full circle, and their sphere of influence had expanded dramatically.

On 4 November 1969, Fire Support Base Buttons was attacked with rocket and mortar fire, which was quickly followed by a wave of NVA soldiers who charged the perimeter in successive assaults. Both brigade and division were well prepared, and in the aftermath of the predawn battle, scores of enemy bodies littered the base's outer perimeter wire.

EPILOGUE

In 1986, the former Lurps and Rangers of the 1st Cavalry Division got together for their first postwar reunion, and from that great event came the company's own LRP/Ranger association. Since then, they have held reunions each year in conjunction with the 1st Cavalry Division's Annual Reunion, and through newsletters and elected board members they have actively sought to reestablish contact with the five hundred plus troopers who served with the unit over the five and a half years of its service in Vietnam. The association has also managed to bring a number of the families in on its activities since 1986, thanks to some of the association's present or past board members; prominent among them are Michael and Bonnie Echterling, George Paccerelli, Doctor Michael Brennan, Robert Gill, Bruce Judkins, Lawrence Curtis, Stanley Freeborn, John LeBrun, and Howard Shute.

BIBLIOGRAPHY

1. Vietnam Studies

Kelly, Col. Francis J. *Vietnam Studies—U.S. Army Special Forces, 1961–1971*. Department of the Army Publication, 1973.

Stanton, Shelby L. *Anatomy of a Division, 1st Cav in Vietnam*. Presidio Press, 1987.

2. Unit Histories, Operational Documents, Etc.

Company H-Ranger newsletters, Jan. 1969–Sept. 1969.

Company E-LRP/Company H-Ranger mission reports, Oct. 1968–Sept. 1969.

Company E-LRP and Company H-Ranger Commander's Order of Battle.

Company H Communications Draft.

Company H-Ranger Operational Results, 1 March to 15 July, 1969.

3. Personal Correspondence

LRP/Ranger Company Commander, Oct. 1968–Sept. 1969.

LOI (Letter of Instructions) for Employment of E Company, 52d Infantry LRP.

4. Other

The Green Beret Magazine, magazine articles, 1967.

INDEX

Don't miss Kregg P. J. Jorgenson's true story of ambushed LRRPs and their Apache Troop rescuers in the NVA-infested jungles of Cambodia:

MIA RESCUE

LRRPs in Cambodia

by
Kregg P. J. Jorgenson

Published by Ivy Books.
Available at a bookstore near you.

For these determined commandos, the endless cycle of stealth, combat, hard-fought battle, and bloody survival was all too real. . . .

THE GHOSTS OF THE HIGHLANDS

1st Cav LRRPs in Vietnam, 1966–67

by
Kregg P. J. Jorgenson

Published by Ivy Books.
Available at a bookstore near you.